PURITANS
AND
RADICALS
IN NORTH
ENGLAND

ESSAYS ON
THE ENGLISH REVOLUTION

ROGER HOWELL, JR.
Bowdoin College

UNIVERSITY
PRESS OF
AMERICA

LANHAM • NEW YORK • LONDON

Copyright © 1984 by

University Press of America,™ Inc.

4720 Boston Way
Lanham, MD 20706

3 Henrietta Street
London WC2E 8LU England

Printed in the United States of America

Library of Congress Cataloging in Publication Data

Howell, Roger.
  Puritans and radicals in North England.

  Includes bibliographical references and index.
  1. England, Northern—Politics and government—
Addresses, essays, lectures. 2. Great Britain—
History—Civil War, 1642-1649—Addresses, essays,
lectures. 3. Radicalism—England, Northern—History—
17th century—Addresses, essays, lectures. 4. Puritans—
England, Northern—Biography—Addresses, essays,
lectures. I. Title.
DA670.N73H69   1984   942   84-10411
ISBN 0-8191-4013-9 (alk. paper)
ISBN 0-8191-4014-7 (pbk. : alk. paper)

All University Press of America books are produced on acid-free
paper which exceeds the minimum standards set by the National
Historical Publications and Records Commission.

Cover illustration:

Small section of W. Hollar's panorama of the Coronation
procession of Charles II, 17th Century England.

FOR ANN

WITH LOVE

TABLE OF CONTENTS

PREFACE

I first visited Newcastle upon Tyne in 1954, almost by accident. I was immediately captivated by the particular spirit of Tyneside, and when, as a graduate student at Oxford some seven years later, I determined to make a study of the little explored topic of the impact of the English revolution on an urban center, Newcastle seemed a natural choice. Its strategic and economic importance gave it a significant place in these unfolding events, and for me it meant the opportunity to return repeatedly to a part of the country of which I was and am very fond. In due course, the thesis was completed and eventually appeared as a book, **Newcastle upon Tyne and the Puritan Revolution: A Study of the Civil War in North England** (Clarendon Press, Oxford, 1967). The publication of that volume did not mark the end of my interest in and work on Newcastle. I have continued to do research on the history of the area, following up in more detail aspects and developments that could only be treated briefly in the thesis. The essays in this volume represent that continuing fascination with the history of the area in the seventeenth century. With the exception of the first essay, which is intended to point to some common themes running through the essays, they have all been published previously and I am grateful to various journals and the societies which sponsor them who have given permission to reprint. The essays themselves were written over a period of nearly twenty years: in that time my perspectives on the revolution have altered; what has remained constant is a conviction that there is much to be learned from a close study of how it unfolded in the localities. From the standpoint of a town like Newcastle, the revolution looked to contemporaries and still looks to the modern observer rather different from the way it appears when viewed from the standpoint of the central government and London. Newcastle's experience should not be thought of as typical of towns as a whole; no one town can be "typical" in such a sense for a series of events as complex as those that made up the English revolution. But even if not typical, the history of Newcastle can be informative about the nature of the revolutionary experience and how it affected the lives of people who were not, on the whole, at the level of those national leaders on whom the textbooks and general accounts focus.

In more than twenty years' research work in and around Newcastle, I have incurred numerous scholarly debts. Many of them are acknowledged in my earlier book on Newcastle. I shall not try to repeat those acknowledgments here. I would only add a word of thanks to those members of the Society of Antiquaries of Newcastle upon Tyne who have contributed many useful comments and criticisms on a number of these essays when they were read as papers to meetings of the Society prior to their publication.

A number of the manuscripts cited in the notes have been rehoused and recatalogued since I first worked on them. The most important such manuscripts are those which were formerly in the Newcastle City Archives and are now to be found in the Tyne and Wear County Archives. Since the manuscripts are easily traced from their former designation, I have not altered the form in which they are cited in the notes. In a few cases, I have updated footnotes or made additions to them in order to provide cross-references in this volume.

Grateful acknowledgment is extended to the first publishers of the essays who have kindly given their permission to reprint them here: The Society of Antiquaries of Newcastle upon Tyne for chapters II, III, IV and appendix, VI, IX, and XII which originally appeared in **Archaeologia Aeliana**; to South Shields Archaeological and Historical Society for Chapter V which originally appeared in the **Papers** of the society; to the United Reformed Church History Society for Chapter VII which originally appeared in the **Journal of the Presbyterian Historical Society of England**; to the Friends' Historical Society for Chapter VIII which originally appeared in their **Journal**; and to Mouton Publishers for Chapter X which originally appeared in M. Rechcigl, ed., **Czechoslovakia Past and Present** (The Hague, 1969).

The most important acknowledgment of all is contained in the dedication.

Roger Howell, Jr.
Brunswick, Maine
September 1983

THE EYE OF THE NORTH:
NEWCASTLE AND THE ENGLISH REVOLUTION

To those in the mid-seventeenth century who might have paused to reflect on it, North East England and Newcastle upon Tyne in particular would have conjured up somewhat contradictory mental images. On the one hand, this area was clearly one of those "dark corners" of the kingdom, a locality that seemed backward and more importantly ill-provided in terms of the spread and hold of Protestant Christianity;[1] "God," as Sir Benjamin Rudyerd observed in 1628, "was little better known than amongst the Indians."[2] On the other hand, Newcastle itself was one of the leading cities of the realm; as the centre of the expanding coal industry, it was in the forefront of the rapid economic development that had accompanied the land transfers of the Reformation period.[3] In population it ranked among the major towns of the nation,[4] but its impact extended considerably further than size alone. It was, as a local enthusiast proclaimed, "The Eye of the North, the Harth that warmeth the South parts of this Kingdome with fire; An Aegypt to all the Shires in the North...for bread."[5] And lest one think that local pride exaggerated its importance, it is worth recalling that William Camden in his **Britannia** employed much the same imagery when he described it, calling it an eye keeping watch on the northern parts.[6]

There was, in fact, more than a measure of truth in each of these pictures. Without doubt, the North East was less "progressive" than the South East; the population was poorer and more thinly distributed, and reformed religion had struck less secure roots and established its clerical provision less effectively. Even in Newcastle itself, for all its economic dominance over the surrounding area and its increasing commercial importance to London, statistical evidence suggests that the town suffered from the problems of poverty to a greater degree than many other provincial centres. In a town of over 13,000 people, fully three-quarters of the population must be classified as poor, while only 5 percent can be labelled prosperous and slightly over 1 percent wealthy.[7] Some further points need to be made about both the wealthy and the poor. It is true that a number of Newcastle men were well known for their wealth. If, in the seventeenth century, there were none whose fortunes corresponded to that of the almost legendary Roger Thornton, the opulent late medieval merchant whose career had made him the Dick Whittington of Newcastle, there were men like Sir Thomas Riddell, Sir George Selby, and Thomas Liddell who were of sufficient wealth to invest in mining at a level equal with or perhaps exceeding that of any other investors in the reign of James I,[8] while the later royalist stalwart Sir Nicholas Cole was described in 1634 as "fat and rich, vested in a Sack of Sattin,"[9] and Sir John Marley, the royalist mayor of Newcastle in the early 1640s was said to be worth £4500 a year.[10] At the very top of the economic pyramid were the powerful coal merchants, the Hostmen, the beneficiaries of recent economic changes that made control of that risky industry the route to power, status, and wealth on Tyneside. At the base of the economic pyramid were the numerous poor, and among them one particular element was of special significance; the rise of the coal industry in the Tyne Valley laid the basis for an extensive Scottish settlement in the area of Newcastle. A survey of 1637-8 made by the coal owners estimated that of some 5,800 men employed in the industry near Newcastle, the majority were Scots and Borderers.[11] While many were migratory workers, others had settled, and, to a government concerned with religious orthodoxy, this presence of Scottish Presbyterians in their midst caused anxiety. When Viscount Conway assessed the situation in letters to Laud and Strafford in 1640 he voiced the fears of many in his comments that the Scots might be of "dangerous consequence" since they were "all as much convenanters as my Lord Rothes."[12]

Even a cursory view of the economic, social, and religious situation of Newcastle points to several themes which are of considerable significance in terms of the role it played in and the manner in which it reacted to the English revolution. It was a centre of industrial and commercial activity in an area that was otherwise regarded as relatively backward and poor. Those who stood at the forefront of these economic developments had secured for themselves, largely from the 1590s on, a local position of wealth, power, and status. It was not only the source of a commodity (coal) that was becoming increasingly vital to the economy elsewhere, particularly to London, but it was also placed in a key strategic position, commanding as it did the intersection of the East-West and North-South military routes. If conditions should become strained between the kingdoms of England and Scotland

2

or even within England itself, it would be, whatever its own loyalties, a source of contention. Added to these circumstances, as one of the "dark corners" of the kingdom, it was precisely the sort of area where in the absence of a vigorous provision by the established state church, old religion could hold on and newer forms of advanced Protestantism could gain converts. The presence of a significant number of Presbyterian Scots underlined the latter danger, while the overt respect given by citizenry and magistrates alike to Mrs. Dorothy Lawson, perhaps the most celebrated of seventeenth century Tyneside Catholics, reinforced concerns about the former[13] and gave credence to such alarmist reports as that of Bishop James in 1615, who lamented the flocking of priests "even in a walled town like Newcastle"[14] or that of the Privy Council in 1629 which maintained that the number of recusants in Northumberland had "increased to such an excessive number as hath given his majesty just cause to be highly displeased therewith and may justly give exceeding great offence to all his well-affected subjects."[15]

Given such circumstances, Newcastle stood in a relation to London that few other provincial towns could expect to emulate. Its importance was clear and undoubted; central authority could hardly neglect it but was rather compelled to seek close working relationships with those who dominated it. The intrusion of the court into the affairs of Newcastle was virtually dictated by the circumstances of its size, location, and dominant position within the coal industry. A key question, however, is how that intrusion was viewed at the receiving end. Did those who held local power welcome the undisguised interest of the court or not? Did such perceptions dictate the loyalties and allegiances of the population when two key components of the centre, King and Parliament, fell out in the 1640s? Did the revolution at the centre produce a corresponding revolution at the local level? And to what extent did the citizens of the area perceive and act on the broader "national" issues, as these forces impinged on them?[16]

Asking such questions is a valid exercise when considering any locality experiencing the unsettling events of the 1640s and 1650s. Answering them for Newcastle does not provide a general model applicable to all other towns, for the developmental stage of local politics, the impact of religious controversy, the nature and actions of the military forces that were in the area, and the general structure of relations to London varied widely.[17] What happened in Newcastle was not precisely duplicated in Norwich;[18] the history of Bristol was identical with neither.[19] Yet certain suggestive themes emerge from a consideration of the Newcastle experience which could well be pursued with respect to other cities.

The problem of the relation of local power to central authority was not posed exclusively by the events of a revolution; it was present all the time, and when those events are placed in a broader historical context the patterns by which loyalties were formed and the reactions of local men to a national crisis become clearer than if they are studied in terms of the revolution alone. Not surprisingly, perceptions grounded in local experience tended to condition attitudes, responses, and allegiances. Indeed at times one has the impression that ill-understood "national" issues have been substantially subsumed into more familiar local ones, and that, under the unlikely banners of King and Parliament, older but more immediate battles, with rather tenuous connections to these labels, are being fought out. When discussion turned to monopolies, it was only to be expected that those which were most visible and close at hand, the Hostmen's control of the coal trade and the town's claim to control over the Tyne River, should become the focus of concern.[20] If the religious policies of Archbishop Laud were the subject in question, they were best understandable to the citizens of Newcastle through their interaction with a local Arminian vicar or by the experiences of a preacher like Robert Jenison who found himself being squeezed out of the church by what seemed to him a narrow and erroneous interpretation of the doctrine of salvation and a constricting attitude towards preaching itself.[21] Perceptions could shift suddenly under the impact of events. A central government that supported a monopoly in town government seemed a friend until support crossed the line into control or that government, for reasons of its own, began to listen seriously to the complaints of those excluded from the monopoly. To Puritans in Newcastle in the late 1630s the Presbyterian Scots across the border or working in the nearby coal mines looked like spiritual brothers in arms; the experience of enduring an occupation of the town by those Scots following the battle of Newburn caused some though not all to change their minds.[22] Scottish Presbyterianism no longer seemed as familiar and friendly as it had at a distance.[23]

4

There were clearly those in Newcastle who responded to the issues raised by a national crisis in a way that transcended purely local considerations and perceptions. On the royalist side Sir John Marley and on the parliamentary side the regicide M. P. John Blakiston, for example, can be identified as men of principle who, while very conscious of local concerns, saw the broader issues and acted on them.[24] The circumstances of revolution brought others with wider perspectives on the implications of these events to positions of prominence in the area. Robert Lilburne is one such example; a North country man himself, he had some close identification with the area, yet his military career in the South of England and in Scotland and his involvement with the politicization of the parliamentary army involved him in issues that went well beyond locally based concerns; indeed they revealed some fundamental ambiguities in the revolution itself.[25] Still others could find themselves identified with the area and involved in its concerns almost as an accidental by-product of the revolutionary events. Thomas Weld had returned to England from the North American colonies on a mission that had no direct connection with Newcastle at all, yet once he migrated to the area, he took an active part in local religious affairs and quickly reflected local perceptions about the danger of radical religious sects such as the Baptists and the Quakers.[26] George Ritschel had distant connections with the town, but his presence in England was the end product of religious persecution in far-distant Bohemia which had chased him from his native land, and his arrival in Newcastle was simply the result of his need to find gainful employment. Still, when he came to the town, he came as part of the response to the perceived problems of improving education in a dark corner of the kingdom, and his activities there represent a conjunction of local concern about the problem and wider perspectives on the issue of education.[27] It is also the case that a local concern could so closely coincide with a national one that the local articulation of it took on, by its very nature, a national importance. Newcastle was hardly the only place in the nation to feel profound unease at the growth of the Quakers and the Baptists. If the local clergy and magistrates hurried to the attack on the basis of events in their immediate vicinity, their expression of concern about the implications of Quaker teaching, for example, illuminates at the same time general societal reactions to the Friends.[28] The interaction of local and national perspectives was always present, and the flow of influence was not

5

unidirectional. If local issues were translated into national terms or helped to make national concerns intelligible and immediate, the broader views likewise provided a context and a generality that lent meaning to the local problem. The case of Thomas Cliffe, who challenged the Newcastle claim to exclusive jurisdiction in the river, was primarily a matter of local interest even though additional parties, such as ship masters trading to Newcastle from other ports, were already involved;[29] when Ralph Gardner took up the case, the argument became part of a general attack on the validity of charters of any kind, echoing wider radical challenges that had arisen during the revolution.[30]

All that said, the local viewpoint was very much to the fore, and for many key individuals it dominated. No history of the English revolution can do justice to its complexity without being sensitive to this point. Making the point does not commit one to what Gerald Aylmer has called the "grass-roots" hypothesis on the causes and course of the revolution.[31] No responsible historian would deny that there were issues which can only be described as national in scope and import. What happened in London and Westminster was important, and it went far beyond such questions as who should be admitted to the inner ring of wealthy merchants who controlled Newcastle or how Newcastle specifically should be provided with a more effective ministry. But for those Newcastle people actually experiencing the events of the middle seventeenth century, the immediate problem and the local perspective bulked large. In doing so, they affected attitudes, political behaviour, and allegiances.

One of the most marked results of this situation was a considerable reluctance in towns to choose sides as the conflict developed or a tendency at least to avoid such a choice until circumstances forced it upon them and made non-involvement or open neutralism impossible. Those who were firmly and ideologically committed on one side or the other as the struggle unfolded were in a minority. The majority favored an accommodation between crown and Parliament, and, if they thought of taking up arms at all, it was primarily for the purpose of protection of property and the preservation of order, rather than to side with one combatant or the other.[32] Many seventeenth century observers were of the opinion that towns had a natural inclination to the parliamentary side, that their merchant communities found the economic policies of the early Stuarts unduly cramping and their religious policies, especially after the ascendancy of Laud, repugnant. No doubt many did find grievances in these areas, but such grievances did not necessarily translate into a propensity to overthrow the state. No doubt too the privileged few realized the obvious connection between their status, the monopoly powers they exercised, and the favor of the crown which bestowed those monopolies, and yet that did not lead to a unanimous or unwavering decision to side actively with the King. For many the key issue was local in its focus, namely the maintenance of their economic activity, and war offered them little attraction in that regard. It took no particular clairvoyance to foresee that if conflict did occur, Newcastle would be a prime military target and that the impact on the coal trade would almost certainly be negative. The Tyne was relatively easy to blockade; the mines themselves were exposed to firing and other forms of destruction. In such circumstances, the most sensible route seemed to many to be that of neutrality. If drawn into the conflict, they saw the next best course to be seeking an early accommodation with those who threatened disruption. As it transpired, Newcastle had little choice about its initial loyalties. Occupied by royalist troops, it became a royalist city. But two important points must be noted here. First, there is a vast difference between choosing sides as a deliberate act of will and choosing sides under pressure. Whatever the citizens of Newcastle might later say about where their loyalties had been at the outbreak of the war, there is ample evidence to suggest that they embraced the royalist cause through necessity, not through fervent cavalier enthusiasm.[33] Second, there is the substantial evidence that a number of key civic leaders, who undertook to manage the city in the royalist interest, were ready and willing, perhaps even eager, to make an early settlement with the Scots and with Parliament when they put pressure on the town by besieging it. There were a number of key figures who served the royalist cause, went on to be bulwarks of the corporation under the Commonwealth and Protectorate, and remained to serve it after the Restoration.[34] The political loyalties of such individuals no doubt seemed inexplicable to their more ideologically committed contemporaries. This is hardly surprising, for such men did not have dominant political loyalties in terms of the "national" issues dividing King and Parliament. Their perspective was more distinctly local. They had engaged the conflict with reluctance; once in it, they were primarily concerned to see that the privileges of the town were preserved and that favorable conditions for their mercantile and industrial activities were restored. This pattern of behaviour, marked by a tendency to neutralism in the initial stages and a willingness to make a settlement with the dominant side in the later stages, was hardly unique to Newcastle.[35] Though each locality had its own specific features which influenced the pattern of events, this general tendency would seem to be an important consideration in explaining loyalties and political affiliations in English towns during the revolution. From this regard alone, it is evident that there exists a need to study the civil war from the viewpoint of the localities as well as from the viewpoint of London and Westminster.

The civil war led to some alteration in the nature of Newcastle government, but the alterations were of a decidedly limited kind. The structure of town government was unchanged; indeed the corporation fought vigorously to see that that was the case. The composition of town government was slightly altered by broadening the circle of those who enjoyed status and power beyond the narrow confines of the inner ring. But there was no "democratic" revolution, no genuine drift to the Left in all of this. If there were whispers elsewhere in the English revolution of a more "democratic" political settlement, they were whispers that were, in the main, unheard in Newcastle. There were towns in the nation--High Wycombe and Bedford are two notable examples[36]--that experienced a drift to the Left in their own local affairs, following in the train of the increasing radicalism of the national revolution, but many of the towns followed the more limited pattern seen at Newcastle. In most cases, town corporations, like that of Newcastle, proved impervious to the pressures of the revolution. If they made changes, they made them at their own initiative in response to locally perceived and understood pressures or they were coerced into them by exterior forces they resented and resisted to the best of their ability. The tendency towards social revolution from within the towns themselves appears to have been rather limited.

There were in Newcastle impacts from the revolution that could not be avoided. The worst fears of those who saw the advent of hostilities as destructive of the town's economic position were indeed realized. The Tyne was blockaded and navigation of it made even more hazardous than it already naturally was by the sinking of ships in the river. Mines were fired and otherwise damaged. At the end of the hostilities, prosperous Newcastle had been reduced to a sorry condition. When the Scots took Newcastle, they reported that there was "in view nothing but many hundreds of almost naked people, wanting all things but misery."[37] The picture may be exaggerated, but statistics drawn from such sources as the records of ships clearing the Tyne or the enrollment of apprentices in the chartered companies of the town confirm the impression of an area whose economy was substantially, if temporarily, damaged.[38] Recovery came relatively quickly with the restoration of the coal trade to London, but it is important to remember that it was a recovery the structure of which was dictated in significant ways by local considerations. Parliamentary leaders in London may have wanted to wrest control of the coal industry from the hands of those they considered malignant; some were indeed removed and new men took their places. But the older economic structures of the region showed great resilience, no doubt bolstered by the fact that even the newest of the new men proved to be just as obdurate in defending local privileges and monopolies as had been the men they had displaced. Only from the outside--from men like Thomas Cliffe and Ralph Gardner--did the call come to alter the economic order of privilege and monopoly in fundamental ways. Such cries for reform at times fell on receptive ears in London, especially during the sitting of the Barebones Parliament, but they were cries on behalf of a lost cause. A case could be made that removing control of the Tyne from the hands of the Newcastle corporation would have served a wider public good. It was not an argument that the Newcastle oligarchs, with their local perspective, accepted, and when the issue was tested, this local view prevailed.[39]

Newcastle faced the end of the revolution and the restoration of the monarchy with many of the same attitudes with which it had faced the revolution itself. The moderates remained in office and accommodated themselves to yet another change in the central government. There were changes in the composition of town government, but the scanty local records suggest that some, at least, of the changes were initiated locally rather than at the behest of the central government. Because it was now singularly appropriate and advantageous, the town cried up its reputation of having been a royalist city at the outset of hostilities. In doing so, it fostered a myth that has lingered on in some of the best modern accounts of

the history of the city.[40] But for all the staying
power of traditional forms of government and economic
relationships, the years of revolution had left an
impact on Newcastle. Very noticeably, the religious
complexion of the area had been altered; the sects had
struck permanent roots, and after the Restoration the
town came to be regarded by the ecclesiastical
authorities in the North as a centre of dissent. There
had been a Puritan movement in Newcastle before 1640,
as the careers of Dr. Jenison and others reveal, but
after 1660 Newcastle was to become the northern focus
of a movement of which it had been but a small part
before 1640. The revolution had stirred radical forces
too; if they were muted in the prevailing localism and
privilege of Newcastle, they were nonetheless present.
Such radicalism was certainly at a discount in the
heady atmosphere of the immediate post-Restoration
years. It took time, a very long time, for Englishmen
to come to terms with the reality of their own
revolution, to accept it and indeed see positive good
in some of what it fostered and achieved. Two hundred
years after the events which are discussed in the
following chapters, Newcastle was a notable centre of
radicalism, and it seems appropriate that a city which
had once sent the regicide John Blakiston to sit in
Parliament should have an avowed radical in Joseph
Cowen to represent it there. Cowen had come to terms
with the revolution and recognized in its leadership
qualities congenial to his own form of radicalism.[41]
His enthusiasm for Cromwell, or more locally for Ralph
Gardner, is distinctly at odds with the attitudes
displayed by many of the seventeenth century masters of
Newcastle, who were, in their pragmatic and localist
ways, never enthusiasts of this sort. But to some of
the people of seventeenth century Tyneside, to John
Blakiston and Thomas Cliffe, for example, his
enthusiasm might well have been understandable.

No one city can provide, in its own history, a
microcosm of the whole revolution. But in the lives of
its citizens, it can provide revealing glimpses of how
the revolution affected people and how they reacted to
it. The capacity to translate large, national issues
into more familiar local concerns is both very human
and very important to understanding what happened. The
story of a Dr. Jenison, for example, is not the whole
story of how Laudianism influenced the growth of
Puritanism, but the struggle of that one individual
with the church authorities contains valuable vignettes
of how larger issues of church and state impinged on
the consciousness of ordinary people. The following

10

chapters are unashamedly local in their orientation and many of them biographical in their structure. They tell only part of a larger tale. But the important point is that it is the part that many participants in these momentous events knew and understood best, and, precisely because this is so, no account of the revolution that submerges it in a wholly national perspective can be complete.

1. On the religious conditions in the North East, see R. Howell, **Newcastle upon Tyne and the Puritan Revolution** (Oxford, 1967), chap. 3. On the "dark corners" of the kingdom, see C. Hill, "Puritans and 'the Dark Corners of the Land'" in **Change and Continuity in Seventeenth Century England** (London, 1974), pp. 3-47.

2. J.A. Manning, ed., **Memoirs of Sir Benjamin Rudyerd** (London, 1851), pp. 135-6.

3. On the rise of the coal industry see J. Nef, **The Rise of the British Coal Industry** (London, 1932). On the impact of changes in land ownership at the time of the Reformation, see H.R. Trevor-Roper, "The Bishopric of Durham and the Capitalist Reformation," **Durham University Journal**, vol. 38 (1945-6), pp. 45-58.

4. For estimates of population, see Howell, **Newcastle and the Puritan Revolution**, pp. 6 ff.

5. W. Gray, **Chorographia or an Exact Survey of Newcastle** (Newcastle, 1818), pp. 37-8.

6. W. Camden, **Britannia** (London, 1607), p. 667.

7. This estimate is based on an analysis of the Hearth Tax returns for the town, P.R.O. SP E179/158/104. For a detailed breakdown of these figures see Howell, **Newcastle and the Puritan Revolution**, pp. 8 ff. and appendix, tables I - III.

8. Nef, **Rise of the Coal Industry**, 1:297.

9. L.G.W. Legg, ed., **A Relation of a Short Survey of 26 Counties Observed in a Seven Weeks Journey, 1634** (London, 1904), p. 32.

10. **Kingdomes Weekly Intelligencer**, no. 44, 14-20 February 1644, p. 342.

11. P.R.O. SP 16/408/57.

12. **Cal. S.P. Dom., 1640**, p. 81.

13. On Mrs. Lawson, see W. Palmer, **The Life of Mrs. Dorothy Lawson of St. Anthony's near Newcastle**

upon **Tyne,** ed. G.R. Richardson (London, 1885). There are modern accounts of her in **Dictionary of English Catholics,** 4:161-5 and Sister Joseph Damien Hanlon, "These Be But Women," in C.H. Carter, ed., **From the Renaissance to the Counter-Reformation: Essays in Honour of Garrett Mattingly** (London, 1966), pp. 371-400. For a general discussion of Catholicism in the area, see W.V. Smith, **Catholic Tyneside 1538-1850** (Newcastle, 1930) and H. Foley, **Records of the English Province of the Society of Jesus** (London, 1878), 5th series, "The Residence of St. John the Evangelist with the Mission of Durham."

14. **Cal. S.P. Dom.,** 1611-18, p. 302.

15. J. Rushworth, **Historical Collections or Private Passages of State** (London, 1659-1701), Pt. II, vol. 1:11-12. Four years earlier the mayor and aldermen of Newcastle had stated that there were only 30 recusants in the town. **HMC, 3rd Report,** p. 39b.

16. A number of these questions are discussed below in Chapter II, "Newcastle and the Nation: The Seventeenth Century Experience."

17. On the problems of constructing a general model, see R. Howell, "The Structure of Urban Politics in the English Civil War," **Albion,** vol. XI (1979), pp. 111-127, and R. Howell, "Neutralism, Conservatism, and Political Alignment in the English Revolution: The Case of the Towns 1642-9" in J.S. Morrill, ed., **Reactions to the English Civil War 1642-1649** (London, 1982), pp. 67-87.

18. On Norwich, see J.T. Evans, **Seventeenth Century Norwich** (Oxford, 1979).

19. On Bristol, see J. Latimer, **The Annals of Bristol in the Seventeenth Century** (Bath, 1970) and P. McGrath, **Bristol and the Civil War** (Bristol, 1981).

20. On the Hostmen's monopoly and the town control of the river, see Howell, **Newcastle and the Puritan Revolution,** especially chapters 1, 2, and 7; R. Howell, ed., **Monopoly on the Tyne 1650-68: Papers Relating to Ralph Gardner** (Newcastle, 1978); and Chapter V below, "Monopoly in the Tyne Valley: The Case of Thomas Cliffe."

21. See Chapter VII below, "The Career of Dr. Robert Jenison, A Seventeenth Century Puritan in Newcastle."

22. On the negative reaction, cf. **A Letre from an Alderman of Newcastle Shewing in Part the Grievances There** in M.A. Richardson, ed., **Reprints of Rare Tracts Chiefly Illustrative of the History of the Northern Counties** (Newcastle, 1847-9), 1:12.

23. On the interaction of Scottish Presbyterianism and English Puritanism, see H.R. Trevor-Roper, "Scotland and the Puritan Revolution" in **Religion, the Reformation and Social Change** (London, 1967), pp. 392-444.

24. On Marley see Howell, **Newcastle and the Puritan Revolution, passim.** On Blakiston see below Chapter IV, "Newcastle's Regicide: The Parliamentary Career of John Blakiston."

25. See below Chapter XI, "The Army and the English Revolution: The Case of Robert Lilburne."

26. See below Chapter VI, "Thomas Weld of Gateshead: The Return of a New England Puritan."

27. See below Chapter X, "A Bohemian Exile in Cromwell's England: The Career of George Ritschel, Philosopher, Schoolmaster, and Cleric."

28. See below Chapter VIII, "Early Quakerism in Newcastle: Thomas Ledgard's **Discourse Concerning the Quakers**," and Chapter IX, "The Newcastle Clergy and the Quakers."

29. See below Chapter V, "Monopoly in the Tyne Valley: The Case of Thomas Cliffe."

30. Howell, **Monopoly on the Tyne**, p. 18.

31. G.E. Aylmer, **The King's Servants** (London, 1961), p. 378.

32. Cf. the evidence cited in Howell, "Neutralism, Conservatism, and Political Alignment," pp. 74-5.

33. On this point see Howell, **Newcastle and the Puritan Revolution**, chaps. 4 and 8.

34. Prominent examples in Newcastle include Robert Shafto, John Errington, and Mark Milbank. Cf. **ibid.**, chap. 5.

35. For examples drawn from other towns see Howell, "Neutralism, Conservatism, and Political Alignment," pp. 67-77.

36. C.G. Parsloe, ed., **The Minute Book of Bedford Corporation 1647-1664** (Bedfordshire Historical Society, 1949); C.G. Parsloe, "The Corporation of Bedford 1647-1664," **TRHS**, 4th series, vol. xxix (1947), pp. 151-165; L.J. Ashford, **The History of the Borough of High Wycombe** (London, 1960), pp. 122-4; R.W. Greaves, ed., **The First Ledger Book of High Wycombe** (Buckinghamshire Record Society, 1956), pp. 132-158.

37. **Parliament Scout**, no. 72, 31 October-7 November 1644, p. 565.

38. For details see Howell, **Newcastle and the Puritan Revolution**, pp. 274 ff. and appendix, tables V-VII.

39. See Howell, **Monopoly on the Tyne** for a detailed discussion of this point.

40. Most notably in S. Middlebrook, **Newcastle upon Tyne: Its Growth and Achievement** (Newcastle, 1950), pp. 70-74, and M.H. Dodds, "The Company of Merchant Adventurers of Newcastle upon Tyne," **Heaton Works Journal**, vol. 6 (1952), p. 271.

41. See below Chapter XII, "Cromwell and the Imagery of Nineteenth Century Radicalism: The Example of Joseph Cowen."

II

NEWCASTLE AND THE NATION:
THE SEVENTEENTH-CENTURY EXPERIENCE

The interaction of local community and central government is one of the pervasive themes of the history of early modern England; it is also, from the standpoint of historical analysis, one of the most perplexing. While never wholly neglected, even by those historians whose focus was on broad national issues of constitutional or religious conflict, local history and the sense of local perspective have increasingly drawn the attention of those investigating the development of politics and political structures in Stuart England. The results have been stimulating and refreshing, and yet some key problems of interpretation remain. From a view of historical development that stressed the centrality of the court and Parliament, there has been a marked shift of interest to the local political perspective, to the realization of the importance of local issues for the vast bulk of the political nation, and towards the view that political attitudes and actions were shaped more by local perceptions of developments than they were by abstract and general concerns with issues of economic, political, or religious liberty so beloved by an earlier generation of historians.[1] The change of emphasis has no doubt served as a healthy corrective, but what has not yet emerged is a satisfactory working model of the interaction of the two perspectives. If a history of seventeenth-century England written from the vantage point of Westminster distorts and exaggerates the picture, the replacement of it by a history written solely from the vantage point of the parish pump does little better. What one needs to know is the manner in which the local issues, local perceptions, and local problems shaped and informed the national perspective as they were expressed and generalized, for example, in Parliament, and conversely how that sense of generality, which is so integral a part of the national perspective, was transferred and perhaps translated back into the framework and language of local politics.[2] That the flow of influence was not unidirectional seems obvious enough; conflict, for example, over a particular local clergyman influenced in major ways the locality's view of national religious policy, but in equally significant fashion a sense of

16

national religious policy informed the locality's interpretation of its own particular situation.[3]

Newcastle in the seventeenth century provides a useful case study of the interaction of local community aspirations and perceptions with the broader issues agitating state and church throughout the century. The pattern of interaction was far from tidy or clear-cut; there were times when the interests of Newcastle coincided closely enough with the intentions of central policy to make a close working partnership seem appropriate and orderly, but equally there were occasions when the divergence became so marked as to raise questions not only about the specific application of policy to Newcastle, but also about the general nature of the policy itself. If there are threads to be found that run consistently through the whole story, they can perhaps be reduced to two. On the one hand, Newcastle, given its sizeable population and its obvious political, economic, and strategic importance, was always a natural area of concern for the central government, whether that government were King and Parliament, King acting alone, Parliament acting alone, or Parliament and lord protector. On the other hand, the Newcastle reactions to such forms of solicitous attention were highly likely to be conditioned by local perceptions of the extent to which they reinforced or diminished the town's cherished sense of liberty and local authority. The stronger the impression of diminution of local liberty and authority, the greater was the possibility that specific local grievance would be translated into a generalized rejection of governmental policy, or, put in another way, the more likely it was that discussion of issues would rise above exclusively local concerns and begin to embrace the characteristics of the "national" issues that dominate histories written from the perspective of the central government. While the consecutive history of the interaction of local and national affairs is beyond the scope of a single paper, a series of case studies drawn from one of the areas where the potential for conflict was high, namely the structure and functioning of local government including the election of members of Parliament, can illustrate well the general nature of these relationships for the period between the accession of James I and the Glorious Revolution.[4]

The latter part of the sixteenth century had witnessed an intense struggle in Newcastle over issues related to the structure of local government. That struggle was basically the result of the increasing dominance in local affairs exercised by a small and exclusive clique of powerful merchants. Almost entirely composed of mercers and coal traders, the inner ring, or "lords of coal"[5] as they were dubbed at the time, were already in a dominating position by the mid-Elizabethan period, well before their control was legitimated and firmly established by charters from the crown; in the period between 1581 and 1591, each of the major coal traders served a term as mayor of the town, eight of those so serving being directly involved in the management of the Grand Lease.[6] This process, by which power in the world of trade was extended directly to the political sphere, was not unresisted, and there was something in the way of a reform group in the 1590s which sought to preserve the rights of the general body of freemen in town government and to rescue what was conceived as the burgesses' share in the Grand Lease from the private interests of the grand lessees. Though the reform movement succeeded in capturing the mayoralty in 1593, its success was neither impressive nor sustained.[7]

Two factors account, in the main, for the limited success of the reform group, and each has a bearing on the complex interaction of central and local government. On the one hand, the reformers were themselves in an ambiguous position. Hardly classifiable among the economically disinherited of Newcastle, they did not seek the destruction of a system of privilege and monopoly; their aim was the far more limited one of widening the inner ring to a slight degree to include others from the upper levels of town life. Yet as allies they could only expect aid from interests which sought a wider destruction of the privileges of the town; the Bishop of Durham and the Lord Mayor and chief traders of London were allies of precisely this stamp. It is not unreasonable to conclude that support of this kind probably did as much to curtail the activities and enthusiasm of the reformers as any overt opposition on the part of the inner ring itself.[8] On the other hand, the reform movement was also faced by a powerful coalition of interests in support of the growing stranglehold of the inner ring on Newcastle politics, for the aspirations of the lords of coal meshed closely with the drift of national policy. Generally speaking, both the Tudor and Stuart monarchs sought to obtain control of the governing bodies of the boroughs, and the most obvious way in which to pursue this policy was to remove the choice of those governing bodies as far as possible from the hands of the whole community of citizens.[9] Thus, at the start of the seventeenth century, crown policy and the desires of the dominant political group in Newcastle were in apparently total agreement. Local circumstances had led to the increasingly powerful position of a ring of related families with interests in the coal trade. They provided exactly the sort of tight and potentially dependent oligarchy that the crown was seeking, a dependency moreover that could be intensified by royal action to support the monopoly position of the Hostmen. The result of this close community of interest is to be found in the charters of Elizabeth I and James I to the town and to the Hostmen.[10]

The pattern of government thus established was to remain the political framework for seventeenth century Newcastle, and political debate was to revolve around its preservation from change, either as the result of local initiatives to widen the base of power or as the result of royal desires to tighten the element of control even further. To forestall the first threat, the inner ring could call on royal support, since the crown had as substantial an interest in maintaining the tight monopoly control as the town oligarchs did; the problem was that recourse to such support from the central government raised the potential for increased royal interference in town affairs. What was, in its origins, a nice conjunction of interests could under stress become something quite different, and that realization obviously influenced in profound ways the interaction of Newcastle government with central government throughout the seventeenth century.

That the stranglehold of the inner ring on town government was the norm for the seventeenth century is graphically revealed by an analysis of town office holding. Such an analysis also reveals clearly that the key to the inner ring was simultaneous position of strength in both the Merchant Adventurers (particularly the Mercers) and the Hostmen, rather than a base in the Hostmen alone.[11] The latter company, it should be remembered, was accessible to any free burgess "of any free mystery" by the charter of James I; the very fact that entry was "open" in this manner meant that the company could not, by itself, serve as the screen that filtered membership into the inner ring.[12] On the other hand, the combination of membership in the Merchant Adventurers and the Hostmen was a striking feature of those who ruled the town throughout the seventeenth century.[13] Between 1600 and 1640, 28 different people held the office of mayor; of these 18 were both Mercers and Hostmen, and 8 others were members of other branches of the Merchant Adventurers and the Hostmen. The remaining two holders of the office were both Merchant Adventurers. Between the Restoration and the Glorious Revolution, 29 different men held the office of mayor; of these 27 were definitely members of the Merchant Adventurers, and at least 20 and probably 22 were also members of the Hostmen at the same time. The same sort of preponderance is seen in other aspects of office-holding as well; those who became sheriffs, both before the Civil War and after the Restoration, reflect the same affiliations, as do members of parliament for the town. It is striking, for example, that of the 8 different men who served Newcastle as a member of Parliament from 1600 to the summoning of the Long Parliament, all were both Merchant Adventurers and Hostmen, and only one was not a Mercer.[14]

The omission of the years 1640-60 from the above analysis was both deliberate and significant. In the confused years of the Civil War and Interregnum, the pattern of inner ring dominance was profoundly challenged. But if the overall nature of the interaction of central government and local government is to be appreciated fully, it must be recognized that there were other occasions outside of those chaotic decades when challenges were raised in equally clear fashion. It should not be thought, for example, that the chartered establishment of inner ring control shut off the sort of protest that had characterized town politics in the 1590s; instead it tended to intensify the cleavages that had marked that decade by making the successors of the reform group of the 1590s a dissident element within the corporation.

The Shrove Tuesday riot of apprentices in the town in 1633 reveals this clearly and also casts some useful light on the central problem under investigation, the interaction of the locality and the central government.[15] Ostensibly the riot had been caused by the construction of a lime kiln on the town drying ground by one Christopher Reasley, a non-freeman who had connections with the inner ring. It is clear, however, that Reasley was the pretext rather than the cause of the troubles, and it is striking that the representatives of the central government suspected this before the town authorities were willing to admit it was the case. Secretary Coke was already referring to the events as "the late seditious riot" before the true circumstances surfaced.[16] What was actually at stake, as Coke shrewdly surmised, was the monopoly of the inner ring and the continuing desire of a reform element in the town to modify it. The surviving evidence suggests that the town authorities felt themselves to be in a somewhat ambiguous position with respect to the central government's interest in the affair. While they welcomed support of their position, they were reluctant to see that support extended to too close an enquiry into their affairs, and the mayor, at least, was clearly less than happy with Coke's suggestions that he should have taken more forceful immediate action; if nothing else, such reprimands appear to have suggested to those in Newcastle a lack of understanding on the part of governmental authorities of the nuances of the local situation.[17] When the real issues surfaced in June 1633 in the form of a petition from 700 or more burgesses to the King,[18] the inner ring was no doubt grateful for the support it received for its position from the royal government, although it seems that, from the perspective of the central government, the events looked rather more sinister than they did from the local perspective. In retrospect, it appears that the petitioners were well within the reform tradition that had been established in the 1590s. In that sense, they were, of course, of considerable concern to the inner ring. But crown authorities saw a deeper significance in the events, drawing attention to a growing population of mariners, colliers, keelmen, watermen and those of mean condition "who are apt to turn everye pretence and colour of greivance into uproare and seditious mutinye".[19]

Although the evidence is by no means unambiguous on this point, it appears that the town authorities, while desirous of royal support for their position, were concerned about the form that support might take in the deteriorating political conditions of the 1630s. The reform group was limited in their manoeuvering by essentially the same concern, for they too had no interest in lessening the independent privileges of the town, yet this is precisely what increasing reliance on the support of the central government might be thought to lead to. What was happening was that the politics of the town were increasingly complicated by the development of national politics as it became clear that opposition to the inner ring and opposition to the policies of Charles I did not always go hand in hand. This point can be illustrated by a number of circumstances. Opposition to the imposition of ship money, for example, tended to pull inner ring and reformers together; resistance appears to have been widespread, with the general body of burgesses rallying behind the inner ring in a determined effort to avoid payment after the first two levies.[20] Attempts by the crown to influence local elections were likewise sternly resisted. In 1639 the King expressly warned the town "that they should be very careful in choosing the mayor for this next succeeding year and by no means admit any factious or seditiously affected person to that place."[21] It is clear that his message was intended to forestall the election of Robert Bewick, a Puritan against whom he had been specifically warned.[22] Yet Bewick was elected and no trace of local discontent about the choice is to be found. That he did not owe his election exclusively to his Puritan opposition to the crown is obvious enough; he was a Hostman and Mercer, a previous holder of the mayoralty, and a member of the inner ring, but that he was elected against the express wishes of the crown is an equally obvious indication of the limits of inner ring subservience to the crown, even at a time of apparently increased agitation over their position.

The municipal and parliamentary elections held within a short time of each other in 1640 provide further examples of the extent to which national politics and local political traditions interacted.[23] The swing in the municipal elections against Puritanism can be attributed to external factors, but not to the machinations of the crown, however helpful the results were for the crown's purposes. The Scottish invasion and occupation had been the critical factor, and the feeling had clearly grown up that Puritan religious sympathies with the Scots had been at least partially responsible for the occupation of the town.[24] The elections to the Long Parliament remain somewhat obscure, but one clear fact does emerge, and that is the widespread support for men of local connection. Of the three candidates who stood in the election, only one was thoroughly typical of inner ring politics, Sir Henry Anderson, and he was returned unopposed. The other seat was contested between John Blakiston, whose close local connections were counterbalanced by the fact that he was not a powerful and wealthy Hostman and the knowledge that he was prominently identified with the Puritan movement, and Sir John Melton, a total outsider to town politics, Secretary to the Council of the North, and a pronounced Straffordian. If powerful external backing was sufficient for Melton to be elected on one return, it should be remembered that the proceedings in the election were under investigation for corrupt practices by the Committee for Privileges when Melton died and that it was subsequently decided

22

simply to amend the return in Blakiston's favour, rather than hold a new election, a strong indication of the popularity of his candidacy in the original election. That an outsider to the inner ring and a Puritan to boot could achieve this level of support in a climate that was clearly anti-Puritan, while a court backer with powerful connections could not attract more significant support, even though aided by the fear that parliamentary reformers would assault the privileged position of the Hostmen, is a telling illustration of the power of local identification and independence in the politics of the period.

The years of the civil wars and Interregnum were to see the pattern of Newcastle politics altered, at times by the application of external pressures.[25] On two occasions in those years, the rights of election of mayor were over-ridden by outside authority. In October 1642 Sir John Marley was elected by mandamus from the King; in 1645 he was removed from office by an ordinance of Parliament and Henry Warmouth substituted in his place.[26] There were, in addition to these actions, various purgings of the town corporation reflecting the shifting fortunes of the war. In April 1643 Henry Warmouth was removed from his aldermancy for neglect of duty,[27] while the following September 35 freemen were disfranchised.[28] Following the reduction of the town to Parliament, the chief royalists such as Marley and Sir Nicholas Cole were ordered purged by Parliament.[29] Such interference in the normal life of the corporation is hardly surprising, given the conditions of the time, but it is not easy to come by evidence concerning the town's reactions to such exterior pressures, which they clearly would have resented and resisted under normal circumstances. What evidence there is, however, suggests that the existing structures of the town showed remarkable resiliency in the face of such pressures, and that, where changes did occur, they were at least in part the result of anticipatory changes stemming from town initiative rather than wholly imposed alterations from outside.[30]

The existence of a substantial and important core of town office holders who not only survived all changes in government but co-operated with each in turn is a case in point. Men whose roots were firmly fixed in the pre-Civil War corporate exclusiveness of the town continued to serve as active members of the corporation while Newcastle was held for the King, reduced by the Scots, subjected to parliamentary control and ultimately the control of the Lord

Protector, and then returned to what was essentially its pre-war political condition at the Restoration.[31] The loyalties of such men might well seem baffling, both to the more zealous partisans of their own age and to subsequent generations of historians because, in a real sense, they had no fixed loyalties with respect to the large and complex questions that were agitating national politics. At the worst, they can be pictured as secular vicars of Bray; looked at in a more positive light, they are men whose concerns for the stability and smooth functioning of traditional local arrangements were paramount.

An analysis of the changes which actually were made during the period reinforces the impression of the persistence that is frequently disguised at first glance because of the patterns by which the labels of the "national" struggle—Royalist versus Parliamentarian, Presbyterian versus Independent—were taken by the participants themselves and super-imposed on the "local" struggle. One certain result of the reduction of Newcastle to Parliament was an alteration, extending throughout the Interregnum, in the old inner ring control of town government. The new governing clique, led by Thomas Bonner and the Dawson family, appears to have established an impressive hold on the mayoralty;[32] in 1656 it was alleged that the Dawsons in collusion with Bonner had managed the election for mayor as they pleased for some years past,[33] and the results of elections seem to validate the allegation. But while the Dawsons had, in effect, ridden to power on the back of the parliamentary victory, they did not represent a totally new impulse in the politics of the town. They could trace their roots to the reform movement of the 1630s, and their behaviour in office was completely consistent with that line of descent. They had no interest in destroying the privileges of the town; their concern was to broaden the base of monopoly control only slightly to include themselves and their most immediate supporters. In practice they proved as uncompromising in their opposition to genuine reformers and as staunchly defensive of the charter rights and independence of the town as any of the older oligarchs they had for the moment displaced.[34]

Between the establishment of the parliamentary corporation in 1645 and the reshaping of town government in the aftermath of the Restoration, two aldermen were removed from office, and the circumstances surrounding their removals can be taken as further evidence for the persistence of local issues

24

disguised in the terminology of national issues. The first to be removed was John Cosins in 1647;[35] although there is some ambiguity about the circumstances of his removal, the chief issue seems to have been the newly created ascendancy of the Dawson group. If Cosins was not a member of the inner ring, his repeated recourse to the town charter as the core of his attack on the Dawsons suggests that he was arguing the case of the inner ring or at least a case with which they could readily identify. Following Cosins' removal, his affairs became much entangled with broader national issues. Cosins himself was a conservative Presbyterian parliamentarian and in the context of a growing split between the Presbyterians and the Independents, exacerbated by disturbances in the army, his report that there was danger the town might be secured against the present government received excited attention in London.[36] But it should not be thought that the issues thus raised were the ones which had led to his expulsion, for it was not until the beginning of July, more than three months after his expulsion, that the Newcastle authorities raised the argument that Cosins intended to bring the Scots back into England, embroiling the nation once more in civil strife.[37] The impression that the root of the trouble was local and connected with inner ring resistance to the Bonner-Dawson clique is further heightened by the minor riot following Bonner's election as mayor the next year; it was triggered off by the actions of Edmond Marshall, a servant and apprentice of Cosins, and appears to have had no connection with broader issues of national politics.[38]

The second alderman removed was Leonard Carr, and his case even more clearly reflects the general pattern which has been suggested. Carr was an established figure in the town and in most ways, other than his origins in Yorkshire, a person typical of inner ring politics; he had become an alderman by 1642, had served as steward and governor of the Hostmen before the Civil War, and had been assistant and governor of the Merchant Adventurers in addition.[39] He had admittedly participated in the defence of the town in 1644,[40] but it is striking that no question of his loyalty appears to have been raised on the occasions of royalist scares in 1648, 1651, and 1655. But in 1657 articles accusing him of royalist sympathies were presented to the Council of State.[41] On close examination, the charges now appear to have been fabrications,[42] but they were sufficient to convince the Council of State; that body directed the mayor and Common Council to remove Carr, which was done on 18th December 1657.[43] The spurious nature of the charges against him and the fact that he was an ill man over 80 years old at the time of his removal suggest that this is something other than the case of an active and loyal corporation reporting on and with the help of the Council of State removing a dangerous royalist. When one realizes that Carr had been an outspoken opponent of the Bonner-Dawson clique,[44] questioning their management of elections and accusing them of extensive abuses of power, all the while continuing to hold an aldermancy and preventing the election to it of one of their own supporters, the whole episode assumes a quite different character and becomes an excuse to eliminate a person who was a problem in local affairs and to the Dawsons rather than in national affairs and to Cromwell. The election of a close supporter of the Bonner-Dawson clique, Ambrose Barnes, to fill the vacancy would seem to complete the picture.[45]

One final observation about the politics of Newcastle in the aftermath of the parliamentary victory needs to be made: despite a clear recognition on the part of Parliament that the town corporation should be reshaped to serve new purposes and new loyalties, the overall form which that reshaping took appears to have been generated as much from below as from above. It is suggestive, for example, that there was a sizeable time lag between Parliament's naming of delinquents to be removed in March 1645 and the local enactment of their disfranchisement in late September 1645.[46] What is even more telling is the evidence which suggests that the parliamentary ordinance for settling the government of Newcastle confirmed an existing situation rather than created a new one. Details of how the town government functioned between the reduction of the town and the parliamentary ordinance are scanty.[47] Part of the resulting obscurity concerns the critical entry into aldermanic office of Henry Dawson and Thomas Bonner, but there is no doubt that they were occupying such places a month or more before Parliament named them.[48] Likewise, one of the aldermen named in the parliamentary ordinance does not appear in the first list of the new corporation, nor for that matter in any subsequent list of town office holders, and it is surely more than coincidence that his place was assumed by a relative of Henry Dawson.[49] Bulstrode Whitelocke was later to assert that the House of Commons took order for settling the magistrates of Newcastle in violation of their charter;[50] on one level that observation was valid, but on another it was

26

misleading. If the breaking of inner ring control and the rise of the Bonner-Dawson clique constituted something in the way of a civic revolution, it was a revolution which in key ways had been engineered from within Newcastle itself and the parliamentary role can more accurately be described as a confirmation of a situation already existing in the town.

The restoration of the monarchy in 1660 and the consequent purging of the corporation in 1662 allowed for the re-establishment of inner ring control. But again, the process by which that control was established must be observed carefully if the delicate interaction of town affairs and central government actions is to be rightly understood. The task of investigation is complicated by the fact that no complete list of members of the town government exists for 1660-61 and thus tracing the changes in membership between 1659 and 1662 is difficult. But the only signed order for the mayoral year of John Emerson shows that at least one of the old inner ring oligarchs, Sir John Marley, who had been purged in the 1640s, had re-established himself in the town government before the actual purging under the terms of the Corporation Act,[51] and there is some additional evidence to suggest that others in this category, Sir Nicholas Cole and Sir Francis Bowes among them, had done the same.[52] The actual purge of 1662 was a relatively limited affair, and again there must be a sizable suspicion that the impetus for the precise changes made came from within the town rather than from without. Five aldermen were removed, all clearly associated with the Bonner-Dawson group; five members of the old inner ring of pre-Civil War days replaced them.[53] Those whose early careers and family connections had cut them out for inner ring politics survived, their activity in the Commonwealth and Protectorate corporation notwithstanding.

The Restoration, then, returned Newcastle politics to its normal seventeenth century stance. The inner ring dominated, grateful no doubt for the general support of the monarchy, but anxious, as before, that this solicitous concern should not interfere in local rights and privileges under the guise of solidifying that support. The increasingly aggressive stance of the later Stuart monarchs towards the issue of royal control of boroughs made that sort of partnership in the long run impossible. The fine line between support and control had always made such conflict a potentiality; the policies of Charles II and James II made it a reality.

27

For the initial part of the reign of Charles II, the political situation in Newcastle appears to have been relatively settled, even though the activities and agitation of dissenters became a prominent part of the scene and inevitably had political overtones.[54] The town had been quick to make a loyal address to the restored monarch, expressing the hope that he would be the instrument to unite a divided church, compose a distracted kingdom, and ease an oppressed people.[55] In the heady atmosphere of the Restoration itself, aggressively overt royalism became the order of the day; at the parliamentary elections a health was drunk to the King and confusion to Zion,[56] while a number of tracts were locally published to stress the deep and continuing loyalty of the town.[57] For his part, the King in February 1664 by a charter of inspeximus confirmed the charters of Elizabeth I and James I with their ancient privileges.[58] As late as 1682, John March, the vicar of Newcastle, could express in a sermon the confident feeling that the magistrates of Newcastle and the monarchy were still working in a pattern of close co-operation, despite the many distractions that plagued national affairs:[59]

"This famous Town, over which you preside, has always been esteemed a place of very great importance...Now a Town of this importance, as it well deserves, so in such times of distraction as we live in, it may justly challenge the greatest care and vigilance of those that are intrusted with the Government of it. And I do heartily rejoice, that I need not fear the least imputation of flattery, whilest I proclaim to the world that as there is not any Town which can equal it for Trade, Populousness, and wealth, so there is none that doe Surpass it, and but very few that equal it in point of Loyalty and Conformity.

This Happiness and Glory we owe in great measure to that Loyalty and Conformity which shine forth in your own Examples; partly also to that great encouragement you give unto the Loyal and Orthodox Clergy of the place, but chiefly to the due exercise of your Authority, in suppressing Conventicles, those notorious Seminaries of Popery, Schism, and Rebellion."

Despite these hopeful comments, a crisis was at hand in the relations between Newcastle and the central government. In the last years of his reign, as he sought to rule without Parliament, Charles II escalated the pressure exerted by the monarchy on the boroughs, and Newcastle was one of the targets of that pressure. The precise nature of the intrigue and in-fighting that ensued escapes us at some key points, but the general outcome of the pressure was clear enough. The attempt to enforce confusing and ultimately unpopular royal policies through the manipulation of the corporation in defiance of its chartered rights led to a repudiation of the Stuart monarchy which the corporation had long claimed to support.

The first act in the unfolding crisis appears to have passed off with surprisingly little overt negative reaction. Early in 1684, Charles II signified to the corporation that he expected a surrender of their charter, "which was to be renewed on condition that the mayor, recorder, sheriff, and town clerk might always be in the King's power to appoint or confirm."[60] While the surrender was not enrolled, the King granted a new charter in 1685, in it constituting several new aldermen and reserving to himself the power to displace the mayor and aldermen at his pleasure.[61] The charter itself did not reach Newcastle until after the death of the King; the proclamation of James II and the arrival of the charter fell within two days of each other. A contemporary tract recalled the two events as being the cause of great celebration;[62]

> "Bells rang, Minstrills play'd, and
>   Cannon did Thunder...
> Pikes, Muskets and Drums, and mony
>   gay Fellowes
> The King's Health was Drunk at ilk
>   Tavern and Ale-house
> Instead of fair water their Fountains
>   sprang Clarret."

The tract labelled the new King "the justest Man on Earth,"[63] and referred to the charter as "their Rule, their Light, and their Guide."[64]

As the unhappy mayoralty of Sir Henry Brabant revealed, the actual situation was far from as stable as these observations might suggest.[65] Brabant himself was a confirmed loyalist, one who, as Richardson observed in the nineteenth century, "carried his attachment to the sovereign to an extent bordering on monomaniacism."[66] His administration appears to have been the source of contention from the very beginning, though it is unclear whether his attitude towards the crown or his rivalry with other town political figures, especially Sir William Blackett, was the root cause of the difficulty. In any case, the clash led to efforts by both sides to the controversy to invoke the aid of the crown in support of their position. The election of the sheriff and Common Council had been suspended by Brabant because of an effort to elect his opponents; he wrote to the Earl of Sunderland to seek royal support and appears to have received it, for he summoned the electors, told them he had the King's support, and asked if they had any reason why the Common Council as named by him should not be sworn. He recalled that Sir William Blackett, speaking for the dissident group, "dissatisfiedly said they had nothing to do, since your Majesty took the power from them, and so departed before the said Common Council could be all sworn."[67]

In an apparent attempt to solidify his position, Brabant called a meeting of all the freemen of the town to explain the nature of the King's interference. According to his account, the meeting was awkward since his opponents "did most wickedly disperse and spread abroad that the Mayor called a Gill [sic] in order to give up their Charter, which made the Mobile much more numerous at and about the Town Court that day than ever was seen before."[68] This uneasiness about the charter suggests that the picture of happy acceptance of Charles II's new charter may be somewhat overdrawn. Despite the obstruction of a significant number of aldermen, Brabant was able to calm the crowd by assuring them there was no further action contemplated with respect to the charter. "They unanimously gave a great shout of 'God bless the King'" and were dismissed without any disorder. "All things," he noted, "looked very serene and peaceable amongst the Commons, of which the far greater number are very loyall, but of late years much disheartened by the overawe of the Magistrates, who make a great many act against their inclinations."[69]

The next stage in the crisis came by an unexpected route. Sir William Blackett, utilizing his position as a member of parliament, appears to have been able to persuade the crown to purge the corporation under the terms of Charles II's charter, in order to reduce Brabant's forces to a minority. Given the fervent loyalty of Brabant himself, the action of the crown at this juncture is difficult to explain, unless it is assumed that Blackett's true intentions and feelings were deliberately misrepresented, as Brabant claimed.[70] Even more puzzling is the failure of the crown to make any reply to Brabant's impassioned petition that the situation be rectified and the ascendancy of the Blackett group curtailed by a royal order continuing Brabant in his mayoralty for an additional year.[71]

The tenseness of the situation and the interaction of local rivalries with national issues was well illustrated in the celebrated struggle during Brabant's mayoralty to erect in Newcastle a statue of James II.[72] It is clear that Brabant himself was the moving force behind the decision to erect the statue, but the Blackett group entered strong objection to the scheme and refused to sign an order for it until Brabant threatened to send a list of those who would not sign directly to the King. At this point, he noted, they agreed, "more out of fear than love."[73] If the opposition to Brabant had its origins in local rivalries, it was by now clearly intertwined with national concerns as well. Blackett may not have hesitated to use the King to purge the corporation, but when it came to erecting a statue to him, his supporters were not slow to declare publicly that "the erecting of the said statue looked like Popery."[74]

In the succeeding municipal elections, the Blackett group had its way. Brabant was not continued in office, and the Blackett-backed candidate Nicholas Cole was elected mayor. Although Cole's mayoralty passed without undue intensification of the growing rift between crown and community, two events falling within it were disturbing pointers to the continuation of crisis. At the end of May the King sent a mandate to the corporation instructing them to admit Sir William Creagh, a notorious papist, to his freedom and he was duly admitted a month later.[75] In September, an address, signed by Cole as Mayor, was sent to the King; though couched in terms of formal loyalty, it clearly expressed deep concern about a growing pattern of interference with civic privileges and overt support of Catholics in the process. It thanked the King for his "repeated acts of grace and bounty vouchsafed to this your ancient corporation" but then added the significant qualification that the thanks were being extended for those acts "not only in the free enjoyment of our liberties and priviledges, but more especially in the full exercise of the professed religion of the Church of England, whereof we are true members, true loyalty

31

being inseparable from the principles of that church."[76]

In the months that followed, the intertwining of local grievance with general national policy was intensified. There is every reason to suspect that Newcastle's antagonism towards the King would have markedly increased even had they conceived the interference with local conditions to be directed against the corporation alone; when they could see it as part of a broader policy, their sense of grievance in like manner broadened. Newcastle's experience in the last years of James II was far from unique; that unhappy monarch was busily unravelling the complex web of support for the monarchy that his brother had so patiently created, and his hand fell clumsily on many corporations and institutions.[77] In Newcastle the net result of his machinations was the alienation of the older governing elite by his interference with the charter, the alienation of the nonconformists by his papist policy, and the eventual restoration of inner ring control in reaction to both these developments.

In 1687 John Squire was elected mayor in succession to Nicholas Cole; as a Merchant Adventurer and Hostman, he was a typical inner ring candidate. At the end of December, James II, acting under the terms of the new charter, moved to reconstruct the corporation into a more pliant instrument of his will. By mandate he displaced the mayor, six aldermen, the sheriff, the deputy recorder, and fifteen of the Common Council. In addition he commanded the electors to choose the recently intruded Sir William Creagh as mayor, along with a carefully selected new set of officials to replace those he had removed.[78] Apparently the electors refused to elect them on the grounds that they were "papists and persons not qualified" but this action had no effect, for Creagh and his colleagues assumed office notwithstanding.[79] Within a month the new corporation had drafted what was described as "a remarkably fulsome address"[80] to the King, but it was not sent, a majority of the Common Council over-ruling it. Despite that setback, the adherents of royal policy appear to have believed that they had succeeded in controlling the corporation for James II. In a sermon preached before the mayor on 29th January 1688, a Jesuit Philip Metcalfe remarked that on the basis of "universal applause" he could only conclude that Creagh "commanded the hearts of all."[81] If Metcalfe was apparently blind to the tension created by royal interference in the town's politics, he did sense that Creagh's religion

32

was a source of contention: "our Prince is pleased with your constant Loyalty; the famous Town of Newcastle with your prudent Government; good Christians with your exemplary life; I wish your Religion were in the same esteem with many as your Person is."[82] Given the consistently anti-Catholic stance of the Newcastle clergy in the years preceding 1688, the latter point was hardly surprising.[83] Even Vicar March, who could not accept the Glorious Revolution in good conscience, had never been able to tolerate the slightest sympathy for the religion of his royal master.

In fact, both religious and political concerns were present. If the traditional elite had been disturbed by the issue of a new charter and the use made of it to date, their concern must have been immeasurably heightened by a further breach of the privileges carried out with the connivance of Creagh and his subservient colleagues.[84] In February a **quo warranto** was served on the mayor; the closeness of the date to that of the failure to carry the loyal address to the King is suggestive. At the beginning of March Creagh and his colleagues surrendered the charter of Charles II, although once again the surrender was not enrolled. Sometime after 9th June and before 22nd September James II granted a further new charter to the town "whereby the ancient custom of electing the mayor &c and burgesses for parliament were changed and the same in great measure put into the power of the mayor and aldermen," a power being "reserved in the King to place or displace."[85] The most plausible reconstruction that can be made of the ensuing municipal elections is that a combination of dissenters who opposed the Catholicism of Creagh and his colleagues and traditional Newcastle political figures who were horrified by the manipulation of the town's charter combined to thwart the continuation of the Creagh group. The design of the latter was to secure the election of Catholics as both mayor and sheriff; the result was a victory for two protestants, William Hutchinson and Matthew Partis. It is certain that Ambrose Barnes played a critical role in organizing the opposition and securing the result, but it is worth remembering that his biographer was at pains to stress that this was no "clandestine election of Dissenters" but rather that many who co-operated "were known to be zealously affected to the Church of England."[86]

The royal policy with respect to Newcastle was clearly in a shambles. Even a corporation already reshaped in the royal interest could not be coerced into the desired results in 1688. The last desperate gamble of reversing the policy of charter interference in October did nothing to alter the situation from the royal point of view. All it allowed was a quiet transition back to inner ring control following the repudiation of the new charters of Charles II and James II.[87] On 5th November Hutchinson and Partis relinquished their offices, to be replaced by Nicholas Ridley, the sheriff of 1682, and Matthew White, both typical inner ring figures; as James Clephan put it, "corporate life had flowed back to its old channels."[88] It was coincidental but appropriate that the soon-to-be William III landed on the same day.

To use the terminology of modern political discussion, one could argue that the political consciousness of Newcastle had been considerably, if perhaps temporarily raised in the events that culminated in the Glorious Revolution. It had been raised in that familiar progression by which specific grievance was generalized and then elevated to the level of ideological opposition. In describing these events with specific reference to Newcastle in the following year, James Welwood noted, "The Accession of a Popish Prince to the throne, the barefac'd Invasion of Liberty and Property, the palpable Incroachments on Laws and Fundamental Constitutions...were Events too great and important not to awaken England out of a Lethargy the reiterated promises of preserving the Protestant Religion as by Law establish'd had cast her into."[89] His analysis is substantially correct. A corporation whose general stance was in favour of the crown because of the support the crown could give to its own peculiar forms of monopoly was turned to opposition when support was replaced by control; a dissenting element excluded from town political life was not long deceived about the true import of James II's interest in toleration and not willing to continue their support at the price demanded. In December 1688 Lord Lumley entered Newcastle declaring "for the protestant religion and a free Parliament"[90] and in May of the following year the statue of James II was pulled down by an unruly mob incited to action by the garrison soldiers.[91]

Not everyone in Newcastle accepted the Glorious Revolution without question. A sermon by Thomas Knaggs preached in June 1689 struck a strongly protestant and loyal note and asked for a blessing on the forces of William and Mary in the war against the French; in his preface to the printed version, Knaggs noted, "A few hot, inconsiderable men among us were very angry after

I preach'd it."[92]   Vicar March, though remaining strong
in his denunciation of papacy, could not reconcile his
view of monarchy with the events of 1688; in July 1690
he was warned by the Common Council that his salary
would be stopped unless he would pray for William and
Mary by name.[93]   But for the bulk of the population the
outcome of these stirring events meant the return to
life as normal, at least so far as political life was
concerned.   At various points throughout the century
local and national politics had intersected in ways
that intensified the nature of political debate.   Local
grievances became the medium through which many
national concerns were perceived, while the issues and
labels of national debate were used to clothe the
continuing local political struggles.   The two
perspectives were deeply intertwined.   If local issues
or the local interpretation of issues continued to be
predominant and concern for the town's chartered
privileges remained to the fore, both were touched,
influenced, and informed by the constant concern of the
national government for the secure allegiance and
peaceful governance of such a populous and economically
important town.

NOTES

1. For a general discussion of this tendency with respect to the years of the English revolution, see R.C. Richardson. **The Debate on the English Revolution** (London, 1977), chap. 7. R. Howell, **Newcastle upon Tyne and the Puritan Revolution** (Oxford, 1967), was an early attempt to apply this perspective. J.S. Morill, **The Revolt of the Provinces** (1976), is an excellent recent study informed by this perspective.

2. This critical point is raised, briefly discussed, but not wholly resolved in R. Ashton, **The English Civil War: Conservatism and Revolution 1603-1649** (London, 1978), chap. 3, esp. pp. 67-70.

3. This situation is amply reflected in the case of Newcastle in the period of the English revolution. See Howell, **Newcastle and the Puritan Revolution,** chaps. 3 and 6.

4. The interaction of local and national perspectives was hardly confined, of course, to the political sphere, and given the relations of political, religious, and social factors, the isolation of the political element for study here has some aspects of artificiality. This paper is not intended to minimize the importance of the other forms of interaction but rather to offer some suggestions about the manner in which the process of interaction worked by examining its specific manifestation within the political sphere.

5. B.L. Lansdowne MSS 66, no. 86.

6. R. Welford, **History of Newcastle and Gateshead** (Newcastle, 1884-7), 3:420. C.H. Hunter Blair, **The Mayors and Lord Mayors of Newcastle upon Tyne 1216-1940 and the Sheriffs of the County of Newcastle upon Tyne 1399-1940** (Newcastle, 1940), pp. 44-6. The grand lessees holding office were William Johnson, William Riddell, Henry Anderson, Henry Mitford, Henry Chapman, Roger Nicholson, William Selby, and George Farnaby.

7. Lionel Maddison was the mayor in 1593; he was said to be in sympathy with the reformers and to have "proved the Townes interest in the grannde lease." B.L. Lansdowne MSS 81, no. 41.

8. The Lord Mayor of London noted in January 1596 that the prominent reformer Henry Sanderson refused to act in any way to the prejudice of the Newcastle corporation and would only testify on behalf of London if the suit were directed solely against the co-partners of the Grand Lease. J.U. Nef, **The Rise of the British Coal Industry** (London, 1932), 2:124. The general difficulties of the reform group over this point are usefully discussed **ibid.**, 2: 121-25.

9. For a brief discussion of this point, see J.H. Sacret, "The Restoration Government and Municipal Corporations," **EHR**, vol. 14 (1930), pp. 232-59 and B.L.K. Henderson, "The Commonwealth Charters," **TRHS**, 3rd Series, vi (1912), pp. 129-62.

10. On the charters and the nature of town government, see Howell, **Newcastle and the Puritan Revolution**, pp. 42 ff.

11. For a more detailed discussion of this point, see **ibid.**, pp. 46-7. In any case it is clear that the Hostmen did not exactly usurp power from the older merchant guilds as some have asserted. For an example of this sort of view, see **A Short View of the Rights of the Freemen of Newcastle upon Tyne in the Town Moor** (Newcastle, 1962).

12. F.W. Dendy, ed., **Extracts from the Records of the Company of Hostmen of Newcastle upon Tyne** (Durham, 1901), Surtees Soc., vol. 105, p. xli; J.F. Gibson, **The Newcastle upon Tyne Improvement Acts.... with an Intro-ductory Historical Sketch** (London, 1881), p. xxxvi. While the Hostmen argued that this provision did not include the 15 bye-trades, this point was not consis-tently enforced; for example, Thomas Turner, a barber surgeon, was admitted on 17th January 1604. Dendy, **Records of the Hostmen**, p. 267.

13. Statistics on the mayors and sheriffs are compiled from Blair, **Mayors and Sheriffs of Newcastle**; M.H. Dodds, ed., **The Register of Freemen of Newcastle upon Tyne** (Newcastle, 1923); and the records of the Hostmen and Merchant Adventurers.

14. Statistics on M.P.s are compiled from C.H. Hunter Blair, "Members of Parliament for Northumberland and Newcastle upon Tyne 1559-1831," **AA[4]**, xxiii (1945); Dodds, **Register of Freemen**; and the records of the Hostmen and Merchant Adventurers.

15. For a detailed discussion of the riot, see Howell, **Newcastle and the Puritan Revolution,** pp. 53 ff.

16. **Cal. S.P. Dom., 1625-49 Addenda,** p. 453.

17. For Coke's criticisms see **ibid.** For the mayor's despondent response see **Cal. S.P. Dom., 1631-33,** p. 585.

18. PRO SP/16/240/27. The text of the grievances is printed in Welford, **History of Newcastle,** 3:313-15.

19. PRO SP 16/245/32. The Council of the North noted that it had decided to look more fully into the matter because they realized the significance of the town to the King. **Ibid.**

20. M.H. Dodds, "Ship Money," **Newcastle Citizen,** vol. 1 (1930), pp. 68-70. Cf. also **Cal. S.P. Dom., 1638-9,** pp. 4-5, 80, 105, 321, 325; **Cal. S.P. Dom., 1639-40,** p. 460; **Cal. S.P. Dom., 1640,** p. 133.

21. **Cal. S.P. Dom., 1639,** p. 480.

22. **Ibid.,** pp. 450-51; the informant was Sir John Marley.

23. For a detailed discussion of these elections, see Howell, **Newcastle and the Puritan Revolution,** pp. 124 ff. The discussion of the elections to the Long Parliament should be supplemented by R. Howell, "The Elections to the Long Parliament in Newcastle: Some New Evidence," **AA4,** xlvi (1968), pp. 225-7, below, chap. iv appendix.

24. For an example of the reaction against the Scots, see **A Letre from an Alderman of Newcastle Shewing in Part the Grievances There** in M.A. Richardson, ed., **Reprints of Rare Tracts** (Newcastle, 1847), vol. I. This letter appears to have been circulated in manuscript form. There are copies in PRO SP 16/466/89; Bodleian Library Tanner MSS 65, ff. 110-11v; B.L. Harleian MSS 1576, ff. 312-13v; William Trumbull MSS, xx, f. 48 (Berkshire Record Office).

25. For a detailed discussion of political life in Newcastle in this period, see Howell, **Newcastle and the Puritan Revolution,** chaps. 4 and 5.

26. A.M. Oliver, **The Mayoralty of Newcastle upon Tyne** (Newcastle, 1910), pp. 21-2.

27. M.H. Dodds, ed., **Extracts from the Newcastle upon Tyne Council Minute Book 1639-1656** (Newcastle, 1920), p. 24.

28. **Ibid.**, pp. 27-8. The order was confirmed at the beginning of October. **Ibid.**, pp. 29-30.

29. They were named in an act of 24th March 1644/5. Newcastle Common Council Book 1645-50, Tyne and Wear County Archives, f. 25. They were also named in the ordinance for the government of Newcastle, 26 May 1644/5. **L.J.**, 7:395.

30. The pattern is not unusual to Newcastle. I have discussed this point in more general terms in R. Howell, "The Structure of Politics in the English Civil War," **Albion**, vol. II, no. 2 (1979), pp. 111-27.

31. Examples among the aldermen would include Robert Shafto, Mark Milbank, and John Emerson. Again, the existence of this middle group, which successfully sought accommodation with successive and conflicting regimes, would seem to be a general feature of urban politics in the period rather than a peculiar Newcastle feature. Cf. Howell, "Structure of Urban Politics," pp. 116-19, 122-3.

32. For a detailed discussion of the Bonner-Dawson clique, see Howell, **Newcastle and the Puritan Revolution**, chap. 5.

33. Newcastle Common Council Book 1650-9, Tyne and Wear County Archives, f. 406.

34. This was revealed clearly, for example, in their struggle with Ralph Gardner. If anything, Gardner seems to have fared less well under the parliamentary corporation than he had when the inner ring predominated. See R. Howell, **Monopoly on the Tyne 1650-58: Papers Relating to Ralph Gardner** (Newcastle, 1978).

35. The effective order for his removal was dated 24th March 1647. Dodds, **Council Minute Book**, pp. 68-9. An order to remove him had been signed as early as 18th February. Newcastle Common Council Book 1645-50, Tyne and Wear County Archives, f. 110. It is interesting to note that Cosins invoked both a "local" and a

"national" argument against his removal. On the one hand, he relied on the charter for his position; on the other, he argued he could not be removed since he was brought in by parliamentary ordinance. **Ibid.**, ff. 124-6.

36. **C.J.**, 5:208. Cosins was not alone in commenting on this subject. Cf. the two letters from Skippon, the parliamentary governor of Newcastle, printed in H. Cary, **Memorials of the Great Civil War 1642-1652** (London, 1842), 1:229-32.

37. **C.J.**, 5:229.

38. Dodds, **Council Minute Book**, pp. 102-4.

39. **Ibid.**, p. 21; MSS Hostmen, Old Book, ff. 185, 187, 188; MSS Merchant Adventurers, Order Book, ff. 1, 18, 26.

40. Cf. E33 (17), **A True Relation of the Late Proceedings of the Scottish Army** (London, 1644), pp. 11-13; **Kingdomes Weekly Intelligencer**, no. 69, 21-7 August 1644, pp. 556-7; E16 (5), **A Particular Relation of the Taking of Newcastle** (London, 1644), pp. 12-13, 9 (2nd pagination).

41. **Cal. S.P. Dom.**, 1656-7, p. 272.

42. On the falsity of the charges, see Howell, **Newcastle and the Puritan Revolution**, pp. 180-81.

43. **Cal. S.P. Dom.**, 1656-7, pp. 226-7; Newcastle Common Council Book 1656-1722, Tyne and Wear County Archives, f. 12v.

44. Cf. Newcastle Common Council Book 1650-9, Tyne and Wear County Archives, f. 406.

45. It is perhaps suggestive that George Blakiston, a younger generation member of an old-style Newcastle political family, resigned from the Common Council in protest at the election. **Ibid.**, f. 467. But it may be that the objection was simply to Barnes's youth. Cf. W.H.D. Longstaffe, ed., **Memoirs of the Life of Mr. Ambrose Barnes** (Durham, 1867), Surtees Soc., vol. 50, p. 99.

46. Newcastle Common Council Book 1645-50, Tyne and Wear County Archives, f. 25.

47. No records of meetings of the Common Council
were kept until 28th March 1645. Dodds, **Council Minute
Book,** p. 25. The financial machinery of the town
appears to have been reestablished more quickly.
Receipts were kept from 22nd November 1644 and payments
from the fourth week of October. Newcastle Chamberlains' Accounts 1642-5. Tyne and Wear County Archives,
ff. 58, 190v.

48. They are among the signatories of a letter to
Speaker Lenthall a month before the first official
notice of their appointment. **C.J.,** 3:714.

49. The alderman so named was Henry Lawson, the
fifth senior member of the Common Council. Dodds,
Council Minute Book, p. 21. William Dawson appears in
his place in the earliest list of parliamentary corporation which dates from the audit of accounts, 4th
October 1645. Newcastle Chamberlains' Accounts 1642-5,
Tyne and Wear County Archives, f. 167.

50. B. Whitelocke, **Memorials of the English Affairs
from the Beginning of the Reign of Charles I to the
Happy Restoration of King Charles II** (Oxford, 1853),
1:348.

51. Newcastle Common Council Book 1656-1722, Tyne
and Wear County Archives, f. 43.

52. **Ibid.,** f. 44.

53. Those removed were George Dawson, Christopher
Nicholson, Henry Rawlings, William Johnson, and Peter
Sanderson. Seated in their stead were Sir James
Clavering, Sir Francis Anderson, Sir Francis Liddell,
Henry Maddison, and Cuthbert Carr. Predictably, the
middle group represented by Robert Shafto, Mark
Milbank, and John Emerson survived.

54. Concern about the dissenters is widely
reflected in the literature emanating from the
Newcastle clergy in the later Stuart period. Cf. for
example, J. March, **The False Prophet Unmaskt** (London,
1683); J. March, **A Sermon Preached before the Right
Worshipful the Mayor, Recorder, Aldermen, Sheriff &c
of... Newcastle** (London, 1677); J. Rawlet, **A Dialogue
betwixt Two Protestants** (London, 1685); and J. Shaw, **No
Reformation of the Established Reformation** (London,
1685). When Thomas Story visited a conventicle at
Newcastle he was most impressed by the political overtones. "Expecting to hear something like Doctrine from

so noted a Man among them," he was disappointed that the message was substantially "suggestions of Jealousy and Dislike against the Government," **A Journal of the Life of Thomas Story** (Newcastle, 1747), p. 3.

55. **Cal. S.P. Dom., 1660-1,** p.4.

56. E1038 (8) **The Lords Loud Call to England** (London, 1660), p. 19.

57. R. Astell, **Vota Non Bella** (Gateshead, 1660); R. Hooke, **The Bishops' Appeale or an Address to the Brethren of the Presbyteriall Judgment** (Newcastle, 1661); R. Thompson, **The Loyall Subject** (Newcastle, 1660 and 1662).

58. J. Brand, **The History and Antiquities of the Town and County of the Town of Newcastle upon Tyne** (London, 1789), 2:193.

59. J. March, **Th' Encaenia of St. Ann's Chappel in Sandgate** (London, 1682), sig. A3-A3v.

60. Brand, **History of Newcastle,** 2:194.

61. Longstaffe, **Memoirs of Barnes,** p. 176 n.

62. G. Stuart, **A Joco-Serious Discourse in Two Dialogues** (London and Newcastle, 1686), pp. 1-2.

63. **Ibid.,** sig. A4.

64. **Ibid.,** p. 3.

65. The following account of events in the mayoralty of Brabant is drawn substantially from **The Eve of the Revolution in Newcastle upon Tyne** in M.A. Richardson, ed., **Reprints of Rare Tracts** (Newcastle, 1847), vol. iv.

66. **Ibid.,** p. 15. The biographer of Barnes recorded that Brabant once declared "if the king should command him to kill a man in cold blood, he took himself bound in conscience and duty to execute his command," Longstaffe, **Memoirs of Barnes,** p. 193.

67. **Eve of the Revolution in Newcastle,** p. 8.

68. **Ibid.,** p. 9.

69. **Ibid.,** pp. 9-10.

70. Ibid., p. 10.

71. Ibid., pp. 13-14.

72. On the statue see M.R. Toynbee, "Fresh Light on William Larson's Statue of James II at Newcastle upon Tyne," AA[4], xxix (1951), pp. 108-17; M.R. Toynbee, "A Further Note on William Larson's Statue of James II at Newcastle upon Tyne," AA[4], xxxiv (1956), p. 91.

73. Eve of the Revolution in Newcastle, p. 13.

74. Ibid.

75. Longstaffe, Memoirs of Barnes, p. 176 n.

76. Ibid.

77. M. Ashley, James II (Minneapolis, 1977) and J. Miller, James II: A Study in Kingship (London, 1977), passim.

78. Longstaffe, Memoirs of Barnes, p. 176 n.

79. Ibid.

80. Ibid.

81. P. Metcalfe, A Sermon Preached before the Right Worshipful the Mayor of the Town & County of Newcastle upon Tyne (London, 1688), sig. A2.

82. Ibid., sig. A2v.

83. For examples of this anti-Catholicism, cf. J. March, A Sermon Preached before the Mayor; J. March, Sermons Preach'd on Several Occasions (London, 1699); J. Rawlet, A Dialogue betwixt Two Protestants; J. Rawlet, An Explication of the Creed, the Ten Commandments, and the Lords Prayer (London, 1679); J. Shaw, No Reformation of the Established Reformation; J. Shaw, Origo Protestantium or an Answer to a Popish Manuscript (London, 1679); J. Shaw, The Pourtraicture of the Primitive Saints (Newcastle, 1652). For the importance of anti-Catholicism in the period, see J. Miller, Popery and Politics in England 1660-1688 (Cambridge, 1973).

84. Longstaffe, Memoirs of Barnes, p. 176 n.

85.   **Ibid.** Oliver gives the date of 24th July for the new charter, Oliver, **Mayoralty of Newcastle,** p. 25.

86.   Longstaffe, **Memoirs of Barnes,** pp. 176 n., 177-8.

87.   Blair, **Mayors and Sheriffs of Newcastle,** p. 79.

88.   J. Clephan, "William Hutchinson Merchant Adventurer," off-print from **AA,** 1880, p. 16.

89.   **Vindication of the Present Great Revolution in England in Five Letters Pass'd betwixt James Welwood M.D. and Mr. John March** (London, 1689), sig. A2.

90.   **Universal Intelligencer,** no. 1, 11 Dec. 1688, quoted in **Destruction of the Statue of James the Second at Newcastle** in M.A. Richardson, ed., **Reprints of Rare Tracts** (Newcastle, 1847), vol. iv, p. 8.

91.   **Ibid.,** pp. 9-17.   The frequently repeated statement of Bourne that the statue was torn down in 1688 is clearly erroneous.   H. Bourne, **The History of Newcastle upon Tyne** (Newcastle, 1736), p. 131.

92.   Longstaffe, **Memoirs of Barnes,** p. 436.

93.   **Ibid.,** p. 438. **Vindication of the Present Great Revolution in England,** p. 25 accuses March of labelling the actions of the Prince of Orange "with the infamous Names of the Rebellion, Damnation and the like."   March himself asserted that passive obedience was "a Principle founded in the Word of God." **Ibid.,** p. 5.

III

KING ALFRED AND THE PROLETARIAT:
A CASE OF THE SAXON YOKE

The theory of the Norman Yoke was for a long period one of the most insistently held left-wing myths in England.[1] Though it was to take many forms, its main outlines were simple. Before the Norman conquest, there had been a free society of equal citizens and government by representative institutions. When William the Conqueror came, he brought with him a royal tyranny and the people lost their rights to the new landlords. Yet beneath the surface, the ideals of the conquered society remained as an inspiration to democratic agitation, and at times the people were able to extract concessions from their Norman overlords as they did with Magna Carta in 1215.

As has been correctly observed, the theory of the Norman Yoke does leave something to be desired as an historical account;[2] its idyllic picture of Anglo-Saxon democracy is an illusion. But as a myth to justify the demands of the people, it was a potent weapon, especially in the seventeeth century. Needless to say, such a theory was stoutly resisted by those in authority. Particularly interesting in this respect is a case in which the myth was, in effect, turned on its head and the Anglo-Saxons made to appear to be the authors of a restricted rather than a popular government. In this portrayal, they were displayed as performing a noble rather than a base act and the impressive figure of King Alfred himself was conjured up to play the role of originator of the civil power of a limited oligarchy.

The case in point appears in the play **The Love-Sick King** by Anthony Brewer, one of a limited number of seventeeth century plays dealing with the Saxon period.[3] Actually, the chronology in Brewer's play is hopelessly mixed; he combines together events from 871, 1016, and 1400 with little regard for historical accuracy or chronology. In the play, King Alfred leads English resistance against the Danish King Canute, and in this he is aided by Roger Thornton, the Dick Whittington of Newcastle upon Tyne. In the end of the play, the Danes are defeated and taken prisoner by Thornton and his men. Alfred (called Alured throughout

the play) is crowned King and then in gratitude confers
a number of privileges on Thornton and Newcastle:

And now to our worthy country-men
It shall be texted to your lasting fame
That your Newcastle strength set England free
In this dayes fair and happy victory
For which and for thy sake (most worthy Thornton)
Wee'l give a lasting honour to the Town
Now beautified by thee with Wals and Towers
To which wee'l add all noble priviledge
Belonging to a Town Incorporate;
And for your former Government of Poretereans [sic]
We here establish it a Mayoralty
And Thornton as the first we here create
Mayor of Newcastle and give thee power
To elect a brotherhood of Aldermen
With choice of Sheriffs to asist thy Government.
Your charters shall be drawn with fullest strength
Even with the fairest Cities of our Land,
This sword confirms it from King Alured's hand;
Bear it before ye still.[4]

Thus is Alfred made the author of Newcastle's closed
corporation. Of particular interest is the reference
that this new arrangement has been made in place of
your former Government of Poretereans. The meaning of
Poretereans is, at best, obscure, but there is a strong
possibility that this is a printer's error for
proletarians, and this reading would, of course, underline the oligarchical implications of the scene.[5]

That this scene was meant to have such a meaning
is further indicated when the history of the play
itself is considered. The date of composition is not
definitely known, but some of the circumstances
surrounding its production do seem clear. In the first
place, it was clearly written for performance in
Newcastle upon Tyne; the local references and the sub-
plot centred on Thornton reveal this much. Moreover,
the play was apparently written to celebrate the visit
of a King to the town and internal evidence makes it
clear that the King in question was James I.[6] King
James I is known to have made two visits to Newcastle:
he stayed in the town from 9 to 13 April 1603 on his
way to his coronation in London, and he later visited
the town between 23 April and 4 May 1617.[7] On both
occasions, the town oligarchy was involved in controversy over its chartered privileges and it would have
been in the interest of the oligarchs to stress a
respectable historical ancestry for their privileged

position. In 1603-04 there was difficulty over the methods of election to town office as provided for in the charter of Elizabeth I;[8] in 1617 there was dispute over the conservancy of the Tyne in the course of which the inner ring of town governors in Newcastle successfully reasserted their right to control.[9]

It seems likely that the 1617 date may be the correct one. In the first place, James' visit in 1603 was both brief and sudden, and it is unlikely that there was time to prepare a stage production. But the visit of 1617 was long enough to allow such a performance and was, moreover, a visit marked by various festivities. In the second place, it would appear that **The Love-Sick King** was written after **The Knight of the Burning Pestle**; this would place it at least after 1607 and probably even later.[10]

One final incident could be noted which also seems to point to the use of the play as propaganda for the ancient foundation of the town's limited government. **The Love-Sick King** was published in 1655. This again marked an occasion when the corporate privileges of Newcastle seemed threatened, this time by Ralph Gardner who had tried to force parliamentary action against the oligarchs of Newcastle during the Barebone's Parliament of 1653 and in 1655 had published his account of these efforts and of the iniquities of the Newcastle Corporation in **Englands Grievance Discovered in Relation to the Coal Trade**.[11] The magistrates of Newcastle used efforts of all sorts to fend off any attempts to break their monopoly or to introduce any democratic element into the government of the town; it appears probable that among these efforts was an interesting use of what might be called the theory of the Saxon Yoke.

NOTES

1. C. Hill, "The Norman Yoke," in **Puritanism and Revolution** (London, 1958), pp. 50-122.

2. **Ibid.**, p. 57.

3. A.E.H. Swaen, ed. A. Brewer, **The Love-Sick King** in **Materialen zur Kunde des Alteren Englishchen Dramas** vol. 18 (Louvain, 1907). See also **Proceedings of the Society of Antiquaries of Newcastle upon Tyne** third series, III, pp. 87-90 and M.H. Dodds, "'Edmund Ironside' and 'The Love-Sick King'," **Modern Language Review**, vol. 19 (1924), pp. 158-168.

4. Brewer, **Love-Sick King**, ed. Swaen, pp. 50-51.

5. This is suggested by Swaen, **ibid.**, p. 61. The O.E.D. notes a few other uses of **Proletarian** or analogous words at this early date, for example by J. Jones in 1579 and by Holland in 1609.

6. See Dodds, "Edmund Ironside and the Love-Sick King," p. 164.

7. J. Brand, **History of Newcastle** (London, 1781), 2:450, 452; R. Welford, **History of Newcastle and Gateshead** (Newcastle, 1884-7), 3:219.

8. R. Howell, **Newcastle upon Tyne and the Puritan Revolution** (Oxford, 1967), pp. 42 ff.

9. **Ibid.**, pp. 29-30.

10. Dodds, "Edmund Ironside and the Love-Sick King," pp. 158, 162.

11. R. Gardner, **Englands Grievance Discovered in Relation to the Coal Trade** [1655] (Newcastle, 1796). On Gardner, see Howell, **Newcastle and the Puritan Revolution**, chap. 7.

IV

NEWCASTLE's REGICIDE:
THE PARLIAMENTARY CAREER OF
JOHN BLAKISTON

In the course of the Civil War, Newcastle gained a
wide reputation for being anti-Puritan and pro-
Royalist. To the Presbyterian John Fenwick, the town
was "famous for thy mocking and misusing Christ's
messengers and ill entertainment of his servants."[1]
William Lithgow, who wrote a spirited account of the
siege of the town by the Scots in 1644, was even more
outspoken. He claimed that the richest and best sorts
of inhabitants were all malignants and most of them
papists, but he did not excuse the lower classes
either, terming them "a masse of silly ignorants" who
lacked knowledge, conscience, and honesty.[2] The
reputation which the town had gained between 1642 and
1644 was widely publicized at the Restoration. A poem
published at Gateshead in 1660 to congratulate Charles
II on the resumption of his "Birthright Power" stressed
that loyalty had never wavered among Newcastle's
citizenry and maintained that "On my first love my eye
was ever bent/Though churlish Keepers did my hand
prevent."[3] The picture is, of course, somewhat
exaggerated. Newcastle had been held for the King, and
since it was virtually the only major port in the hands
of the royalists, it had assumed a great significance
for their forces. Its royalism was, however, in many
ways the result of the occupation of the town by the
Earl of Newcastle rather than the product of overwhelming sympathies. There were men in the town who
were loyal to the Parliament: thirty-five freemen were
disfranchised in September, 1643, because they had
"refused to hould wth our Soveraigne Lord the
King...and [had] beene incendiaries and treated with
seuerall men of another nation to invade this kingdome
and to possesse themselves of this Towne."[4] Even Sir
John Marley, who as mayor had the chief local responsibility for keeping the town safe for the crown, admitted that there were dissident elements among the
population.[5] When the Earl of Newcastle first
attempted to garrison and fortify the town, he was
stoutly resisted by the labourers in the coal trade.[6]
It is perhaps suggestive that the Earl changed his
appeal slightly but significantly when he came from
Durham to Newcastle. At Durham, he had beat the drum

for the King; at Newcastle, it was struck up for King and Parliament.[7]

It may seem ironic, nonetheless, that the most famous political figure of Newcastle during the Interregnum was a strong Puritan and an active parliamentarian, but to view John Blakiston as a republican anomaly in the politics of a royalist town is to misinterpret both Blakiston himself and the politics of the town. Blakiston's immediate ancestry contained little that foreshadowed his career as a radical. He was the second son of Marmaduke Blakiston, prebendary of Durham and vociferous Arminian.[8] His father was a frequent target of Puritan attacks, not only for his Arminianism but also for pluralism and for having secured the vicarage of Northallerton for his son Thomas.[9] Peter Smart, another prebendary of the cathedral, was the most outspoken of his critics, claiming that Blakiston had six livings of which he had bargained away all but two; at neither of the two which he had retained had he preached for seven years. Smart concluded scornfully, "You thinke you doe service ynough to God and the Church, yf you sit now and then in your stall, like an idle drone (as allwaies you have ben), to heare piping and chaunting and observe devoutly your son Cosin his new ceremonies."[10] Little is known of the early life of John Blakiston, and there is no information which dates his repudiation of the Arminian views of his father or his own acceptance of Puritanism. He entered on a commercial career in Newcastle, married there in November, 1626, and by 1632 had secured a place at the bottom level of town office-holding as one of the chamberlains.

By this time, he was already a Puritan, and he continued to be an active leader of the movement in the 1630s, participating in the securing of the unofficial lecturer William Morton and being castigated in the local High Commission Court for his attacks on the vicar of the town, Yeldard Alvey.[11] Blakiston's position politically was enhanced by the growing Puritan strength, and, in 1640, when elections for the Long Parliament took place, he became a candidate. The election was a confused one. In the first place, it is necessary to appreciate the extent of the electorate. In the second place, the actual results must be clarified since the election led to a dispute. The original returns are lost, and this is, in fact, no easy task. In the third place, the town was occupied by the Scots, and it is important to ascertain what role, if any, they played in the polling. One thing is certain; the elections created great interest and excitement. The town companies appear to have appointed representatives to meet together in order to draw up statements of their grievances to be presented to the members.[12] There has been some doubt expressed about the extent of the franchise at Newcastle,[13] but every available indication suggests that it was a freeman borough and that the electorate was large.[14] Three candidates presented themselves to this aroused body of freemen: Sir Henry Anderson, Sir John Melton, and John Blakiston.

They were men who differed considerably in background and outlook. Anderson was an elderly man who had already held high municipal office and had had considerable parliamentary experience.[15] He was a powerful Hostman, and, as such, was far more in touch with the governing classes of the town than Blakiston. Blakiston, of course, had some contacts with Newcastle political life. He was not, as one contemporary pamphlet charged,[16] a mere shopkeeper, but he was not a part of the inner ring of Hostmen and Mercers who had dominated municipal politics since before 1600. The third candidate, Sir John Melton, was a complete outsider. This in itself hindered his chances, for the town rarely elected anyone without close Newcastle connections to represent them in Parliament. The closest contact which he had with the town was through his post as Secretary of the Council of the North, but he was further hampered by being a pronounced Straffordian. He had attempted as early as 1635 to influence Strafford to procure the summons of a Parliament, and there can be little doubt that he was Strafford's personal candidate in the election.[17]

Despite the odds against him, Melton was returned as one of the two members in a violently disputed contest. It is important to ascertain the order of events since they have frequently been treated in a misleading fashion by later writers. The **Old Parliamentary History** and Alderman Hornby, who followed it, stated that Melton and Anderson were elected and that, after Melton died, a new writ was issued which resulted in the election of John Blakiston.[18] The editors of the official returns confessed, on the other hand, that they were unable to determine the order of the elections.[19] Bean, in his study of the parliamentary representation of the northern counties, appears to have been the first to establish the correct sequence of events, namely a disputed election for one of the places between Blakiston and Melton, and an undisputed return of Anderson for the other place.[20]

Although some more recent accounts have suggested other possibilities,[21] this would seem to be the correct view. The **Journals of the House of Commons** and various parliamentary diaries appear to demonstrate conclusively that Anderson's election was never in question. Within a week of the first sitting of the Parliament, he was acting and speaking as a fully qualified member; the earliest reference to his activity was on 10 November, 1640, when he made a relation of the state of Newcastle, Northumberland, and Durham, and concluded with an attack on the Book of Canons, suggesting that it should be burned by the common hangman.[22] There are, in addition, other traces of his speaking and participating on committees in the first month of the Parliament's life.[23] There is, moreover, a clear statement that the dispute was over the election of Melton; this was made when there was a motion for a new writ for electing a burgess in place of Melton who had died in the interval between the election and 17 December, 1640.[24] Melton does not appear to have taken his seat in the Parliament at any point; Blakiston first appears as a sitting member on 27 April, 1641 when he was appointed to the committee to consider the act for the reformation of abuses in ecclesiastical courts.[25]

Two further points about the election should be cleared up, namely the nature of Newcastle's two representatives, Anderson and Blakiston, and the extent to which the Scots may have interfered. It is misleading to talk as if Newcastle had returned at least one royalist in 1640. Anderson was later disabled from sitting in the Parliament as a result of joining the King's forces,[26] but to talk of him as a royalist or even as a moderate royalist in 1640[27] is to miss the point that the parties, if such there were, were not drawn in that year on the lines of royalist and parliamentarian; if anything, they were divided into reformers and non-reformers, perhaps even more explicitly into Straffordians and non-Straffordians. On this division, Anderson and Blakiston clearly form a pair, for Anderson's parliamentary career was consistently anti-Straffordian,[28] and even in 1648, he was still professing a moderate reforming faith when he wrote "I have alwayes conceived & still do, that the Regall Power ought to be limited by the Law: And if it be debarr'd of its due course in the execution thereof, God defend, but the people upon generall complaint should have remedy therein."[29]

The one point that remains to be cleared up is the extent to which Blakiston may have owed his election to undue influence on the part of the Scots. It was alleged in a pamphlet at the Restoration that he owed his seat entirely to their interference, and this charge has been repeated by later writers.[30] All suggest that this was to screen himself from paying £6000 which came into his hands as the executor to the executor of Sir John Farmer who had bequeathed the sum for charitable uses. While it is not impossible that the Scots did exert some influence on the election, several factors would indicate that this was unlikely. In the first place, the Scots were seemingly quite careful to maintain the good will of those Newcastle citizens who supported them. They plundered ruthlessly outside of the town, but they seem to have restricted their plundering inside the walls.[31] In the second place, there is some negative evidence. Not all hostile contemporary references to Blakiston mention the role of the Scots in his election.[32] Moreover, no comment about the Scots interfering in his election can be traced in 1640-1; this is especially notable in its absence from the manuscript address to the leaders of the Scottish army which was scattered in the streets of Newcastle. This document accused the Scots of many things, but influencing the elections was not one of them.[33] Finally, it is clear that Blakiston was no pawn of the Scots. He was later referred to caustically as one of the "little Northern Beagles" who cried out loudly against the Scots and their depredations in the North in 1644.[34]

Blakiston did not make initially as much of an impact on the House of Commons as his more experienced colleague Anderson. There are scattered references to him in the **Journal** during the remainder of 1641, but it is apparent that it was Anderson who was more deeply involved in the work of the House, both in minor business and in more major affairs such as the disbanding of the army.[35] Something of the relative respect accorded to the two may be indicated in D'Ewes's journal. On 30 December, 1641, D'Ewes noted a speech by Anderson on the present dangers; two weeks earlier when Blakiston had spoken on a similar theme, D'Ewes had recorded only that he "withdrew out of the howse whilest hee was in speaking, it being between one and two of the clocke in the afternoon."[36] Blakiston's parliamentary career, in other words, began in an unspectacular fashion once he had won the fight to secure his seat. It was not long, however, before he became the more active of the two Newcastle members.

The reasons for this do not seem too difficult to discern. Sir Henry Anderson had been extremely diligent during that period of the Long Parliament's life which was concerned with dismantling the apparatus of the Stuart state, with opposition to Straffordian policy, with the removal of Star Chamber, ship money, and the Council of the North. Once this work was completed, the unity of the House began to break up. The moderate reformers, such as Anderson, wished to hold to the constitutional position that had been created by the process of destruction. The radicals wished to push on with vigour and to attack, among other things, the position of the church. It is accurate, in some senses, to speak of the episcopal party which grew up to face this opposition, but it is also important to note that some men, such as Hyde, slipped into the royalist party in an attempt to preserve the constitutional position that had been reached.[37] There is some reason to think that Anderson's development was similar to this. Although he was not removed from the House until 1643, his activity there appears to have declined after the end of 1641. He continued to be appointed to a few committees,[38] and he twice acted as a teller, once in January, 1642 and once in May, 1643,[39] but it is apparent, even from a casual perusal of the **Journal**, that it was Blakiston who was becoming the more conspicuous of the two.

It is not possible to follow in precise detail Blakiston's parliamentary career. He did not keep a diary himself, so one is forced to rely on the official records and the mentions made of him by others. Evidently, he became recognized as one of the most belligerent of the war party, more outspoken than Pym who can be associated frequently with the middle group in the House.[40] Although his personal contribution to the money raised in June, 1642 for the defence of Parliament was not a large one, it is worth remembering that Anderson did not contribute at all.[41] On the other hand, Blakiston did advance a sizable amount for the Irish land venture in addition to the amount which he advanced for the town.[42] Even more indicative of his growing importance in the House is the increasing frequency with which his name is mentioned in the **Journal**. Between April and December, 1641, Blakiston had served on six committees to consider bills of various natures.[43] Between March and December, 1642, he had served on 17. In 1643, he served on 35 such committees, and by June of that year, he was acting as chairman of a more permanent one.[44] In 1644 the number of committees on which he participated increased to 44.

His extended activity in the House is further revealed by the fact that he became a teller in a division; significantly, the vote concerned a matter of religion and Blakiston's co-teller was Oliver Cromwell.[45]

Religion was one of Blakiston's chief concerns, and a number of the committees to which he was appointed in this period reveal that interest. He served on the committee to consider the act for reformation of abuses in ecclesiastical courts, on the Covent Garden Church committee, on one to consider depriving the bishops of their places in the House of Lords, and on at least eleven other committees whose concern was primarily religious.[46] Of these, the most significant was that for plundered ministers of which Blakiston became a member in November, 1644.[47] This committee had wide powers of dealing with scandalous ministers, of providing for the taking of the Solemn League and Covenant, and of dealing with questions of lay preaching, heretical doctrine, and preaching without a license.[48] Blakiston is also to be found asking ministers to preach before the House of Commons and giving the thanks of the House to those who did so.[49] There is further an almost certain connection between Blakiston and the general movement against some of the more unpopular clerics of Durham and Northumberland in 1642. On 25 March, 1642, it was ordered that the petition preferred by Blakiston concerning Durham, Northumberland, and Newcastle be referred to the Committee for Scandalous Ministers.[50] The exact contents of this petition are unknown, but it obviously concerned ecclesiastical matters, and it is suggestive that there are at least four petitions involving Durham and Northumberland clergymen which can be dated to about this time.[51] Blakiston's hand was no doubt strong in the decision to send for the Newcastle Arminians Alvey and Wishart as delinquents. Although the complaints against these two took the form of a petition by the burgesses and other inhabitants of Newcastle, Blakiston was one of the two men who attested the validity of the articles.[52] It also seems probable that Blakiston exercised considerable influence on the choice of representatives to the Westminster Assembly from Durham and Northumberland; the two Puritan preachers of Newcastle with whom he had had close contacts in the 1630s, Dr. Jenison and William Morton, were chosen to represent Durham.[53]

Blakiston's work was not, of course, entirely concerned with religion. At various points when the position of Newcastle closely touched the position of the Parliament, he played an extremely active role on committees. This is shown, for example, in June, 1642, when the town was garrisoned for the King by the Earl of Newcastle. He was then appointed to a committee on 20 June to consider information received from the town and to another on 27 June to consider the state of the business in the North. On 8 July, he reported to the House about arms and horses being brought into the town, while in September he is found propounding to the Committee for the Navy what ships were available and suitable to ride at the mouth of the Tyne to see to the defences of Newcastle.[54] Between the summer of 1642 and the reduction of the town in 1644, Blakiston is to be found serving on many similar committees. In October, 1642 he was one of those considering how two troops of horse might be raised and paid for in Durham and Northumberland. In December, 1642 he was on a committee to consider raising money for the supply of the North, and in February, 1643 he served on a similar committee, while in March he was attempting to secure the release by **habeas corpus** of several Puritans and parliamentarians who were imprisoned at Newcastle.[55] In 1644, he likewise appears on a number of committees dealing with Northern affairs and with the provision of coal to London. As a war measure, trade to Newcastle was prohibited as long as the town remained in royalist hands. It was fitting that when the town was reduced to Parliament Blakiston was ordered to bring in an ordinance for re-opening the trade.[56]

One can catch other glimpses of Blakiston's activities in these years. In 1643, he handled much of the business connected with the making of a new Great Seal for the Parliament.[57] Although he was more bellicose in his views than Pym, he is found on one occasion jumping to his defence by presenting information to the House against a Mr. Shawberry who had called the Puritan Leader "King Pym and Rascal."[58] Blakiston even attracted the notice of the Royalist newspaper **Mercurius Aulicus** as a result of his strong views on the position of the House of Commons. According to this account, Blakiston "lately told the Lower Members openly, that the Lords had been suffered too long to domineer, and we see (said he) how often they have been defective." Thus, the account concluded, "these two pretended Houses having graspt at all England as a Monopoly for themselves, doe now tug hard to defraud one another, the Lower stickling to heave out the Higher."[59]

The reducing of Newcastle to parliamentary hands opened a new phase in Blakiston's career. One of the most important tasks facing Parliament was to ensure the safety of Newcastle once that town was under their control. The lesson of the first Civil War had been well-learned; London's reliance on Newcastle for its coal supply placed the northern town in a unique relation with the capital, and it was apparent to all that the Newcastle trade must not be cut off again.[60] It is not surprising, then, to discover that Blakiston devoted an increasing amount of effort to the problems of Newcastle politics. It seems certain that the political life of the town continued to operate well within the framework of the old struggle between the inner ring of the Hostmen and Mercers and the rest of the freemen for control of corporation offices,[61] but Blakiston brought, or rather attempted to bring, to the local struggles the awareness of national politics which he had gained during his years at Westminster. Although he had served his town in Parliament, Blakiston had not held major town office before 1644. This was changed by the parliamentary ordinance disfranchising the mayor and others of Newcastle in May, 1645; by its terms, Blakiston was appointed an alderman.[62] He continued to play an active role in the House of Commons, but it is apparent that he was also devoting much of his time to the affairs of the corporation. His involvement in local politics became even greater in the following year when he was elected mayor of the town.

It is worth tracing Blakiston's local political career in some detail at this point. It should be admitted from the start that he was not in a position to be present in the town for any extended periods since his duties in the House of Commons precluded this. Consequently, he was never able to dominate its political life nor to bring it completely to the awareness of national politics which he had come to possess. On the other hand, he did take as active a part in the corporation's affairs as his parliamentary career allowed. In October, 1645 he was given leave by the House to go to Newcastle, obviously in connection with his election as mayor.[63] He was certainly still in Newcastle in the following January and cannot be traced as definitely back in the House of Commons before 11 March.[64] It is also very important to note Blakiston's further leaves of absence from the House. In 1646, 1647, and again in 1648 he was given permission to withdraw from the House near the beginning of September.[65] The only explanation for this absence at

the same time in successive years is that he was
returning to Newcastle to participate in the municipal
elections and to keep an eye on them. Thus it would
appear that even when he was absent from the town for
most of the year, he was determined to keep a close
watch over its affairs. On the one other occasion when
Blakiston was excused from the House, in March, 1648,
he does not appear to have gone to Newcastle.[66] But it
is probable that he was engaged on town business, for
two matters which closely concerned the town and on
which he is known to have been consulted were then at a
critical stage.

The first of these was the projected purchase of
the Grand Lease by the corporation. The fortunes of
the town were obviously closely linked to the
collieries lying within the manors of Gateshead and
Whickham, but the decision to sell church lands to the
profit of the state threatened the town's interest
there severely, especially since the Common Council of
London had decided after a stormy meeting to purchase
the manors themselves.[67] The expressed desire of
Newcastle to purchase the lease antedated London's
decision by two years, for as early as 1646 the corporation had exchanged letters with Blakiston on the
subject and had summoned the stewards of the town
companies to see if they would lend money for the
purpose on the security of the corporation.[68] The
agitation over the purchase had reached its peak in
March, 1648, and the town was able, with the aid of
Blakiston, to fight off the threat from London. A
strongly worded petition to the Lord Mayor and Common
Council of London contained an intimation that London
interference would lead to a disastrous interruption in
the coal trade,[69] and this appears to have worked.
Only a small portion of Gateshead manor seems to have
been sold outside the corporation, and at the
Restoration Bishop Cosin complained that the control of
Newcastle over the Grand Lease was so strong that no
episcopal profit could be extracted from it unless a
concurrent lease were granted.[70]

The second piece of town business on which
Blakiston was almost certainly engaged at this period
was the procuring of a new master for the Grammar
School. The master who had come to replace the
royalist Amor Oxley after the reduction of the town had
decided to retire. Blakiston's aid in securing a
replacement was eagerly solicited. It is well to
remember the importance with which the Puritans viewed
education. As the Common Council itself expressed it,

"the Scholes of this Kingdom have byn and are the Nurseries and Seedeplotts of Learninge and good Education."[71] William London, the Newcastle bookseller, expressed the other side of this picture in a well-known passage when he drew attention to the great interruptions to education which a period of disorder had brought to the North; commenting on "the present want of Studious Gentlemen" in the area, he concluded that "these Tempestuous Winds of a civil war" had made learning "too great a stranger to these parts."[72] Given these conditions and the general Puritan concern with education, it is not surprising that Blakiston took an interest in procuring a new schoolmaster. What is of more significance is the schoolmaster he attempted to procure, Hezekiah Woodward, a notable exponent of the importance of elementary education and a close associate of the advanced educational thinkers Hartlib and Comenius.[73] Blakiston's attempt to secure Woodward for the town broke down, apparently as the result of a dispute over the proper method of teaching Latin, but it is probable that Blakiston had some influence on the eventual choice of George Ritschel, a Bohemian refugee, since Ritschel was also a member of the Hartlib-Comenius circle.[74]

Blakiston did not turn his attentions to what were essentially municipal affairs only on the occasions when he sought leave of absence from the House to do so. There are frequently recurring references in the minutes of the Common Council to letters received from him, and it is apparent that he kept in close touch with the Puritan corporation. He also played a major role in the beginning of the Commonwealth agitation over the town's rights and liberties in the Tyne. These were to result eventually in the celebrated onslaught of Ralph Gardner in the 1650s, but the forces were already taking shape around the issue of Sir Henry Vane's ballast shore. The town had seen to the destruction of this, but Vane objected on the grounds that such action constituted a breach of his privileges as a member of Parliament. He was joined in protest by shipowners and masters trading to Newcastle.[75] If the references to this affair in the books of the Common Council are a true guide, Blakiston played an active role in combatting any attempt to break down the town's privileges. He may not have been acting in the long run in the best interests of the Tyne Conservancy, but he was acting precisely in the way a burgess loyal to the interests of his town was expected to act.

Blakiston's attention to local affairs overlapped with an interest in national affairs in connection with a new parliamentary election. After Sir Henry Anderson had been removed from the House, Blakiston sat as the town's sole representative. There were frequent demands, following the reduction of the town to parliamentary hands, that this situation should be rectified. As early as December, 1644 there were demands that writs be issued for a new election,[76] and in September, 1645 Blakiston himself indicated in a letter that these would be sent down speedily.[77] Nothing was done, however, and a year later Blakiston was violently attacked in the House for withholding the writs.[78] It seems clear that the accusation was, at least in part, true, but Blakiston defended himself by asserting that he had been acting in the best interests of the state. He argued that Newcastle was still full of delinquents and that an election would thus be dangerous. He seems to have won the House to this view; at least they agreed that no election should be held until after the King had been removed from the town. It is also apparent that he was not the only person who was blocking a new election; the mayor and other members of the governing body of the corporation backed him completely on this point.[79] In addition, it should be noted that the election was allowed as soon as conditions permitted.[80]

Blakiston continued at the same time to show a lively interest in national affairs. It seems certain that he was becoming more and more attached to the Independent cause; he was one of those who joined Speaker Lenthall in fleeing to the army at the end of July, 1647.[81] He was also gaining a wide reputation as a religious radical; in 1648 a newspaper rather unfairly referred to "Blakiston the reformed Pedler of Newcastle" as an "Anabaptisticall" sectary.[82] The judgment was based on his attitude to the bishops, for he had argued that since "the Bishops were set up here in this kingdom by a Law...therefore now the inconveniencie of them is found, they may be put down by a Law." Analysis of the committees on which Blakiston served between 1644 and Pride's Purge reinforces the view that he was still devoting a large part of his parliamentary time to matters of religion. He served on committees dealing with the sale of bishop's lands, with the abolition of deans and chapters and the sale of their lands, with the reconstruction of damaged churches, with the maintenance of ministers, with the determining of scandalous offences, with the problems of pluralism and division and unification of parishes, as well as a large number of other committees of a similar nature.[83] He continued to be asked on frequent occasions either to invite ministers to preach before the House or to convey the thanks of the House to them for their pains.[84] His stature in the House is likewise revealed by two major appointments; in October, 1645, he was added to the Committee for Privileges and in July, 1646 he became one of the conservators of the peace between England and Scotland.[85]

The final stage in Blakiston's parliamentary career was opened by Pride's Purge in December, 1648. The forcible exclusion of unsure spirits from the House was a necessary adjunct to the furthering of the revolution. Blakiston once again became the town's only representative; his colleague Ellison cannot be traced in the records of the House after the purge. It is of some significance that at this time the one clear radical outcry of the Newcastle corporation during the Interregnum can be heard. In October, 1648 the mayor, aldermen, Common Council, and other well-affected persons of the town set their hands to a strongly worded petition calling for speedy justice on all the incendiaries and actors in the Civil War.[86] The mayor, aldermen, and Common Council backed up this petition with an additional one of their own, arguing against a personal treaty with the King and rebuking the Parliament for being ignorant of their own freedom and birthright "which they are willing to sell for a Messe of Pottage, so that they may enjoy a Slavish Peace."[87] When one remembers these petitions and the enthusiastic welcome which the town gave to Cromwell in October,[88] it becomes apparent that Blakiston was not acting in a unilateral fashion when he participated in the trial of the King. Blakiston was one of the most active of those who sat in judgment on the King; he attended every meeting of the court, was present when the sentence was passed, and signed the death warrant,[89] but before one condemns him completely for this, one should remember two things. In the first place, the evident duplicity of Charles I was an ever-present danger to Parliament. If we accept the principles of government for which the Parliament was striving, we cannot condemn their action completely. In the second place, Blakiston was acting with the full support of the Newcastle corporation. Nothing is more damaging to Newcastle's reputation as a royalist centre than its reaction to the death of the King; after his execution, a letter from the town stated that the prevailing view of Charles there was that he was "not onely weak but

61

very wilful and obstinate, and for Religion, the
simplest of all carnal men of his principles in the
world except Doctor Juxon...nothing can we see in him
tending to a true Christian or the power of
godliness."[90]

In the months between Pride's Purge and his own
death, Blakiston became one of the most active members
of the Rump. He served on 37 committees from 13
December, 1648 to 30 April, 1649;[91] these included some
of the major bodies of the House, such as those for the
excise and the army. His active participation in the
affairs of the Rump Parliament raises the question of
his relationship with Sir Henry Vane the Younger, who
became in many ways the leading exponent of the Rump's
powers.[92] It is difficult to prove that Vane and
Blakiston had very close connections; Blakiston's role
in preserving the interests of the town against Vane's
father in the case of the ballast shore on the Tyne may
well have told against this. But there is one
reference which would indicate that his relations with
the Vane family were, in fact, close in this period.
The Leveller, John Lilburne, in the course of a typical
diatribe against the Vanes referred to Blakiston as
"one of Vane's creatures for the many thousand pounds
sake of the Common-wealth's money he has helped him
to."[93] One can conclude that Vane and Blakiston were
at least associated enough to become the targets of
similar attacks. Lilburne's bias against Blakiston is
obvious. One should place the statement in its proper
perspective, for it was precisely in this period of
intense parliamentary activity that the Newcastle
burgess came under fire from the Leveller leader and
more particularly from Lilburne's brother George.
These attacks contained two main charges, namely that
Blakiston had furthered the cause of delinquents in the
North and that he was busily stuffing his own pockets
with profits extorted from private individuals and from
the commonwealth.[94] This was not the first occasion on
which charges of double-dealing were levied at
Blakiston. John Musgrave, a disgruntled pamphleteer
whose reliability is far from being above question, had
made such charges in 1645 and 1647, but they had never
been substantiated.[95] It should be remembered that
Blakiston's family connections placed him in an awkward
position. He had a large number of delinquent relatives, some of them in the church, and there may be
some truth in the complaint that he went out of his way
to protect them. This appears, for example, to have
been the case with his brother Thomas, the vicar of
Northallerton. There is certainly a suspicion that

62

Thomas was, in his views, much after the likeness of his father Marmaduke Blakiston; certainly pre-war Puritan comment would suggest this. It is striking, however, that he was not removed from his post until well after John Blakiston had died, and the implication of protection is obviously present.[96]

It is impossible to assess with complete confidence the accuracy of the various charges that were made against Blakiston, but it seems plausible to suggest that most of them were false. The accusation that he had placed malignant preachers in livings in the North is highly unlikely in view of what is known of his own religious development, and, in any case, the three preachers who were specifically named by Lilburne in the attack were apparently appointed by order of Parliament rather than by direct action on Blakiston's part.[97] There may be more truth in the accusation that Blakiston had taken over some of the property belonging to his relatives in order to protect it from sequestration, but there is little evidence that Blakiston grabbed other property on dishonest terms. It was charged that he purchased Durham Castle as the result of shady dealing. This seems unlikely; it is not even established that he purchased it under any conditions.[98] The corporation of Newcastle was not convinced of the truth of the charges. They wrote to Speaker Lenthall in May, 1649 in defence of their burgess, pointing out "how it hath pleased God in mercie even in a declining age to preserve Mr. Blakiston in an acceptable way of sinceritie and faithfullnesse to ye commonwealth and how unapt he is to cramme himselfe wth ye riches of a ruined countrie or seeke after great things notwithstanding his many losses."[99] Final resolution of the matter was not achieved; in the midst of the agitation over the charges, John Blakiston died.

Some no doubt saw this as a judgment of God on a man who had dared to participate in the trial and execution of a king. This was hardly the view of the Parliament that he had served and the town he had represented. The former voted his widow and children a large sum of money in respect of his personal losses and in gratitude for his services; the latter likewise made a payment to his widow "takinge into their due consideracion his great paines and ffaithfulnes about their Occasions and the many good services he performed for this Corporacion."[100] The eventual collapse of the English republic and the restoration of the monarchy brought with it a blackening of the reputation of all

63

the regicides including Blakiston. Pamphlets such as
The Mystery of the Good Old Cause portrayed them as
dishonest, scheming, and unsavoury. Blakiston's own
town began to stress its royalist past and conveniently
forgot the attachment which it had once shown to him
and his ideas as well as the services which he had
performed for it in municipal politics, education, and
religion. The biased picture of these men, enshrined
in the Rev. Mark Noble's **Lives of the English Regicides**
which was published at the end of the eighteenth
century, continues to shape the reactions of many
people to them. They were, of course, determined and
often desperate men, engaged in the violent business of
revolution. Not all of them were, by any means, above
reproach; perhaps John Blakiston himself was not when
things came to a conflict between family interest and
the interests of the state. But to accept Noble's view
as the final judgment on Blakiston is to do a major
figure in Newcastle's history a great injustice. One
should remember the note written by a descendant of
Newcastle's regicide into his copy of Noble's book:
"This 'Life' is in every respect strikingly inaccurate
& cannot be depended on."[101] That judgment is
perfectly correct; John Blakiston was certainly a
regicide, but he was also one of the most active,
imaginative, and faithful members of Parliament to have
served the town.

APPENDIX

THE ELECTIONS TO THE LONG PARLIAMENT IN NEWCASTLE:
SOME NEW EVIDENCE

The history of the election of members to
represent Newcastle in the Long Parliament in 1640 is
considerably confused.[1] The original returns for the
election being missing, it is difficult to reconstruct
the sequence of events, although a number of attempts
have been made. It is known that there were three
candidates in the field: Sir Henry Anderson, Sir John
Melton and John Blakiston. The most plausible
construction on the basis of evidence hitherto
available was to suggest that Anderson was returned
unopposed, while Blakiston and Melton contested the
second place. Melton was declared the victor, but the
legality of his election was subsequently disputed; he
died before the issue was resolved and Blakiston was
then seated in his place.

This interpretation of the sequence of events is
confirmed by previously unnoticed comments on the
election recorded in a letter from the Scottish
preacher John Nevay to Lady Loudon, dated from
Newcastle on 19 October, 1640.[2] The letter is also of
some significance in assessing the political and
religious stance of the candidates in the election.
Anderson is not mentioned by name, but he is certainly
the anonymous successful candidate referred to who had
sat in Parliament before and was "against poprie but
for the power of godlines hath little of thatt." Nevay
goes on to record that for the other seat there was a
great contest between those "yt voyced for on Mr.
Blackstone" and those that favoured Melton. Nevay
notes that Melton had been made a burgess of the town
for the purpose of the election and that he contested
the seat with the recommendation of the Earl of
Northumberland. Melton carried a close contest by 60
votes.

Nevay's account considerably clarifies the story.
The sequence of elections is confirmed, and moreover,
the positions of both Blakiston and Melton are made
clearer than has been the case in the past. It was
alleged at a later date that Blakiston owed his
political rise to the backing of the Scots. It is
obvious from Nevay's letters that he had a general
sympathy for Blakiston, but there is no direct evidence

65

that the Scots took any steps at all to aid Blakiston
while he was actually contesting the seat. The story
of Blakiston's reliance on Scottish support can be
dismissed as a fabrication by later propagandists.[3] It
has also been asserted[4] that Melton, who had had close
contacts with Strafford in the past through his post as
Secretary to the Council of the North, was Strafford's
own candidate in the election. Nevay's statement that
Melton had the patronage of the Earl of Northumberland
would suggest that this view is false. It is
interesting to note that Nevay had hopes for Melton as
a supporter of the Scottish position. "He is ane able
man, & it is thot may syde with ye better p[t]." From
Nevay's comment, it would appear that the town of
Newcastle was even more solidly anti-Straffordian and
"reformist" on the eve of the Civil War than has been
indicated in the past. Anderson and Blakiston were
both strongly anti-Straffordian, but Melton apparently
was not so much an outsider to this attitude as his
previous connection with Strafford would lead one to
suspect.

The problem of when Blakiston assumed his seat in
Parliament still remains. However, in letters to Lady
Loudon and the Presbytery at Irvine, Nevay affords
proof that Blakiston was in London soon after the
assembling of the Parliament. On 16 November, Nevay
reported in letters to both that a communication had
been received in Newcastle from Blakiston "who should
have bein burgesse to the Parliament from this place."
In his letter, Blakiston, who had been observing
affairs at London, reported on the early activity of
the Long Parliament, including the petitions to set
Burton, Prynne, and Bastwick at liberty.[5]

66

1 For a fuller statement of what follows see R. Howell, **Newcastle Upon Tyne and the Puritan Revolution** (Oxford, 1967), pp. 125 ff. and **A.A.** 4, xlii, pp. 210 ff.

2 The letter is contained in a book of transcripts of letters, mainly from John Nevay to Lady Loudon and to the Presbytery at Irvine. The volume is now in the library of Princeton University (Gen. MSS. Misc. John Nevay). I am grateful to Professors Lawrence Stone and Elmer Beller for drawing my attention to this manuscript. On Nevay who was a Covenanter and nephew of Andrew Cant, see **DNB**.

3 I have discussed other evidence on this point in **A.A.**4, xlii, pp. 213-14.

4 Howell, **op. cit.**, p. 127.

5 The petition concerning Burton and Bastwick was read in the House on 7 November, **C.J.**, 3:22. A petition on behalf of Prynne was presented by his servant John Browne on the same day. J. Rushworth, **Historical Collections** (London, 1706), 3:250.

NOTES

1. J. Fenwick, **Christ Ruling in the Midst of His Enemies** in Richardson, **Historical Reprints** (Newcastle, 1847-9), vol. 1, p. 9.

2. W. Lithgow, **A True Experimental Relation upon the Siege of Newcastle** (London, 1645), p. 14.

3. R. Astell, **Vota non Bella** (Gateshead, 1660), p. 7.

4. M.H. Dodds, ed., **Extracts from the Newcastle upon Tyne Council Minute Book 1639-1656** (Newcastle, 1920), pp. 27-29.

5. Bod. Clarendon MSS, State Papers 26, fols. 118-118v. This account of military proceedings in the North between 1642 and 1645 was apparently written by Marley in about 1648.

6. **The Parliament Resolution for the Speedy Sending of an Army to the North, also the True Relation of a Fight Performed at Newcastle** (London, 1642), p. 2; **Sir John Hothams Resolution whereunto is annexed Joyfull Newes from Newcastle** (London, 1642), sig. A 4v.

7. **LJ** 5: 170.

8. It has been stated, as in **A.A.**[4], xviii, p. 67, that he was the son of Sir William Blakiston of Gibside, but this is incorrect. John Blackiston of Gibside died in 1647 when the future regicide was obviously still alive. See H.M. Wood, ed., **Wills and Inventories from the Registry at Durham**, pt. iv (Durham, 1929). Surtees Soc., vol. 142, p. 307.

9. P. Smart, **A Catalogue of Superstitious Innovations Brought into Durham Cathedral** (London, 1642), pp. 31-32; **Articles of Impeachment Proved upon Oath before the Lords delivered in writing by Nicholas Hobson and Robert King** (London, 1642), p. 24.

10. G. Ornsby, ed., **The Correspondence of John Cosin** (Durham, 1869-1872), Surtees Soc., vols. 52, 55, 1: 185. Marmaduke Blakiston's daughter Frances had married Cosin in 1626.

68

11. **A.A.**[4], xli, pp. 143-147; W.H.D. Longstaffe, ed., **The Acts of the High Commission Court within the Diocese of Durham** (Durham, 1858), Surtees Soc., vol. 34, pp. 155-167.

12. MSS Butchers' Co. Minute Book 1626-1722, f. 157; MSS Soc. Antiq. Newcastle, M 13/D 10, f. 45.

13. See W.A. Taffs, **The Borough Franchise in the First Half of the Seventeenth Century** (London M.A. thesis, 1926, unpublished. Bod. MS Eng. Hist. d. 233), pp. 305-306.

14. **Perfect Occurrences of Every Daie Journall in Parliament**, no. 14, 2-9 April, 1647, p. 107, for example, refers to "a great meeting of the whole body of Freemen, for the choosing of a Burgess to sit in Parliament." **Moderate Intelligencer**, no. 142, 2-9 December, 1647, p. 1051 gives the electorate as 361, while a newsletter of 1659 gives it as 1239. C.H. Firth, ed., **The Clarke Papers** (London, 1891-1901), 3: 174.

15. **A.A.**[4], xxiii, p. 139.

16. **The Mystery of the Good Old Cause Briefly Unfolded** (London, 1660), p. 4.

17. **DNB**, s.v. Melton, Sir John.

18. H. Hornby, "An Attempt towards Some Account of the Ancient and Present State of the Town of Newcastle," MSS Duke of Northumberland 187/A202, f. 87, citing **Old Parliamentary History**, 9:35.

19. **Returns of the Names of Every Member Returned to Serve in Each Parliament** (London, 1878), 1: 491 and n.

20. W.W. Bean, **The Parliamentary Representation of the Six Northern Counties of England** (Hull, 1890), pp. 564-565.

21. M.F. Keeler, **The Long Parliament** (Philadelphia, 1954), p. 59 suggests, for example, that there were two returns, one naming Anderson and Melton, the second naming Blakiston and one of the other two. See also D. Brunton and D.H. Pennington, **Members of the Long Parliament** (London, 1954), pp. 61-62, 202.

22. Bod. MS Film 39, Diary of Thomas Peyton, p. 9; Cambridge Univ. Library, MS Kk.vi. 38, p. 28.

23. **CJ** 2: 39; J. Rushworth, **Historical Collections** (London, 1659-1701), pt. iii, vol. 1: 66; Bod. Rawlinson MS C 956, fols. 35, 62v, 73; Sir S. D'Ewes, **Journal**, ed., W. Notestein (New Haven, 1923), pp. 25, 43, 51, 56, 73, 81.

24. **CJ** 2: 53; Rushworth, **Historical Collections**, pt. iii, vol. 1: 120.

25. **CJ** 2: 128.

26. **CJ** 3: 227 (4 September, 1643); he was appointed to a committee as late as 7 August 1643. **Ibid.**, 3: 196.

27. Brunton and Pennington, **Members of the Long Parliament**, pp. 62, 126, use both terms.

28. This judgment is based on an analysis of the committees on which Anderson served. He moved a series of charges against Strafford on 21 November, 1640. D'Ewes, **Journal**, ed., Notestein, pp. 51, 539.

29. H. Anderson, **A Meanes to Reconcile the Present Distempers of these Times** (London, 1648). He expressed somewhat similar views in 1643. **HMC 5th Report**, appendix, p. 115.

30. **The Mystery of the Good Old Cause**, p. 4; **The History of King Killers or the Fanatick Martyrology** (London, 1720), vol. 1 (June), p. 77; M. Noble, **The Lives of the English Regicides** (London, 1798), 1: 91.

31. **A Letre from an Alderman of Newcastle Shewing in Part the Grievances There** in Richardson, **Reprints**, vol. 1, pp. 8-9.

32. See **The True Character of the Educations, Inclinations, and Several Dispositions of all Those Judges upon the Life of Our Late King** (London, 1660), p. 2.

33. Bod. Tanner MS 65, fols. 37-38v. The earliest reference I have traced to the Scots' interference is in 1648. **A List of the Names of the Members of the House of Commons** (London, 1648), **BL** 669 f. 12 (103).

34. "Memoirs of Holles" in F. Maseres, ed., **Select Tracts Relating to the Civil Wars** (London, 1815), 1: 227-228.

35. **CJ** 2: 84, 153, 172.

36. Sir S. D½Ewes, **Journal**, ed., W.H. Coates (New Haven, 1942), pp. 300, 364.

37. On this point, see B.H.G. Wormald, **Clarendon** (Cambridge, 1951), pt. 1.

38. For example, to the Committee for Ireland in April, 1643. **CJ** 3: 47.

39. **Ibid.**, 2: 366; 3: 102.

40. J.H. Hexter, **The Reign of King Pym** (Cambridge, Mass., 1941), p. 20, n. 30.

41. Bod. Tanner MS 63, f. 59. Blakiston advanced £50.

42. **C.S.P. Ireland, Adventurers 1642-59**, p. 76; Keeler, **Long Parliament**, p. 109.

43. The following figures are taken from **CJ, passim.** They include comittees to consider bills as well as more permanent bodies such as the Committee of Adventurers for the reducing of Newcastle.

44. **CJ** 3: 146. The committee is simply referred to as Blakiston's committee. There is another reference to it **ibid.**, 3:315. It is possible that it was the committee for sorting petitions of which Blakiston was certainly chairman in December, 1644. **Ibid.**, 3: 723.

45. **Ibid.**, 2: 470. The vote concerned a lecturer for St. Giles in the Fields.

46. **Ibid.**, 1: 128; 2: 191, 467, 816, 893, 895; 3: 37, 60, 271, 340, 470, 579, 699, 705.

47. **Ibid.**, 3: 699, **BL** Add. MSS 15669, f. 1v.

48. On its work, see W.A. Shaw, **A History of the English Church during the Civil Wars and under the Commonwealth** (London, 1900), 2: 194ff.

49. **CJ** 3: 182, 639, 642.

50.   Ibid., 2: 496.

51.   The Petition and Articles Exhibited by the
Parishioners of Pont Island and Others in Northumberland against Dr. Gray (London, 1642); The Petition of
the Parishioners of Ackeliffe, Durham (London, 1642); A
Most Lamentable information of Part of the Grievances
of Mugleswick Lordship (London, 1642); The Petition of
John Salvin (London, 1642).   The last petition can
almost certainly be dated in March, 1642. The Mugleswick petition is somewhat earlier; the incumbent
Bradley was sent for as a delinquent 22 February. CJ
2: 449.

52.   CJ 2: 127, 128, 151, 636.

53.   A Catalogue of the Names of the Divines
Approved of by the House of Commons for each County in
England and Wales (London, 1642), sig. A 2v.

54.   CJ 2: 638, 646, 657, 776.

55.   Ibid., 2: 806, 895, 985, 996-997.

56.   Ibid., 3: 690.

57.   Ibid., 3: 226, 269; BL Stowe MS 184, f. 58.

58.   CJ 2: 478.

59.   Mercurius Aulicus, no. 29, 20 July, 1644,
p. 1088.

60.   The price of coals in 1643 had risen to 20s.
above the legal price by May. Mercurius Aulicus, no.
21, 21-27 May 1643, p. 277.   The dangers were well
pointed out by Alderman Adams of London, CJ 3: 171.
See also the comments in Artificiall Fire or Coale for
Rich and Poore (London, 1642) and in Sea-Coale, Char-
coale, and Small-Coale (London, 1643).

61.   The desires for a limited extension of town
government had been expressed earlier by Henry
Sanderson, customer of the port in the 1590s and during
the Shrove Tuesday riots in 1633.

62.   LJ 7: 395.

63.   CJ 4: 306.

64. He wrote a letter from Newcastle to the House in January. **Ibid.**, 4: 403. On 11 March, his presence in the House was recorded. **Ibid.**, 4: 472. In April, a deputy mayor, Henry Dawson, was appointed in his place. Dodds, **Council Book 1639-56**, pp. 62-63.

65. **CJ** 5: 286, 663; 6: 20.

66. He was given leave on 9 March; he was again present in the House on 20 March. **Ibid.**, 5: 489, 505.

67. **The Kingdomes Weekly Account of Heads of Chiefe Passages in Parliament**, no. 9, 1-8 March, 1647/8, p. 68.

68. Newcastle Council Book, 1645-50, fols. 75, 82-83.

69. Dodds, **Council Book 1639-56**, pp. 86-87.

70. Several parcels of Gateshead manor were sold to James Baylis in April, 1648, for £63.15.10. **BL Add. MSS 9049**, f. 6v. For Cosin's fears, see Ornsby, **Correspondence of Cosin**, 2: 94.

71. Dodds, **Council Book 1639-56**, p. 60.

72. W. London, **A Catalogue of the Most Vendible Books in England** (London, 1658), sig. B 1-1v.

73. **DNB**, s.v. Woodward, Hezekiah; A. Wood, **Athenae Oxonienses** (London, 1813-20), 3: 1034-1037; Newcastle Council Book 1645-50, f. 227.

74. Ritschel had acted as Comenius's literary agent. There is a good account of his career before he came to Newcastle in R.F. Young, **A Bohemian Philosopher at Oxford in the Seventeenth Century** (London, 1925). See also below, Chap. x.

75. On Vane's case, see R. Gardner, **England's Grievance Discovered in Relation to the Coal Trade** (Newcastle, 1796), p. 57; Newcastle City Archives, Foreshore Case Documents, Box 49, 7/40-45, 47-49; **PRO SP** 16/492/37; **CJ** 4: 461; Newcastle Council Book 1639-56, fols. 91v.-92, 95, 96-96v; Council Book 1645-50, fols. 58, 61.

76. **CJ** 3: 715.

77. **C.S.P. Dom.**, 1645-7, p. 124, 9 September, 1645.

78. **BL** Add. MSS 10114, f. 18v. Diary of John Harington, 11 September, 1646.

79. **London Post**, no. 1, 14-31 December, 1646, pp. 4-5.

80. The election was temporarily delayed by an error in the wording of the writ. **CJ** 5: 86. When it did take place, the result was disputed and a second election had to be held before Robert Ellison was chosen. **Perfect Occurrences of Every Daie Journal in Parliament**, no. 14, 2-9 April, 1647, p. 107-108; **Kingdomes Weekly Intelligencer**, 20-27 April, 1647, p. 610; **CJ** 5: 255; **Moderate Intelligencer**, no. 142, 2-9 December, 1647, p. 1051.

81. Rushworth, **Historical Collections**, pt. iv, vol. 2: 755. On this incident, see S.R. Gardiner, **History of the Great Civil War** (London, 1911), 3: 334 ff.

82. **Mercurius Pragmaticus**, no. 35, 21-28 November, 1648, sig. Bbb 3v.-4.

83. **CJ** 4: 97, 211, 218, 275, 276, 425, 502, 516, 608, 719; 5: 84, 602; 6: 81; **LJ** 8: 359; 10: 471.

84. **CJ** 4: 36, 224, 226, 663; 5: 287, 545.

85. **CJ** 4: 300; T. Birch, ed., **Thurloe State Papers** (London, 1742), 1: 79.

86. **Moderate**, no. 14, 10-17 October, 1648, pp. 115-116.

87. **Ibid.**, p. 120.

88. B. Whitelocke, **Memorials of English Affairs** (Oxford, 1853), 2: 429, 431.

89. J. Nalson, **A True copy of the Journal of the High Court of Justice for the Tryal of K. Charles I** (London, 1684), p. 129. According to Nalson's list, only four others (J. Carew, Sir J. Danvers, A. Scroop, H. Smith) attended all the sessions and signed the warrant.

90. **Moderate**, no. 30, 30 January-6 February, 1649, pp. 295-296.

91. **CJ** 6: **passim.** There appears to be some overlapping in these appointments and the actual number of effective committees on which he served may be somewhat smaller.

92. On Vane, see R. Howell, "Sir Henry Vane the Younger and the Politics of Religion," **History Today,** 1963, pp. 275-282.

93. J. Lilburne, **The Legall Fundamentall Liberties of the People of England** (London, 1649), p. 19.

94. Much of the following is based on **To every individual member of the honorable House of Commons, the Humble Remonstrance of George Lilburne** (n.p., 1649). This was answered by T. Shadforth, **Innocency Modestly Vindicated** (London, 1649); T. Saunders, **An Additional Answer to a Pamphlet Called a Remonstrance written by Mr. George Lilburne** (n.p., 1649); **The Vindication of Edward Colston to a Most False and Scandalous Remonstrance** (London, 1649).

95. J. Musgrave, **A Word to the Wise** (London, 1645), p. 5; J. Musgrave, **A Fourth Word to the Wise** (London, 1647), p. 2.

96. Thomas Blakiston did, however, claim to have parliamentary sympathies. See A.G. Matthews, ed., **Walker Revised** (Oxford, 1948), p. 389.

97. Shadforth, **Innocency Modestly Vindicated,** p. 7.

98. Colston who was supposed to have aided in the transaction utterly denied it and queried whether Blakiston had made the purchase. **Vindication of Colston,** p. 6. In the records of the sale of bishops' lands, it is noted as being sold to Thomas Andrews, Lord Mayor of London in May, 1649. **BL** Add. MSS 9049, f. 16.

99. Bod. Tanner MS 56, f. 22.

100. **CJ** 6: 280; Dodds, **Council Book 1639-56,** pp. 107-108.

101. This copy of Noble, which formerly belonged to the Rev. R. Blakiston, is owned by K.V. Thomas, St. John's College, Oxford.

V

MONOPOLY IN THE TYNE VALLEY:
THE CASE OF THOMAS CLIFFE

Agitation over the rights and privileges which the town and county of Newcastle exercised in the Tyne Valley was already a well-established practice by the middle of the seventeenth century. The town claimed rights in the river from Sparhawk to Hedwin Streams, or from the mouth of the river to a point well above the town. These claims rested firmly on a frequently confirmed charter which had been granted by King John. Their monopoly rights within that jurisdiction were based on a statute of 1529 which provided that no merchandize could be shipped or delivered within the river except at Newcastle. Claims such as these had always been disputed by rivals to the power of the Newcastle oligarchs. Before the Reformation, the Prior of Tynemouth had repeatedly asserted that the priory had the right to carry on its own shipping at adjacent North Shields. The Bishop of Durham had established a conflicting claim as early as 1393 when a royal charter had confirmed his rights to half the river with the power to load and unload. The growth of the coal trade and the consequent increase in the amount of shipping in the river and port greatly intensified the dispute, and the general reaction against monopolistic practices which was a feature of the seventeenth century added to the complaints against the town of Newcastle; the early part of the century was marked by a series of law suits which called into question the town's rights in the river. These suits culminated in the **Quo Warranto** proceedings against the town in the fourth year of the reign of Charles I. The town, however, was able to withstand these charges because of the buttress of chartered privileges which had been accumulated. Even legal defeat did not, however, stem the attacks of those who questioned the Newcastle monopoly, and during the confused period of the Civil War and the Commonwealth, agitation flared once again. The best known example of this is the spirited attack of the Chirton brewer, Ralph Gardner, who repeatedly petitioned the central government to call in the charters of Newcastle and thus break their monopoly; he published a scathing attack on the town entitled **England's Grievance Discovered in Relation to the Coal Trade.** He was not, however, alone in making his attacks, and was, in fact, preceded into the battle by a humble shipwright of

Shields, Thomas Cliffe. Although Cliffe's struggle often has been overlooked, it formed an important part of the seventeenth century battle for the right to exercise a trade freely in the Tyne Valley.

Cliffe was not a native of the Tyne Valley. He had come to Shields from Ipswich where he had served as an apprentice to one Robert Bull, a shipwright. Having, as he put it, "attained to some measure of perfection in his trade," he attempted to set himself up in business in Shields. In attempting to do so, he soon found himself in severe difficulties with the Newcastle corporation and the Newcastle Company of Shipwrights which claimed to have the sole privilege of that trade within the town and port; one should remember that they defined the limits of the port as extending from the mouth of the Tyne to some miles above Newcastle. Cliffe's first and major struggle with the corporation stemmed from an incident in 1646. The town's River Court Books record the affair in prosaic fashion. On 23rd March, he was summoned to appear along with two others at the next meeting of the court. On 6th April, he appeared and was ordered to pay a fine. The case was actually far more spectacular than these brief mentions would suggest; this is shown in the fuller accounts of it which were given by Cliffe's follower, Ralph Gardner. Gardner quoted in his book the deposition given by Henry Harrison, the master of a ship which was cast on the rocks near Tynemouth Castle during a storm. The master managed to get ashore with some difficulty and secured the aid of Cliffe and three of his men "to save the said ship from perishing, which ship had been quite lost if the said master should have run to Newcastle to have agreed with the free carpenters, whose excessive rates and demands often surmount the value of the ship in distress and their tediousness in coming and going that distance [means] that often the ships in distress are quite lost."

Cliffe and his men were able to save the ship. They got her off the rocks, brought her to the lower end of North Shields and laid her on the sand to mend her. While the three carpenters were at work on the ship, watched by Cliffe's wife and daughter, a deputation from the town of Newcastle arrived, led by two sergeants of the town and a number of free carpenters. They came with purpose "to seize upon all the aforesaid workmen for daring to save any ship from sinking in that river, with command to carry them to prison." As the men were being carried away, the two

77

women, who had been watching, began to vilify the
Newcastle officers whereupon "Thomas Rutter with a club
by several blows upon Ann Cliffe's body and head,
knockt her down to the ground; the other sergeant John
Hall by several blows with a rule or truncheon broke
Ann Wallice her arme." The incident attracted the
attention of some of the garrison of Tynemouth Castle,
and, as they came upon the scene, "both the said
sergeants fled to Newcastle where they were protected
from the hand of justice." The affair was a disaster
for Cliffe. His wife died from the blows that she had
received, demanding of her friends on her deathbed that
"as they would answer it at the last day, they should
require her blood at the hands of Rutter, he being her
death." The shipwrights who had been arrested were
kept in prison, and Cliffe himself was harassed by
legal procedures, forced to pay a fine for working in
the river while not being a freeman of the town, and
compelled to enter bond never to work in such fashion
again.

Cliffe did his best to bring the Newcastle
officers to judgment. He tried to bring the case to
law, having the officers of the town, Thomas Rutter and
John Hall, indicted; the indictment was found by the
Grand Jury, but the power of the Newcastle magistrates
was such that he could obtain no redress against them.
Cliffe was, however, a determined and committed man,
and he refused to give up the practice of his trade and
succumb to the pressures exerted by the Newcastle
monopolists. For its part, Newcastle could not let his
challenge go unanswered; consequently, they began a
suit against Cliffe and some others for violating the
privileges of the town by their continued practice of
the trade of shipwrights. Most of the other unfree
shipwrights who worked in the Tyne Valley did not have
the determination of Cliffe; the majority of them seem
to have given up resistance and to have compounded with
the Newcastle Company of Shipwrights. Cliffe, however,
proved to be far more obdurate. Possibly his resolute
attitude was due to the death of his wife; more probably, it was due to the fact that he began to receive
outside aid in the form of money from shipmasters who
traded to Newcastle and wished to see the monopoly
broken. The interests of these shipmasters were easily
apparent, for the Newcastle monopoly meant not only
possible danger to their ships in going up the river to
the town, but also highly inflated charges for services
rendered. The dangers in navigating the river as far
as Newcastle are too well-known to require any elabora-
tion; the inflated charges of the monopolists are

perhaps less well known. Henry Harrison provided evidence of this in testimony which he gave before a Committee on Trade at a slightly later date. He referred to a case when he had been in command of the **Apple Tree** of London which had lost its rudder as it came into Tynemouth harbour. He went to a freeman of Newcastle to ask him to repair it but was told that the charge would be at least 40s. even if Harrison provided the timber. He then went to Cliffe who performed the necessary repairs for a noble.

Cliffe, backed by the money and by the testimony of shipmasters such as Harrison, engaged in the legal battle with considerable vigour. The suit against Cliffe was heard in 1649 at Gateshead under a commission from the Exchequer Chamber to William Astel, Ralph Delaval, Ralph Gardner, and William Coulson. It is interesting to note that both Delaval and Gardner were later to emerge as significant foes of the Newcastle corporation over many of the same issues which were heard in Cliffe's case; both of these men served as members of the abortive Court of Sewers which investigated Newcastle's conservatorship of the river in 1659.

The arguments of the Newcastle witnesses were based on three main points: the chartered privileges of the town in the river, the rights of the Newcastle Company of Shipwrights to exercise a monopoly within that jurisdiction, and the assertion that breaking the monopoly of the town would be harmful to the whole nation. The first two arguments had a considerable degree of legal validity; they had formed the core of Newcastle's defence in similar cases since at least the sixteenth century. The third argument was more far-fetched, stating that if the monopolies which the town trades exercised were allowed to be broken, this would lead to the depopulation of Newcastle and eventually to an inability on the part of the town to pay the fee-farm and other duties. Ill-founded as it was, this sort of argument was to come to play an increasingly important part in Newcastle's defence of its privileges during the Interregnum. The arguments in defence of Cliffe were based largely on the utility of having shipwrights other than those of Newcastle resident at Shields. The deposition of Richard Hall of North Shields was typical of those which were offered by the witnesses for Cliffe. Hall testified that Cliffe had been at North Shields for about twenty years and that during that time he had practiced only the trade of a shipwright. He further stated that he had heard many mariners say that they would like to have Cliffe continue in his trade at North Shields. Several of the witnesses for Cliffe were willing to go a bit further in their argument; they argued that not only was it useful for Cliffe, and others like him, to be free to practice their trade at the mouth of the river, but also that the jurisdiction which Newcastle claimed was unfounded and that such jurisdiction properly belonged to the Earl of Northumberland. The witnesses also revealed (albeit on the most part reluctantly) that Cliffe was in receipt of outside funds in order to sustain his case against Newcastle. Richard Taylor, an anchorsmith of North Shields, stated that he had not contributed himself but that he knew two shipmasters who had contributed and that he had seen them pay Cliffe money on that account, although he could not remember the sum which had passed hands. The brother of the defendant gave the names of several of the people who had contributed. Not all of them are now identifiable, but it is not surprising to find that they were largely strangers to Newcastle and that at least one of them was a shipmaster who had been in trouble with the Newcastle River Court.

The aftermath of the hearing at Gateshead is not entirely clear. Ralph Gardner asserted that the trial was transferred to the common law to be tried at York during the Hilary Assizes in 1651 and that the verdict went for Cliffe. The mayor and burgesses of Newcastle denied in 1653 that this was so. Cliffe himself stated after Hilary term, 1651, that the suit was still pending and had been for six years. Although he claimed to have spent many hundreds of pounds, all that he had obtained was the judge's expressed desire that he should have liberty to follow his trade; since the Newcastle magistrates refused to give way on this, nothing was accomplished and the suit dragged on.

Cliffe's case brought clearly into prominence the question of the Newcastle monopoly in the Tyne. It did this both by the hearing at Gateshead and by the hearings which it stimulated before the central government. As Cliffe's case dragged on, the shipmasters who were backing him presented a petition to Parliament against the town of Newcastle. The petition was referred to the Council of Trade. The depositions that were taken there show clearly the conditions to which the traders objected: the incon- venience and danger of going upriver to Newcastle to cast ballast on the town's licensed shores, the decay of the river, and the delays caused to those who used

80

unfree facilities at Shields. By the time of these hearings in 1651, Cliffe's own case was becoming a thing of the past. But the hearings form an important link in the history of the agitation against the Newcastle monopoly. Cliffe himself appeared as a witness to testify to the practices of the Newcastle corporation and the damage that these practices had done to traders in the river and port. Another witness who appeared was one of the men who had heard Cliffe's case in Gateshead in 1649; this was Ralph Gardner who was to plague the corporation over this very issue for the rest of the Interregnum. Gardner, like Cliffe, was to draw to himself the support of the shipowners who traded to Newcastle, and the hearings in 1651 over Cliffe's case are the first clear example of Gardner's co-operation with this important source of support. This underlines once more the extent to which Cliffe was Gardner's most significant predecessor.

For Cliffe himself, the argument with the Newcastle corporation ended less happily. While Gardner took up his case, Cliffe, at last defeated, was forced to leave the Tyne. As he testified, "I dare not go home by reason of their threats to put me where I shall never see sun nor moone more if they light on me." Behind him, he left a sturdy record of individualist resistance to the monopolists of Newcastle, and for this Thomas Cliffe should not be forgotten by the inhabitants of Shields.

Note

This essay was originally published without footnotes and is reprinted here in that form. It is based largely on materials in the Newcastle City Archives and in the Public Record Office, as well as information contained in Ralph Gardner's famous attack on Newcastle, **England's Grievance Discovered in Relation to the Coal Trade** (1655). The relevant documents from the city archives have subsequently been published in R. Howell, ed., **Monopoly on the Tyne: Papers Relating to Ralph Gardner** (Newcastle, 1978); the introduction to this volume (pp. 8-11) contains an abbreviated account of Cliffe's case with full references to the manuscript material.

VI

THOMAS WELD OF GATESHEAD:
THE RETURN OF A NEW ENGLAND PURITAN

During the period of the English Civil Wars, the Newcastle region was singularly blessed by the ministry of able and devoted Puritan preachers: Jenison, Hammond, Sydenham and others successfully nurtured the growth of religious noncomformity in the region, and it was one of the lasting changes wrought by the period of disturbance that Newcastle became a centre of dissent in North England.[1] Among the Puritan clergy who labored in the area, Thomas Weld of Gateshead deserves special mention. A man whose career was significant enough to merit inclusion in both the **Dictionary of National Biography** and the **Dictionary of American Biography,** Weld was among the most prominent of that too little studied generation of Puritans who returned from New England during the troubles to involve themselves in the task of reformation in their native country. Though distinguished, Weld was also controversial. His own Gateshead parishioners came to comment that Mr. Weld, "assuming a peculiarity and inclosure of some donative and irrefragable power instated upon him by greater authorities, acts diametrically contrary to the constitutions of our own and all other Christian churches."[2] The American historian, James Savage, referred to Weld as a "virulent pamphleteer" and an "overcunning writer" resorting to the "sneaking device" of an "extraordinary instance of bibliographical disingenuity" for "a shield of his own cowardice."[3] The truth is that Weld, in an active career on both sides of the Atlantic, never shunned controversy, delighted in theological bickering, and was eager to strike out against any who deviated from the narrow path which his own theological convictions had shown to him. Persons as diverse as Archbishop Laud, Anne Hutchinson, Thomas Ramsay the False Jew of Hexham, and James Nayler the Quaker propagandist, were all subjected to his wrath.

Very little can be gathered about the early career of Thomas Weld, though the meagre information in the **Dictionary of National Biography** that he was born about 1590 in the South of England can be somewhat supplemented.[4] He was actually born in 1595 in Sudbury, Suffolk, the fourth son of Edmond Weld, a well-to-do mercer, and Amy his wife. Weld matriculated

83

at Trinity College, Cambridge, and was graduated B.A. in 1613/14 and M.A. in 1618. He was ordained deacon at Peterborough 1 March 1617/18 and priest the following day. He then served successively as Vicar at Haverill, Suffolk and Terling, Essex. Exercising his ministry in this school of English Puritanism, Weld followed the familiar path indicated to him by other nonconforming divines. The first few years of his ministry at Terling, which commenced about February 1624/5,[5] seem to have been relatively peaceful, and between 1625 and July, 1631, Weld and his first wife, Margaret Deresleye, were blessed by the birth of four sons.[6] But as Weld's theological convictions became more openly expressed and as the church at the same time attempted to enforce a stricter conformity to Laudian ideals, Weld's parish came to the attention of the clerical authorities. A paper survives in Laud's handwriting, dated 25 November 1630, and entitled "The Names of Such Ministers In Essex As Are Not Conformable;" included in this list is "Mr. Thomas Weld, Vicar of Terling."[7] During the next year, Weld was fined £20 by the Ecclesiastical Commission for an unspecified offense.[8] Weld was, in fact, to receive noticeably sharp treatment at Laud's hands. The records of the High Commission contain a brief summary of his case:[9]

> "An intimation was sent from this Court to be published in the parish church of Tarling that Mr. Welles should appeare heere this day upon pain of being deprived: An oath was made that it was soe published, and the intimation was likewise read to the Court, reciting that William Bishop of London had heertofore convented him and given him thereupon a canonicall admonition and tyme for halfe a yeare to consider whether he would subscribe, and that afterwardes the said Thomas Welles was not satisfied and being put to it whether he would subscribe he refused, that there upon he was excommunicate and afterwards was scited to appeare in the Consistory at Paules, and he came not and that therfore the Bishop of London was forced to complaine to this Court, and the Court sent this intimation, &c. which beeing heere read and testifyed upon oath to be published as was required, and the said Mr. Welles not appearing, the Kinges Advocate desired for this contumacy, he might be deprived, &c. Which by the unanimous consent and sentence

84

of the Court was donne: And a sentence ready
drawen was then read to that purpose."

The deprivation of 1631 impressed itself strongly
on Weld. Twelve years later, he made a special visit
to Laud in the Tower to berate him for what he had
done. Laud, writing of this latter confrontation,
commented on Weld in icy terms:[10]

"On Thursday, December 28, which was
Innocents day, one Mr. Wells, a New-England
Minister, came to me, and in a boisterous
manner demanded to know, whether I had
Repented or not? I knew him not, till he
told me he was Suspended by me, when I was
Bishop of London, and he then a Minister in
Essex. I told him, if he were Suspended, it
was doubtless according to Law. Then upon a
little further Speech I recalled the Man to
my Remembrance, and what care I took in
Conference with him at London-House to recall
him from some of his turbulent ways; but all
in vain: And now he inferred out of the good
words I then gave him, that I Suspended him
against my Conscience. In conclusion he told
me, I went about to bring Popery into the
Kingdom, and he hoped I should have my Reward
for it. When I saw him at this heighth, I
told him, he and his Fellows, what by their
Ignorance and what by their Railing and other
boisterous Carriage would soon actually make
more Papists by far, than ever I intended;
and that I was a better Protestant than he,
or any of his Followers. So I left him in
his Heat."

For the moment, however, Weld was in no position
to answer back to Laud. He appears to have gone off
briefly to Amsterdam[11] and on 5 June 1632, he arrived
in Boston to take up residence in the Massachusetts Bay
Colony.[12] Something of Weld's reputation must have
preceded him; he is known to have been in touch with
John Winthrop, Jr., as early as 1630/31,[13] and one of
Winthrop's correspondents had given him a lively
account of the excommunication and short-lived arrest
of Weld in a letter of January, 1632.[14] In any case,
within a month Weld had been established as first
pastor of the church at Roxbury. As John Winthrop
noted in his history, "After many imparlances and days
of humiliation, by those of Boston and Roxbury, to seek
the lord for Mr. Welde his disposing, and the advice of

those of Plimouth being taken, etc., at length he resolved to sit down with them of Roxbury."[15] In the following November, John Eliot, the noted apostle to the Indians, was joined with Weld at Roxbury as teacher.[16] It is interesting to speculate on the extent of Eliot's influence on Weld, for certainly the desire to foster the propagation of the Gospel among the Indians became one of the strong motives in Weld's life.

Within a short period, Weld established himself as one of the leading ministers in the Bay Colony, and in many of its affairs he played a prominent role. He was a zealous partisan in the fierce Antinomian controversy and took a strict line against the followers of Mrs. Anne Hutchinson.[17] Convinced of their errors, he attempted to change their minds; that failing, he railed at them and that failing too, he participated prominently in the trials of the Antinomian leaders. Weld was later to refer to the Antinomian controversy as "the sorest tryall that ever befell us since we left our Native soyle."[18] On the whole, however, Weld found the New World to be the Puritan paradise for which he had hoped. Like many of those who took part in the Great Migration, Weld wrote back to his parishioners in England to tell them of the joys of New England. In a letter of 1633, Weld described his Atlantic crossing in near-lyrical terms:[19] "In spite of Devills and stormes, as cheerful as ever, my wife all the voyage on the Sea better then at land...att sea my Children never better in their lives." And the Colony, so he urged his former parishioners, was just where the godly should desire to be: "Such groves, such trees, such a aire as I am fully contented withall and desire no better while I live.... I find three great blessinges: peace, plenty and health in a comfortable measure...I know no other place on the whole globe of the earth where I would rather be then here: We say to our freends that doubt this Come and see and tast. Here the greater part are the better part." Weld made his own contributions to seeing that the reality did something to match the propaganda. A person with an intense interest in education, he struggled to improve the facilities in the Bay Colony, and in 1638 he became an overseer of Harvard College.[20] He was also closely involved in the production of the Bay Psalm Book, the first volume printed in the American colonies. Inspired in part by a new metrical version of six psalms brought to Boston in July, 1638, by John Josselyn, Weld, John Eliot, and Richard Mather undertook a full metrical translation of the psalms to supersede Sternhold & Hopkins. **The Whole Book of Psalms Faithfully Translated Into English Metre** appeared in 1640, an important if not always, in a literary sense, a graceful production.[21]

By 1640, however, the affairs of the Bay Colony had attained something of a desperate quality.[22] Despite financial assistance from England and the immigration of thousands of people into the Colony in the 1630s, the Colony was becoming distinctly poorer. The balance of trade was unfavourable, the colonists having virtually no products to sell to the home markets. Supporters of colonization in England increasingly looked elsewhere in their financial ventures; the prospect of vast profits in the West Indies led many former supporters of New England schemes, like Lord Brooke, the Earl of Warwick, and Sir Arthur Hesilrige, to turn their investments southward away from the apparently profitless Massachusetts Bay. The flow of migration to the Colony slackened, and the reverse flow of emigration from the Colony began, intensifying the economic depression and endangering the Colony's credit. By the autumn of 1640, the Colony had begun to debate the idea of sending agents to England to seek financial support to protect the Colony's chartered interests and to participate in the reformation of church and state that seemed so imminent. There were those who argued that this was not a sound course; Winthrop opposed sending agents "for this consideration, that if we should put ourselves under the protection of the parliament, we must then be subject to all such laws as they should make, or at least such as they might impose upon us; in which course though they should intend our good, yet it might prove very prejudicial to us."[23]

By the following February, however the Court of Assistants had voted "to send some chosen men...with commission to negotiate for us...both in furthering the work of reformation of the churches there which was now like to be attempted, and to satisfy our countrymen of the true cause why our engagements there have not been satisfied this year...and also to seek out some way for procuring cotton from the West Indies, or other means that might be lawful and not dishonorable to the gospel, for our present supply of clothing, etc."[24] The agents selected were Thomas Weld, Hugh Peter, pastor at Salem and like Weld a Cambridge Puritan harried out by the Laudians, and William Hibbins, a prominent Boston merchant. The governor wrote to the Salem and Roxbury churches asking for the release of

Peter and Weld; though the Roxbury church acquiesced in this plan, there was marked opposition at Salem, both on grounds of state policy and on the grounds that it was unseemly to send ministers on such a mission.[25] The opposition at Salem, spreading throughout the Colony, threatened to create dangerous divisions and the plan was temporarily abandoned, but by the spring of 1641, with the economic situation continuing to deteriorate, the scheme was revived and once again Weld, Peter, and Hibbins were chosen to act for the Colony. The Salem objections being this time silenced, the trio hastened to depart. Since no ship was immediately available for England, they left on 3 August for Newfoundland to catch passage in the fishing fleet.[26] In Newfoundland they were again delayed for lack of shipping; both Peter and Weld used the opportunity to preach to the seamen on the island who, it is recorded, "were much affected with the word taught, and entertained them with all courtesy."[27] After three weeks passage was secured, and following a voyage which, according to Winthrop, was marked by foul weather and continual storms, the agents reached England.

It is important to understand the intentions of the agents. Though no known copy of their instructions survives it seems reasonably clear what the intentions of the Colony in sending Weld, Peter, and Hibbins were. They were to explain to the Colony's creditors why payments could not be made now as in former years; they were to secure what aid they could--in either money or supplies--for the Colony, for Harvard College, and for missionary efforts among the Indians. They were to seek any form of honorable support for the commerce of the Colony by approaching parliamentary leaders and other influential friends. Finally they were to further the work of reformation in the English churches. Though some authorities have denied that this was officially a part of their mission, the evidence of Winthrop's journal seems irrefutable on this point.[28] It is also indicative that Edward Johnson, writing in 1652, commented that Weld and Peter "so soon as they heard of the chaining up of those biting beasts who went under the name of spiritual lords" returned to England where "what assistance the Gospel of Christ found there by their preaching is since clearly manifested."[29] This specific part of their instructions was, in the long run, to prove fatal to their efforts as agents and was to change materially the life of Thomas Weld. That the Colony's confidence in its agents was in most respects justified is true enough; Weld and Peter were skilled controversialists and both were deeply committed to the ends for which they had been sent. Yet there was one chief difficulty; the Colony had not been quite clear in its own mind whether priority was to be given to the material or the spiritual parts of the commission. But the nature and inclinations of both Weld and Peter were such that it was nearly inevitable that they would be carried away by the work of destroying the Laudian regime at the expense of their other interests.

The England to which Weld and Peter returned in 1641 was vastly different from that which they had left less than a decade before. In September, 1641, the country stood at the end of a euphoric summer in which it seemed as if a revolution had been peacefully achieved.[30] Star Chamber, High Commission, ship money had all been destroyed. The architect of "thorough" Strafford had been curbed, and Laud was in the Tower awaiting similar treatment for his ecclesiastical policies. Yet already disturbing signs had come to the surface, notably in ecclesiastical affairs, and it would not be long before the triumphant forces, splitting among themselves, allowed the King to create a party, to draw the moderates like Hyde to his side, and to begin that slow, insensible process by which the country slipped into a civil war.[31] During those chaotic and confusing days, the agents began their work for the Colony. It is not necessary to follow out in full detail their efforts on behalf of Massachusetts Bay, but several points are important to note. In the first place, though there existed little effective parliamentary machinery for regulating the colonies, the agents were able to gain the Parliament's ear in an effort to remove restraints on New England shipping which had been imposed by a Laudian commission; in August, 1643, the Parliament declared all restraints removed from ships, persons, and goods bound for New England.[32] They also met with some measure of success in seeking money and supplies from wealthy friends of the Colony. During their first winter, they made contacts with donors of various sorts, mainly London businessmen who had invested in the Colony before. For example, a group headed by Robert Houghton, a Southwark brewer and former donor, gave £500 in cloth and other useful commodities. This was shipped in 1642 to the Colony, sold at a profit of £80, which was divided equally between President Dunster for the college and Captain Sedgwick, and the principal returned to England by the next ship.[33] But even in these early transactions, difficulties arose. In one attempt to raise

89

money Weld and Peter signed a bond for £110, and when the transaction failed, they were forced to pay the price of the bond out of their own pocket.[34] Still, by the end of the first year abroad, Weld and Peter had gathered nearly £2,000 in total for Massachusetts Bay, no small accomplishment in view of the chaos of the time.[35] But Peter first and then Weld began to find themselves drawn by inclination and temperament into the developing struggle.

The part which Weld played in the unfolding events of the war is very sketchily recorded, though there was no surprise in the fact that he vigorously espoused the parliamentary cause. Weld was active in the campaign to see that no accommodation that did not fully grant Puritan demands was reached with the King.[36] He played an active part in soliciting funds to transport children and orphans, many of them refugees from the Irish rebellion, to New England and succeeded in raising nearly £875 for this purpose.[37] With such a sum, it should have been possible to arrange for the transportation of about a hundred children, but unforeseen difficulties arose--delays in shipping, costs of clothing, medical expenses. Weld estimated that more than £300 of the fund was dissipated in such fashion.[38] In the summer of 1643, twenty children were safely transported and others followed. But over £200 of the money sent to the Massachusetts Court for the care of the children was misapplied, some £150 going to President Dunster of Harvard to defray costs of his house, £50 to John Winthrop, Jr., for expenses, and more to pay for soldiers to go to Providence in 1643.[39] Though the financial records are anything but clear, there is evidence to suggest outright fraud, especially in the case of the merchants, Emmanuel Downing and Nehemiah Bourne, who received some £712 according to Weld's accounts for the care and transportation of children and who appear to have pocketed some portion of this without any services performed.[40] As Weld reported in his account to the General Court in 1647, Massachusetts had "little benefitt by all these moneyes and lesse Considering how great trouble the Court hath had about it."[41] This was the unfortunate story of many of the agents' efforts on behalf of the Colony. They assisted John Winthrop, Jr., in attempting to raise funds to establish an ironworks in the Colony; Weld witnessed the agreement and appears to have invested in the project, but a whole series of unfortunate developments brought this scheme too to ruin, and William Hubbard was to write of it a few years later that "instead of drawing out bars of iron,

for the country's use, there was hammered out nothing
but contention and lawsuits, which was but a bad return
for the undertakers."[42]

There can be no denying that Weld was labouring in
unfruitful fields. In the first year, the good will of
friends had been substantially exhausted, and it was
felt that further efforts would require a more
strenuous campaign of publicity. Accordingly, the
agents persuaded President Dunster of Harvard to send
an account of the first commencement, a description of
the college, and a summary of its rules and regulations
so that they could demonstrate this was no paper
institution, as a similar college in Virginia had
turned out to be after its proponents had raised money
for it in England. In the winter of 1643, Weld and
Peter assembled this and other material sent to them
from the Colony, made some additions of their own, and
published the collection under the title of **New
England's First Fruits** in the early spring of 1643.
Here at least Weld did have some success. Following on
his plea that "all things in the Colledge are at
present, like to proceed even as wee can wish, may it
but please the Lord to...stir up the hearts of his
faithfull, and able Servants in our owne Native Country
and here... to advance this Honourable and most hopeful
worke,"[43] Weld secured £100 from Lady Ann Moulson, a
fervent Puritan and wealthy widow of a former Lord
Mayor of London. The donation was to be used for needy
scholars, and it became the first scholarship
established at Harvard College. Weld, it might be
noted, not only signed the bond for the money, but also
arranged that the stipend should go to his son John
"till he attain the degree of a Master of Arts."[44] In
conjunction with Peter, Weld secured perhaps an
additional £200 in books, money, and other supplies for
the college and the advancement of learning.[45] He had
less success in raising funds for the conversion of the
Indians, a cause to which he was personally deeply
committed. Despite an encouraging annual gift of £20
from Lady Armine, Weld could only solicit meagre
additional gifts for this purpose.[46]

By the late summer of 1643, it was apparent to
both Peter and Weld that their usefulness as agents for
the Colony, at least in a fund-raising capacity, was
nearing or at its end. In fact, they intended to
return in that year in one of the ships hired to
transport the poor children, but as Weld later wrote,
"providence appeared clearly to o[r] consciences to stop
us in o[r] way, more than once or twice: in o[r] ful

91

intentions and preparation for ye voyage putting such
crosbarrs in our way that in deed we could not with
good conscience break thorow them."[47] What exactly the
circumstances were, other than the fact that Weld did
not choose to risk a winter voyage, is not completely
clear, but it would seem that a major consideration was
the desire of Weld to participate more fully in the
parliamentary and Puritan cause in England. In a
letter which he wrote to the General Court in
September, 1643, Weld revealed the extent to which he
had become involved in the last of his commissions, the
work of reformation in England.[48]

> "The p^rsent condition of this kingdome,
> y^t is now upon the Verticall point, together
> wth ye incredible importunities of very many
> godly Persons, great & smale (who hapily
> conceive we by o^r p^rsence doe more good here,
> then we o^rselves dare imagine y^t we doe) have
> made us, after many various thoughts, much
> agitation, & consultation wth god, & men,
> vnwillingly willing to venter o^rselves upon
> Gods Providence here, & be content to tarry
> one six moenths longer from yr & o^r churches
> most desired p^rsence with whom o^r hearts are,
> w^thout the least wavering, fixed; Things can
> not long stand at this passe here, as now,
> but will speedily better or worse. If
> better, we shall not repent us to have bene
> spectatours & furtherers of o^r Deare Cuntries
> good, & to be happy messingers of ye good
> newes thereof vnto you. If worse, we are
> like to bring thousands wth us to you.

> "If yr selves were here & favor all
> things as they stand, & hard all argum^ts on
> both sides, we p^rsume you would advise, at
> p^rsent, not to disert the cause of Christ, &
> discourage so many 1000^ds at once, as will
> (say they) be weakned by o^r departure; The
> greatest Venter is o^r owne, but the Lord
> Jesus, whom we seeke herein, whose o^rselves,
> tallents & lives are, is able to carry us on
> Eagles wings, by the helpe of yr praiers,
> above all dangers & feares & bring us safly
> into yr bosomes wth a blessing by ye next
> Opportunity."

Even before he wrote this letter, Weld had joined
with Peter in contributing to the controversial
religious literature of the Presbyterian-Independent

struggle. It would appear that their inspiration came largely from New England, through their editing and publishing of works written by Richard Mather and others of their Massachusetts colleagues.[49] The New England basis of their efforts created certain difficulties. Particularly was this the case in regard to policy towards toleration. On this point the Independent ministers of old and New England differed sharply. While in England the Independent circles stressed toleration to win converts and to protect themselves from the Presbyterians, in New England Independent churches, the whole principle was abhorred. Peter managed to engage in this pamphleteering without unduly compromising his position or raising charges of hypocrisy. Weld did not; in 1644 he was induced by Presbyterian plotters to edit, with additions, Governor Winthrop's manuscript account of the Antinomian troubles.[50] The book, by emphasizing Congregational intolerance in New England, seriously compromised the Independent's position in England and emphasized the ambiguities of Weld's position in the Independent fold, an ambiguity which he was later to demonstrate at Gateshead in an even more spectacular fashion.

It was at this time that Weld undertook his last recorded major action on behalf of Massachusetts. Parliament had created the Earl of Warwick governor-in-chief and Lord High Admiral of all the colonies in America. At the same time they had created a committee of seventeen of whom a majority (defined as nine plus the Earl of Warwick) were empowered, in effect, to rule the colonies and to control their charters.[51] Within six weeks of the creation of the Warwick commission, Weld applied to it for a patent to the Narragansett territory. He appears to have been acting on his own, without direct authorization from the Colony, in order to forestall the efforts of Roger Williams, who had recently arrived seeking a legal basis for his government in Rhode Island. Weld did receive a patent on 10 December 1643, but it had been signed by only nine of the commission, and when Williams secured a charter in March of the next year, properly signed and sealed, the battle was lost.[52] Apparently Weld knew that he had been outmanoeuvered from the very beginning, since he did not send his patent to Massachusetts until 1645, and only then in an effort to show he had tried to counter Williams.[53]

Though Weld continued to oversee a few commercial transactions for Massachusetts, his services had come to an end. After the failure of the Narragansett patent, he turned over part of the Colony's business to John Pocock and other London friends of Massachusetts, and he urged the General Court that Pocock and his group be designated the official agents.[54] This was done in October, 1645, and at the same time a sharp note was sent back to Weld: "The howse of Deputies think it meete y^t as Mr. Peeters & Mr. Weld being sente ouer as persons fitt to negotiate for ye Countrye, having bine long absent desire they may understand ye Courts minde, that they desire their presence heere & speedy returne."[55] The tone of the note was indicative of the fact that misunderstanding and suspicion had come to characterize Weld's relation with Massachusetts Bay by 1645. From the Massachusetts side there was disappointment; the large collections of 1642 had raised hopes which Weld's efforts had not been able to satisfy. There was also a feeling that Weld had become so involved in the struggle between the Independents and the Presbyterians that he had been neglecting the real interests of the Colony. From Weld's side, there was great displeasure and mounting suspicion about the use which the Colony was making of the goods and materials being sent over. That the Colony misapplied the funds is obvious. Though the financial records are far from complete, there is ample evidence that the Massachusetts General Court persistently failed to honour contracts made by the agents with donors in England.[56] They acted in this way even to their closest friends, such as John Pocock. In 1642 Weld and his colleagues purchased cloth from him to the value of £150, agreeing to make payment within six months. The Colony sold the goods in question at a healthy profit, but neglected to transmit any money to Pocock. Weld and Peter repaid him £100 out of the money they were collecting for the Colony, but the remaining £50 went unpaid until 1656, much to Pocock's irritation and Weld's discomfiture.[57] Situations of this sort led to charges against Weld and Peter of embezzling the funds. To attempt to clear themselves, they opened their accounts to public inspection at John Pocock's shop in Watling Street, but even if they could show what they had done with the money, they could not account for what had happened to it after it had left their hands.[58] In part, the confusion was procedural; there was no real system for transferring money and supplies to the colonies, and Massachusetts Bay did not appoint its first auditor of accounts until October, 1645, after Weld had been discharged.[59] But the trouble was also clearly connected with the role that Weld had played in the Independent-Presbyterian struggle. It seems clear that the most vociferous English critics

94

were London Presbyterians, seeking to discredit Weld and Peter, and through them, the Independent cause. It is suggestive that the charges of embezzlement came largely from the pen of that cantankerous Presbyterian, Thomas Edwards, and appeared first in his **Gangraena**.[60] It is suggestive too that Weld identified a major group of his critics as being "divers ministers who used to meet at Sion College."[61]

Though Weld did his best to clear his name and bury these accusations, they followed him to Gateshead. The whole affair was renewed with considerable bitterness in 1649 at the time when the New England Company was being organized. This parliamentary effort, a companion piece to the Commission for Propagating the Gospel in Wales and in the northern counties, was better conceived than the solo efforts of Weld and Peter, and it had a wide parliamentary backing. But the new corporation found it difficult to raise contributions at the start because the old tales of embezzlement by the Weld-Peter mission were revived. William Steele, the president, wrote to the Commissioners of the United Colonies, saying that their work had been made difficult because of "the ill management of former gifts bestowed on ye Countrey of New England of which no account hath been given to ye donors and som personally Reflecting upon Mr. Wells and Mr. Peters, som upon our selves the Corporation as if wee had so much per pound of what is collected and might feast our selves liberally therwith wheras through mercy wee never yet eat or drank of the fruit or charge of yt."[62] Weld tried vigorously to clear his name; he sent full accounts to the Colony in 1645, forwarded a detailed relation of his efforts in April, 1647, and prepared a manuscript entitled "Innocency Cleared" for the press, but it was not until 1651 that the General Court finally audited and approved Weld's accounts.[63] His efforts and those of Steele on his behalf finally silenced his critics and cleared his name. As he wrote to Steele from Gateshead in January, 1650,[64] he was grateful for his "friendly, faithful and loving defense of me and Mr. Peter." The efforts, Weld maintained, had been worthwhile: "Glad am I that I have opportunitye hereby, to make my just defence to yo^w and by yo^w to the Corporation or to any others... that itt may appeare those guifts given for the good of Newe England were not in vaine...I am sure my Conscience knowes, and how much I am like to bee a looser will not see, yet I blame not those Godly Soules there in New England but looke higher and sitt downe contented if any way I have bene serviceable." Still,

95

when all was said and done, Weld was discouraged and somewhat cynical. Though still deeply committed to the goals of fostering the godly, improving Harvard, and converting the Indians, he closed his letter to Steele by stating, "I shall learne some points of wisdome, I hope not to meddle noe more in this."

This is not the place to attempt a full analysis of the result of Weld's and Peter's efforts for Massachusetts Bay. But it should be noted that they had some success. Under the most unpropitious circumstances, they had obtained reasonably large contributions for the Colony, the college, the poor, and the Indians. By lobbying Parliament, they obtained relief from the excise and other duties levied on the Colony's commerce. They helped to give to the Colony a prestige in England which it enjoyed at no other time in its existence. And they did all this without compromising the Colony's position in regard to its own charter, proceedings against which were stilled until the Restoration period. There was failure admittedly to forestall Roger Williams, but Weld missed success here by a narrow margin. As one historian has written, "No subsequent Massachusetts agents to England in the seventeenth century obtained so great material benefits for the Colony."[65] The real failure lay in a different direction, the instructions to the agents to further reformation in England. These efforts not only diverted them from their material task, but led them, and especially Peter, to points of theology and ecclesiastical policy which placed them at odds with the Colony and would, as Thomas Edwards pointed out, have caused the colonists to "trod them down as mire in the street."[66]

Though Weld saw his relations with Massachusetts Bay severed, he did not find himself at loose ends. He had entered too fully into the maelstrom of English events for that. He may have maintained for a period a clerical position of some sort in London. Edwards refers to him as halting "between Giles Cripplegate and New England, between Master Walker and the money for the poor children's sending over to New England."[67] In 1646 he served a short spell as rector at Wanlip, Leicestershire, and on 1 February 1649/50, he was installed at St. Mary's, Gateshead, where he was to serve out the Interregnum as a zealous supporter of the Cromwellian cause.[68] His arrival in Gateshead was a boon to the Puritan cause, even if it gave less comfort to a Presbyterian like Edwards, for Gateshead had stubbornly elected a delinquent preacher, probably

Elizason Gilbert, in 1647, and his anti-Puritanism apparently did much to encourage the malignants of Newcastle who were widely suspected of having a hand in his choice.[69]

Weld's career at Gateshead is noteworthy in two respects. In the first place, he displayed himself as a prolific propagandist of strict Puritanism and lashed out at the more left-wing sects, notably the Quakers and the Baptists. In the second place, his version of a gathered church created great tension in the parish, as he systematically excluded from full membership in the church any parishioners he suspected of being ungodly. This was to develop into a major confrontation between the parish and the ecclesiastical authorities in 1657.

It is interesting to note that although Weld remained in essence an Independent, some of his first published work while in the north involved editing sermons of Cuthbert Sydenham, who appears to have been in Presbyterian orders. That this could be the case illustrates the essential veracity of Sydenham's own picture of the Newcastle clergy of both Presbyterian and Independent persuasions working closely together.[70] The work in question was Sydenham's **Hypocrisy Discovered in its Nature and Workings**, which was published in 1654 with a preface by Weld. Weld displayed there some of his characteristic attitudes. He indulged in sharp attacks on Quakers and Arminians and criticized those who "alledging to be scandalized by your walkings are turned to embrace the gross abominations of popery."[71] More than a hint of the stress on Puritan morality which swept the Newcastle region in the 1650s is indicated in Weld's mention of "the loathsome fashions of many of you with powdered haire, painted faces, naked breasts and such phantastick garbes, that yet would go for choice Saints and Christians."[72] Weld also included a warm tribute to his fellow preacher, indicating he was capable of praise as well as vituperation: "You may see his tender bowels towards the poorest soules under any of the workings of God, his unwearied paines, even to the visible wasting of his owne bodily strength in the work of the Ministery, and his great care over the flock over which the Holy Ghost had made him overseer, all of these did bespeake him a vessell fitted for his Master's use, and it is not unknown to those in chiefest places his otherwise usefulness to the people of God in

this nation. Thus did he serve his generation with
these many talents his God had furnished him with."[73]

The spirit of co-operation with other local clergy
manifested here was typical of Weld's literary
productions while at Gateshead. He seldom wrote alone
but most often in conjunction with his two closest
ecclesiastical colleagues, Samuel Hammond and William
Durant, and in particular they joined together to
resist the Quakers and the Baptists. It is significant
that a large proportion of the books published in
Newcastle in this period fell into this category of
controversial writings: just under one-half the books
published in the town between 1652 and 1662 were
concerned with the Quakers and the Baptists, and in
1653, when more books were published in Newcastle than
in any other year during the Interregnum, all five of
them meet this description.[74] It is not necessary here
to trace out the shadowy beginnings of Baptism in the
Tyne Valley, but one incident which closely involved
Weld deserves discussion.[75] This was the bizarre
episode of the False Jew.[76] The Baptist preacher in
Hexham, Thomas Tillam, had proudly proclaimed the
conversion of a Jew, Joseph ben Israel, to the Baptist
faith. The convert turned out to be, however, a
Scottish Catholic named Thomas Ramsay. Ramsay had been
born in London, educated in Edinburgh and Glasgow and
then gone via Germany to Rome, where he had passed time
in a Dominican monastery and a Jesuit College. He had
then been sent by papal order on a special mission to
Germany where he had worked closely with the
Anabaptists. Returning to Rome, he was circumcised to
act like a Jew and then sailed from Hamburg to Shields
in 1652, using the name of Thomas Horsley. Under the
alias of Joseph ben Israel, he remained in Newcastle
for a short period, making some contacts with the
Baptists there before going on to Hexham to ensnare
Tillam. He had been sent north to create dissension
among the sects, and he succeeded admirably. Under
questioning by the clergy of the Newcastle region, in
which Weld played a prominent part, the whole shabby
story came out. Weld took an active role in
publicizing the story, notably in the tract, **A False
Jew**, published in 1653. The case allowed Weld and his
colleagues to indulge in two of their favourite games:
embarassing the extreme sects and warning against the
Catholic danger. "Deare Brethren," they warned, "keep
the doore strictly, let none come over the wall, nor do
not you breake it downe to let such in."[77] They
stressed that "this wretched Counterfeit told us that
the method of the Popish Emissaries at present in

98

England is to undermine the churches by closing with errours and crying up notions."[78] They argued against the danger of the Baptist reliance on the single ordinance of baptism; this, Weld argued, would undo all "for it will...make men under-valew grace in comparison of that ordinance."[79]

Weld and his colleagues were able to turn the affair into a highly successful assault on the Hexham Baptists. Ramsay was arrested and sent to London.[80] Tillam, despite efforts to defend himself in print, was locally discredited, and his relations with Baptist congregations in London severely strained. The "child of the devil...from Rome," as the Baptist records of Hexham refer to the False Jew,[81] had enabled the Newcastle clergy to cast Tillam into a position from which he and the Hexham congregation could not easily recover. Within a short period the Hexham congregation was split into two factions, and Tillam himself left, defeated, in 1656. The decay of the Baptist community, slow at first, became more and more rapid until shortly after 1660 they could write, "The church here began sadly to decline their duties, break off their meetings, and forget their Rock, whereupon miserable effects ensued to be their portion, so that most of them returned to folly...little of a (right) spirit yet remained in them to return unto the Lord."[82] Weld could congratulate himself that he, just as he had in Massachusetts Bay when faced by the Antinomians, had struck a crushing blow for the godly party.

Weld's dispute with the Quakers, though it led to a greater volume of paper, was less successful, in part because he faced a more formidable antagonist in James Nayler, in part because the Quaker community struck more permanent roots, aided in this by the patronage of Sir Arthur Hesilrige's crony and secretary, Anthony Pearson.[83] The techniques of attack by Weld and the Newcastle clergy on the Quakers were similar to those they employed against the Baptists: discredit their theological position and imply there were dangers of popery being raised. In **The Perfect Pharisee Under Monkish Holiness**, published at Gateshead in 1653, Weld and his colleagues set out to present a view of what they considered to be the doctrines of the Quakers. If the end product is a thoroughly distorted picture of what Nayler, Fox, Pearson, and others did believe, it still affords a picture of the enemy which the Newcastle establishment assumed it was fighting. It is hardly necessary to list the seventeen positions which they attributed to the Quakers and supported by quotations often violently ripped from context. Their nature is illustrated by the assertion that the Quakers postulated an equality of man with God. The principles with which they taxed the Quakers were a more accurate presentation; they were the same charges that so often provoked difficulties between the Quakers and the government, namely that they would not salute anyone, that they would not give any outward token of reverence to those in authority, such as magistrates and parents, and that they claimed no man should bear the title of master.[84] To Weld, the Quakers were new Pharisees, separating themselves from the rest of humanity "upon an account of a conceit they had of their owne surpassing holinesse."[85] The tract concluded with a typical appeal to the faithful to remain firm: "And now, Brethren, you, for the establishing of whose Faith in a speciall manner we have Published this, having forewarned you of grievous Wolves entring in upon you; not sparing but endeavouring to make havocke of the Flocke and of the Faith once delivered to the Saints. We commend you to the Lord and the Word of his Grace, which is able to build you up, and to give you an Inheritance amongst all them that are sanctified."[86]

James Nayler was not one to let such attacks go unanswered, and Weld and his colleagues soon found themselves in a virulent pamphlet war with the Quaker leaders.[87] In their second onslaught, **A Further Discovery of That Generation of Men Called Quakers,** published at Gateshead in 1654, they attempted to draw parallels between the doctrines of the Quakers and those of the papists, especially in connection with the doctrine of justification. "It is as claere as the noone day...that the Papall Apostasy and state is the Anti-Christ so often prophesied of in scripture. Now it is as plaine that the very distinguishing Doctrines and practices of these men are such as are the maine principles of that man of sinne in opposition to Jesus Christ."[88] The remainder of the argument was less imaginative and in the main was a repetition of their assertions in their first tract. Weld could take less satisfaction from this struggle than he could from his encounter with the Baptists. In characteristic fashion, Nayler got in the last word, and there is some evidence, notably in the visitation records of Bishop Cosin, that the Quakers had managed to settle themselves permanently in some places in Northumberland and Durham, including Gateshead.[89]

Weld was, however, diverted from these confrontations with the sects by difficulties in his

100

own parish.[90] In his attempt to establish a godly church, Weld began to cast out of his congregation those who differed from his New England, Independent views. A crisis was reached in 1657. By then it was alleged he had "interpretatively excommunicated and actually excluded above a thousand soules from the benefit of the sacraments, with out any legall proceeding, hearing, or sentence denounced against them in any civill or ecclesiasticall judicature, and have so kept them under the same penall suspention above eight years together, against the rules of law, religion and conscience; nor will indulge the favour of administering the sacraments to any of his parish, but to eight women and two men, weak and unstable persons, that are sublimed his converts."[91] The Presbyterian element in Gateshead, alarmed at this sort of Independent ascendancy and intolerance, demanded the establishment of a Presbyterian lecturer at Gateshead. The parishioners who complained stressed their willingness to undertake the charge of the lecturer themselves, "preferring their spiritual improvements before secular interest."[92] It is noteworthy that this petition for the installation of a Presbyterian lecturer was signed by all four serving churchwardens of the parish. They appear to have had in mind enlisting one of the Newcastle Presbyterians--Cole, Prideaux, or Knightbridge--until they secured someone on a more permanent basis. Weld, under pressure, seems to have agreed initially with this plan, but he then changed his mind and precipitated increased difficulties by withdrawing his approval. On 30 November 1657, his dissident congregation pressed him to sign an agreement which would have allowed a Presbyterian lecturer at Gateshead once a fortnight, with the administration of the sacrament once a month and a promise that he would not interfere in any way in the choice of the lecturer. He was further asked to disclaim forever any power of displacing the lecturer without the free and unanimous consent of the whole parish of Gateshead. It was Weld's refusal to admit the lecturer on these terms--and the refusal scarcely need occasion any surprise--that led in turn to the publication of complaints against him. A petition against him was presented to the Northern Commissioners on 3 March 1658; after they considered it, they returned answer that they were not empowered by their Commission to take cognizance of it.[93] Their verdict is not surprising. Weld was a prominent and respected person, who appears himself to have worked closely with the Commission. Moreover, he had powerful friends, including notably Sir Arthur Hesilrige, who exercised

101

great authority in this area. Weld had carefully cultivated Hesilrige as far back as 1654, when he stated publicly that God had made Sir Arthur "a terror to the enemies of his Son" and brought him "among us when his enemies were very high and turbulent" and had drawn out his heart "in being an instrument to procure the three yeares commission for propagating the Gospell in these foure Northerne counties."[94]

The upshot of the attempt to force Weld's hand was totally unwanted and unexpected by the petitioners. Not only was the petition disallowed by the Commissioners, but the whole affair appears to have been employed as a pretext for a purge of the four and twenty of the parish, a change affecting secular, as well as religious, administration. Utilizing the aid of his ecclesiastical colleague, Hammond, and the support of some of the inhabitants of Gateshead, Weld petitioned the Council of State against the four and twenty of the parish, accusing them of assuming without right a power to govern the rest and of hindering the work of reformation. He urged that these "known oppressors of godliness" be removed and that those whose names appeared in an annexed list be allowed to act in their stead.[95] By a Council order of 22 June 1658, his wishes were carried out.[96] Among those who were purged by this successful tactic were the four churchwardens who had created difficulty for him.

As events in England moved towards the Restoration of the Stuarts, Weld's career at Gateshead came to an end. He performed one last characteristic, if fruitless, service in the north by becoming closely involved with the foundation of Durham College. Although strongly attacked by the Quakers for his interest in this institution, which Fox at least saw as sinful, he was appointed in the letters patent of Oliver Cromwell of 15 May 1657 one of the first visitors of the college to hold office for two years.[97] His interest in this educational experiment is a logical counterpart to his earlier work for Harvard College. His concern for education was a lifelong work, and there is every indication that he himself, for all the blustering of his pamphleteering, was a learned man; the catalogue of the library, which he sold to John Eliot for the use of the New England Company in 1651, is indication of that.[98] When exactly Weld left Gateshead is uncertain. He appears to have withdrawn prudently to London shortly before 1660. In any case his successor, John Ladler, read the thirty-nine articles to the congregation on 26 August 1660; he had been presented to the living by the King somewhat earlier in the year, there being no Bishop of Durham in whom the patronage was vested between Morton and Cosin, who was not consecrated until December, 1660.[99] In March, 1661, Cosin, in his capacity as Bishop, formally instituted the new incumbent.[100] In London Weld took little, if any, part in events. The only trace to be found of his activities is his signature to the Congregational ministers' renunciation of Venner's insurrection of January, 1661.[101] He died about two months later, survived by his third wife. He had buried the first at Roxbury and the second at Gateshead.[102]

In a career spanning the two sides of the Atlantic, Thomas Weld had left his mark both in Massachusetts Bay and in England. His achievements may not have been great, but it is clear he was a formidable follower of the Puritan way, as his enemies from Anne Hutchinson to his own Gateshead parishioners could testify. A man of broad interests and concerns, including education and conversion of the Indians, he was also marked by a narrowness of vision that turned him from the toleration the English Independents were developing to a simple but unattractive bigotry. Though more prominent than many, this Interregnum clergyman of Gateshead may well have been typical of both the aspirations and the shortcomings of many of those Puritans who returned home from New England in the 1640s to build a new Jerusalem in old England to match their Bible Commonwealth in North America.

NOTES

1. For a discussion of the Puritan movement in Newcastle in this period, see R. Howell, **Newcastle upon Tyne and the Puritan Revolution** (Oxford, 1967), chaps. 3 and 6. For a detailed study of Jenison, see R. Howell, "The Career of Dr. Robert Jenison, a Seventeenth Century Puritan in Newcastle," **Journal of the Presbyterian Historical Society of England,** vol. XIII, no. 2, 1965, pp. 14-25, reprinted as Chapter VII below.

2. W.H.D. Longstaffe, ed., **Memoirs of the Life of Mr. Ambrose Barnes** (Durham, 1867), p. 377.

3. J. Winthrop, **The History of New England from 1630 to 1649,** ed. J. Savage (Boston, 1853), 1:298-299, n. 1.

4. **Dictionary of National Biography,** s.v. Weld, Thomas.

5. Weld's entries in the Terling Register commence 13 February 1624/5, T.W. Davids, "The Rev. Thomas Weld," **New England Historical and Genealogical Register,** October, 1882, p. 405.

6. John (baptized 6 June 1625); Thomas (baptized 26 July 1627); Samuel (baptized 8 October 1629); Edmund (baptized 8 July 1631), **ibid.**

7. S.P. Dom., Charles I, vol. 175, no. 104.

8. Miscellanea Exchequer Queen's Remembrancer, List of Fines exacted by the Ecclesiastical Commission, 16 November 1631, quoted in Davids, "Thomas Weld," p. 406.

9. S.R. Gardiner, ed., **Report of Cases in the Courts of the Star Chamber and High Commission** (Westminster, 1886), p. 260.

10. W. Laud, **The History of the Troubles and Tryal of William Laud To Which is Prefixed the Diary of His Own Life** (London, 1695), pp. 213-214.

11. Laud stated in the Court of the High Commission that Weld had gone to Amsterdam. Gardiner, **Report of Cases in the Courts of Star Chamber and High Commission,** p. 264. Henry Jacie wrote to John

Winthrop, Jr., that Weld had gone to Bergen, **Winthrop Papers** (Boston, 1943, Mass. Hist. Soc.), 3:60.

12. Winthrop, **History of New England**, I:93.

13. The accounts of John Winthrop, Jr., for 1630-31 record the receipt of a payment of £13.7.0 from Weld, **Winthrop Papers**, 3:6.

14. **Ibid.**, 3:60.

15. Winthrop, **History of New England**, 1:98.

16. **Ibid.**, 1:111.

17. On the Antinomian controversy, see D.D. Hall, **The Antinomian Controversy 1636-1638** (Middletown, 1968); E. Battis, **Saints and Sectaries** (Chapel Hill, 1962); C.F. Adams, **Three Episodes of Massachusetts History** (Boston, 1896); C.F. Adams, ed., **Antinomianism in the Colony of Massachusetts Bay** (Boston, 1894); D.B. Ruttman, **Winthrop's Boston** (Chapel Hill, 1965). There is a full bibliography on the controversy in Battis, **Saints and Sectaries**, pp. 349-365.

18. **A Short Story of the Rise, Reign and Ruine of the Antinomians** (1644), Preface, printed in Adams, **Antinomianism**, p. 71.

19. B.L. Sloane MSS 922, fols. 90a-93b, quoted in C. Bridenbaugh, **Vexed and Troubled Englishmen 1590-1642** (New York, 1968), p. 449.

20. **Dictionary of American Biography**, s.v. Weld, Thomas.

21. **Dictionary of National Biography**, s.v. Weld, Thomas.

22. For a good discussion of the state of the colony, see R.P. Stearns, "The Weld-Peter Mission to England," **Publications of the Colonial Society of Massachusetts**, December, 1934, pp. 188-246; R.P. Stearns, **The Strenuous Puritan** (Urbana, 1954), chaps. 6-7.

23. Winthrop, **History of New England**, 2:30.

24. **Ibid.**

25. The opposition was led by John Endecott. See his letter to Winthrop, **4 Coll. Mass. Hist. Soc.**, vi. 138-141. See also Winthrop, **History of New England,** 2:31.

26. Winthrop, **History of New England,** 2:37-38.

27. **Ibid.,** 2:38.

28. Winthrop noted that the agents were "to be ready to make use of any opportunity God should offer for the good of the country here, as also to give any advice, as it should be required, for the settling the right form of church discipline there." **Ibid.,** 2:37.

29. E. Johnson, **Wonder-Working Providence** (1652), ed. Poole, p. 224, cited by Stearns, "Weld-Peter Mission," p. 194, n. 1.

30. On the mood of England in the summer of 1641, cf. H.R. Trevor-Roper, "Three Foreigners: the Philosophers of the Puritan Revolution," in **The Crisis of the Seventeenth Century** (New York, 1968), pp. 264-265.

31. The phrase is Bulstrode Whitelocke's. He wrote that the country had "insensibly slid into this beginning of a civil war by one unexpected accident after another as waves of the sea which have brought us thus far, and we scarce know how." B. Whitelocke, **Memorials of the English Affairs** (Oxford, 1853), 1:176. On the passage of the moderates to the King's side, cf. the case of Hyde, discussed in detail in B.H.G. Wormald, **Clarendon: Politics, History, and Religion 1640-1660** (Cambridge, 1951), part 1.

32. **C.J.,** 3:207.

33. Stearns, "Weld-Peter Mission," p. 199.

34. Bod. Rawlinson MSS c934, f.5., printed in G.D. Scull, "Rev. Thomas Welde's 'Innocency Cleared'," **New England Historical and Genealogical Register,** January, 1882, p. 64.

35. Stearns, "Weld-Peter Mission," p. 201.

36. **Ibid.**

37. Cf. **ibid.**, pp. 214 ff. Weld mentions the figure of "Eight hundred and odd pounds." Scull, "Welde's 'Innocency Cleared'," p. 64.

38. Stearns, "Weld-Peter Mission," p. 215.

39. **Ibid.**, p. 215, n. 5.

40. **Ibid.**, p. 216. Cf. the following entries in Weld's receipts and disbursements: £50 to Bourne "for 30 passengers agreed wth for and not put aboard;" £91 to Bourne and Downing "for losse that some passenge ye Chil: runne away." There are other similar entries. J.H. Tuttle, "Thomas Weld's Receipts and Disbursements," **Publications of the Colonial Society of Massachusetts,** December, 1911, p. 125.

41. G.D. Scull, "The Society for the Propagation of the Gospel in New England and the Rev. Thomas Welde," **New England Historical and Genealogical Register,** April, 1885, p. 182.

42. W. Hubbard, **A General History of New England** (Boston, 1848), p. 374.

43. **New England's First Fruits** (1643), quoted in Stearns, "Weld-Peter Mission," p. 218.

44. On the scholarship see A.M. Davis, "The First Scholarship at Harvard College," **Proceedings of the American Antiquarian Society,** n.s.5, pp. 129-139 and A.M. Davis, "The Lady Moulson Scholarship at Cambridge," **Proceedings of the American Antiquarian Society,** n.s.8, pp. 274-280.

45. Weld noted receipt of £231 for the college and the advance of learning. This included Lady Moulson's gift. But there are other entries in his confusing accounts relating to educational purposes, such as Roxbury School. Tuttle, "Thomas Weld's Receipts and Disbursements," pp. 124, 126.

46. **Ibid.**, p. 125.

47. Scull, "Welde's 'Innocency Cleared'," p. 68.

48. W.B. Trask, "Rev. Thomas Welde's Letter, 1643," **New England Historical and Genealogical Register,** January, 1882, p. 39.

49. Stearns, "Weld-Peter Mission," pp. 221 ff.

107

50. A Short Story of the Rise, Reign and Ruine of the Antinomians, printed in Adams, Antinomianism, pp. 67-233.

51. C.H. Firth and R.H. Rait, eds., Acts and Ordinances of the Interregnum (London, 1911), 1:331-333.

52. Stearns, "Weld-Peter Mission," p. 233.

53. Ibid.

54. Winthrop, History of New England, p. 260.

55. Mass. Archives, cvi. 4a., quoted in Stearns, "Weld-Peter Mission," p. 235.

56. On this point, see Stearns, "Weld-Peter Mission," p. 237.

57. Ibid., p. 237, n.4.

58. Cf. Scull, "Welde's 'Innocency Cleared'."

59. Mass. Records, II, 141-144, cited in Stearns, "Weld-Peter Mission," p. 237.

60. Cf. T. Edwards, Gangraena (London, 1646), pp. 40-42; T. Edwards, The Second Part of Gangraena (London, 1646), pp. 84, 289-290.

61. Scull, "Welde's 'Innocency Cleared'," p. 65.

62. "Records of the United Colonies of New England," quoted in Stearns, "Weld-Peter Mission," p. 238.

63. Tuttle, "Thomas Weld's Receipts and Disbursements," p. 126.

64. Scull, "Welde's 'Innocency Cleared'," pp. 63-64.

65. Stearns, "Weld-Peter Mission," p. 245.

66. Edwards, Gangraena, p. 53.

67. Edwards, Second Part of Gangraena, p. 84.

68. For Weld's stay at Wanlip, see **Dictionary of American Biography.** Weld came to Gateshead in February, 1650, following a petition on his behalf by the parishioners, **C.J.** 6:354; Gateshead Vestry Book, p. 159.

69. On this incident, see Howell, **Newcastle and the Puritan Revolution,** p. 228.

70. C. Sydenham, **The Greatness of the Mystery of Godliness** (London, 1654), dedication to William Johnson. See Howell, **Newcastle and the Puritan Revolution,** pp. 145 ff. on this phenomenon.

71. Longstaffe, **Memoirs of Barnes,** p. 366.

72. **Ibid.**

73. **Ibid.**, p. 367.

74. R. Welford, "Early Newcastle Typography 1639–1800," **A.A.**[3] iii (1907), pp. 56–58.

75. On the early history of the Baptists in the Tyne Valley, see Howell, **Newcastle and the Puritan Revolution,** pp. 248 ff.

76. **Ibid.**, pp. 250–251; E.A. Payne, "Thomas Tillam," **Baptist Quarterly,** n.s., vol. 17 (1957–58), pp. 61–66.

77. T. Weld and others, **A False Jew** (London, 1653), p. iv.

78. **Ibid.**

79. **Ibid.**

80. **Cal. S. P. Dom. 1653–4,** pp. 73, 101, 428. In March, 1660, a Thomas Ramsay was given a pass to France, but whether or not this was the same man is not clear. **Cal. S. P. Dom. 1659–60,** p. 572.

81. B. Underhill, ed., **Records of the Churches of Christ Gathered at Fenstanton, Warboys, and Hexham 1644–1720** (London, 1854), p. 292.

82. **Ibid.**, p. 297.

83. On the early history of the Quakers in Tyneside and the importance of Pearson, cf. Howell, **Newcastle and the Puritan Revolution**, pp. 254 ff.

84. T. Weld and others, **The Perfect Pharisee under Monkish Holinesse** (Gateshead, 1653), pp. 31-34.

85. **Ibid.**, p. 49.

86. **Ibid.**, p. 51.

87. On this, see Howell, **Newcastle and the Puritan Revolution**, pp. 257 ff. See also below, Chapter IX.

88. T. Weld and others, **A Further Discovery of that Generation of Men Called Quakers** (Gateshead, 1654), p. 11.

89. G.L. Turner, "Presentations in Episcopal Visitations 1662-1679 Durham," **Journal of the Friends' Historical Society**, vol. 13 (1916), pp. 20-21.

90. Longstaffe, **Memoirs of Barnes**, pp. 375-382; Howell, **Newcastle upon Tyne and the Puritan Revolution**, pp. 263-266.

91. Longstaffe, **Memoirs of Barnes**, pp. 380.

92. **Ibid.**, p. 375.

93. **Ibid.**, p. 382.

94. **Ibid.**, p. 366.

95. **Cal. S. P. Dom. 1657-8**, p. 251.

96. **Cal. S. P. Dom. 1658-9**, pp. 69-70. The order is copied in Gateshead Vestry Book, p. 242.

97. "The letters Patent of Oliver Cromwell for Founding a College at Durham," **Allen Tracts** (Darlington, 1777), no. 44. For the Quaker attacks on Weld and others, see **Some Quaeries to be Answered in Writing or Print by the Masters, Heads, Fellows, and Tutors of the Colledge they are setting up at Durham** (n.d., n.p.).

98. G.D. Scull, "Documents of the Society for Promoting and Propagating the Gospel in New England," **New England Historical and Genealogical Register**, October, 1882, pp. 371-373.

110

99. Longstaffe, **Memoirs of Barnes**, p. 386.

100. **Ibid.**

101. **A Renuntiation and Declaration of the Ministers of Congregational Churches and Preachers of the Same Judgment Living in and about the city of London against the late Horrid Insurrection** (London, 1661).

102. Davids, "Thomas Weld," pp. 405-406.

VII

THE CAREER OF DR. ROBERT JENISON,
A SEVENTEENTH CENTURY PURITAN IN NEWCASTLE

In March, 1640, Thomas Triplet wrote to Archbishop
Laud to complain about a Puritan preacher named Husband
who had been active in Sunderland. Husband, he claimed
had done great mischief in the town, and, were he
allowed to continue, it would soon be a proverb "that
Sunderland is Husbandied as Newcastle Jenisonied."[1]
His assertion reflects the extent to which Dr. Robert
Jenison, the Puritan lecturer at Newcastle, had by 1640
stamped the impress of his personality and theology on
the North. By that year, Jenison had become prominent
enough to attract the attention of the central
government. Secretary Windebank was convinced that
Jenison had dealt subversively with Scottish Covenanters;[2] the Commissioners for Causes Ecclesiastical
within the Province of York were certain that he had
committed numerous breaches of discipline, including
refusal to wear a surplice when reading the service and
administering communion to persons not kneeling.[3] The
attention which Jenison attracted on the eve of the
Civil War has caused that period in his life to be both
well-known and well-documented. Far less has been
written about his earlier career and about his activities in the North after the Civil War. This would seem
to be a serious oversight, for Jenison was obviously of
extreme importance in the growth of the Puritan movement in the Newcastle region, and he was, after the
Civil War, the most important Presbyterian leader in
the town.

Fortunately, it is possible to document his career
both before and after 1640 in rather more detail than
has hitherto been done. His early writings not only
afford a picture of his theological development, but
they also contain a certain amount of biographical
material; this is particularly true of the preface to
The Height of Israels Heathenish Idolatrie which
appeared in 1621. Moreover, there are a number of
letters surviving which he wrote to his Cambridge
tutor, Samuel Ward, the master of Sidney Sussex
College.[4] After 1645, his career can be traced in some
detail in the Common Council Books of the town of
Newcastle. By using materials such as these, it becomes possible to make a far clearer appraisal of the
work which Jenison performed in the North.

Jenison was himself from Newcastle; more than that, he had strong local connections with some of the powerful families of the area, being the younger son of a prominent townsman.[5] His father Ralph Jenison had died in 1597 while serving as mayor and had previously served as sheriff. His uncle William Jenison had been sheriff in 1568, had twice served as mayor and in 1571 as a member of parliament. Jenison himself was born about 1584. The details of his earliest education are not entirely clear other than that he was trained at the Grammar School in Newcastle before going up to Cambridge. Even in his youth, Jenison was not growing up into a society free from Puritan influences. Newcastle is not usually thought of as an early centre of the Puritan movement, but it is apparent that puritanism not only had a long history in the town but that it was gaining strength in the period in which Jenison was a boy there.[6] The shortcomings in the religious provision of the area were already a subject of much comment, and there can be little doubt that Jenison was acquainted to some degree with puritanism before he went to Cambridge.

Nevertheless, his Cambridge experience was a crucial one, and Jenison himself underlined the importance of this in the preface to **The Height of Israels Heathenish Idolatrie.** At Cambridge, he came under the influence of Samuel Ward, who appears to have been his tutor at Emmanuel. Ward, who became the master of Sidney Sussex in 1610, was generally recognized as a moderate Puritan of Calvinistic views, strongly attached to the Church of England but equally strongly opposed to any "popish innovations."[7] Under the influence of Ward, Jenison inclined to the ministry from his first year at the university. He had his first chance to practice his calling when he served for a short period as domestic chaplain to the Earl of Kent. Somewhat earlier, he had become a fellow of St. John's College, Cambridge, and the death of his patron threw him back on the fellowship for his financial support. At this point, however, he received an unexpected call to his native town of Newcastle:[8]

When I thought not on Newcastle (but inclined towards my fellowship for my better furnishing) Newcastle thought on me and the letters of your late, worthy, learned, and reverend Pastor as also of others well affected to the Gospell of Christ...gave me a call to come unto it. Unto which call,

113

considering the Premises, how could I be disobedient?

Jenison may have come to Newcastle slightly earlier than has been thought. The Earl of Kent died in 1614, and Jenison's own statement implies that the invitation from Newcastle followed closely upon this event. In any case, he was clearly in Newcastle before the death of William Morton in July, 1620, since the latter had taken a direct part in procuring him for the place.[9]

Once in Newcastle, Jenison did not lose contact with his former tutor Ward. He maintained an intermittent correspondence with him between 1620 and 1640, and these letters provide an interesting picture of the Puritan movement in the town and of the spiritual development of Jenison himself. Jenison can be regarded as a Puritan in 1620; it is more doubtful whether he can be regarded as a Presbyterian. The path of his spiritual development was to lead from the one to the other. Three factors seem especially crucial to this development. One was certainly the issues which most concerned Jenison: fear of Catholicism and the question of salvation. A second was his struggle with the growing strength of the Arminian faction in the northern diocese. The third was deprivation from his lectureship and the experience of the English Civil War. After the war, Jenison emerged clearly as a Presbyterian; thus it is of extreme importance to look carefully at his career in the period just before the war to see if the seeds of this development can be found.

From the very first, Jenison appears to have been in bitter conflict with the Arminians of the area, particularly with the Durham authorities. It should be remembered that the high church party was very clearly in the ascendancy at Durham under the leadership of John Cosin, Francis Burgoyne, Marmaduke Blakiston, and William James, all prebendaries of the cathedral. It was not without point that the Puritans protested that "both towne and countrye began to imytate [the Laudians] to the shame of our church and the complaynt of all well affected people in the King's dominions."[10] Jenison was outspoken from the very beginning of his ministry in Newcastle. In his first work, **The Height of Israels Heathenish Idolatrie,** his strong views about the dangers of popery were considered to be risky by his printer, who made some unauthorized changes in the text in order to moderate the attack.[11] While the

114

printer may have feared the worst from Jenison's already marked Puritan leanings, his congregation in Newcastle found his teaching to their liking. On 26 December, 1622, at a vestry meeting at All Saints, a motion was made by the church-wardens to Sir Peter Riddell and the rest of the Four and Twenty that "Whereas Mr. Doctor Robert Jenison now present Lecturer whose paines and labours in this parish is extraordinary amongst us, for better incuradgment of his sayd paynes we whose names be here under written ar content willinglie to pay quarterlie those severall sumes under mentioned for his stypand."[12] Puritanism had, it would seem, an appreciative following in Newcastle, for Jenison had earlier commented that he found in the town recompense beyond his deserving, "especially in regard of that liberall yearely stipend which lately your Worships appointed mee out of the Common Treasury."[13]

Jenison appears to have turned on frequent occasions to his old tutor Ward for advice. In the summer of 1622, a post of afternoon lecturer in the town became vacant when scandalous sexual behaviour on the part of the incumbent, Mr. Jerome, necessitated his hasty removal from Newcastle. The mayor in that year was William Jenison, the lecturer's cousin, but a man of rather different religious views, a man, he wrote to Ward, "who I thinke you knowe to be popish, though nowe and then hee comes to churche."[14] A deputation from the town was sent to the universities to find a replacement but Jenison feared that the new man might well be cast in the theological image of his cousin rather than in that of himself. His suggestion that the deputation take advice from Ward had been set aside brusquely, and he gave Ward to understand that the mayor inclined towards one Naylor of Caius College, a man who "inclines to Arminianisme which will not be so fit for us here."[15] He asked Ward to keep an eye on the deputation and to send instant word about anyone it seemed prepared to select. Whether or not Ward did so is unknown.

When Jenison next wrote to Ward in 1624, the situation in Newcastle had somewhat changed. The vicar of the town, Mr. Powers, who appears to have inclined to Jenison's side, had died, and the fear on the part of the Bishop of Durham that Jenison might become vicar had introduced an element of enmity and hostility into his life in the town. Jenison disclaimed any intention of seekng the post; he termed the bishop's worries "a needlesse fear, yf he had knowne mee as well as I knowe

115

judging of right and wrong, on the apparent
excellence and high character of
individuals. There is a right and a wrong
in matters of conduct, in spite of the
world; but it is the world's aim to take our
minds off from the indelible distinctions of
things, and fix our thoughts upon man ...
But if Scripture is to be our guide, it is
quite plain that the most conscientious,
religious, high-principled, honourable men
... may be on the side of evil ... For in
the world's judgment, even when most
refined, a person is conscientious and
consistent, who acts upon his standard,
whatever that is, not he only who aims at
taking the highest standard....[18]

These are, of course, words of the highest Christian
wisdom. Cited in the context of a discussion of evil,
they serve to remind us that the Christian view of
evil is not permeated by some Manichean view of the
inevitable, unyielding force of an abstract, necessary
fate -- be it capitalism, or matter, or tyranny, or
phobia -- but by our free will choices over the
"indelible distinctions of things," whereby we can
strive to substitute our standards for God's.

Evil is not to be identified with any worldly
system, with any matter as such. Rather, it arises
from myriads of human wills freely choosing and
rejecting standards of God as given to us in nature
and grace. These are the standards which, when
chosen, serve to define best what we are and want,
what best our destiny. The metaphysical problem of
the "existence" of evil as such, then, is not opposed
to but supportive of this Christian analysis. The
question might be posed: Ought God to have chosen
another world? Belloc's witticism -- "How odd of God
to choose the Jews" -- might well be to the point
here. Philosophically, we have long wondered whether
God as Absolute Good created the best possible world.
On the assumption that the existence of various evils
creates insolvable problems to this thesis, it was
concluded either that God was less than absolutely
good (and thus not God) or that He did not create the
best of all possible worlds (hence a rather
parsimonious sort of deity).

Still another possibility, of course, might be
that God did indeed create the best world possible.
But within this best world, considerable evil, though

"[we] received as it were presse-money from God, to fight valiantly, constantly, and faithfully under his banner, against all his and our enemies (after which it is high treason against his Maiestie to revolt or give over); resolve therefore now of constancie to hold out to the end."[24] The second work which he mentioned in this letter was a more substantial treatise and more typical of his learning. This was **The Christians Apparelling by Christ**; it was at this time in the hands of the printer and was published in the following year. A long work of over 500 pages, it argued for the necessity of "putting on" Christ, outwardly by baptism and profession and inwardly by faith.[25]

By August, 1624, the situation in the town was somewhat clarified. The appointment of Dr. Thomas Jackson as the vicar of the town had removed the fears that Jenison would himself become vicar. On the other hand, the appointment set the stage for the remainder of Jenison's pre-Civil War struggles with the Anglican church. Jackson was an important member of the Arminian wing of the church,[26] and that branch of the church was to control the pulpit in Newcastle up to the outbreak of the Civil War, for Jackson was succeeded by Yeldard Alvey, a man Prynne called "the Arminian and superstitious Vicar of Newcastle."[27] Jenison was prepared to let matters ride in 1624. He expressed to Ward his doubts about Jackson, but did point out that the Bishop of Durham had not troubled him in a recent visitation. In the same letter to Ward, he stoutly maintained both his innocence from any earlier charges brought against him and his present conformity. Nonetheless, he did indicate one of the difficulties that would come to the fore in the crucial decade of the 1630s, the question of kneeling when taking communion.[28]

> I be not so urgent as hee expects (otherwise then in my preaching) to force them at Allhallowes to a conformitie in kneeling: seeing, I conceive, that taske of debarring such from the communion belongs more to the Doctor being o^r vicar (& it accounted a chappel depending on St. Nicholas) or to his curate, then to mee, seeing I only assist & helpe to administer upon good wil, the communicants commonly being many; & I only a Lecturer. What the canon injoynes me I am not unwilling to performe.

Jenison was clearly not yet the Presbyterian he was to become; he was a Puritan inside the Anglican church, not a separatist. The 1630s were to produce a change in this attitude.

In the 1630s Jenison began to formulate his doctrinal ideas more clearly. Increasingly, he turned from the anti-popery type of tract which he had written in the past to consider the question of salvation. This was in many ways due to the presence of the Arminians Jackson and Alvey, who preached on this subject a doctrine which Jenison could not accept. Increasingly, too, Jenison consulted his former tutor Ward on matters of doctrine. In 1630, for example, he sought Ward's aid in interpreting the doctrine of predestination which he was disputing with Jackson.[29] This incident is of particular interest because it shows Ward working as the centre of a network of correspondents. Ward wrote to two others, Thomas Gataker and John Davenant, both men of clear Calvinist affiliations, to consult with them about it, and the results of the inquiry were then passed back to Jenison.[30] At this point, it would appear that Jenison's theology was very close to that of Ward; his letters and published works repeatedly stress the dangers of "popish innovations" and the salvation of the elect.

In 1631, the struggle between Jenison and the Arminians came out into the open. Shortly before Easter, Jenison indicated to the vicar, Yeldard Alvey, and to the mayor his intention of preaching on Good Friday.[31] The following day he began to hear rumours that he was not considered sufficiently orthodox on the doctrine of the church concerning general grace. The Arminians, in the period before Easter, expounded their views on the subject from the pulpit. On Good Friday, Jenison answered them. He protested that he did not do this from a spirit of wilful opposition but in an attempt to reach a fuller explanation and reconciliation of difficult passages of scripture. Preaching on the text of **Ephesians** 5:2, he queried the Arminian position. "Christ is the head and husband of his Church, and these are holy ones, the elect people of God whom the Holy Ghost doth sanctify.... He is a savior of all, but especially of those yt beleeue.... Do all beleeue? No, all men haue not faith." Christ's merits, he argued, are available to all believers, but to believe is not given to all. "And so Christs death hath purchased a possibility of saluation for all men, if all men can beleeue. But we say againe, yt Christ

118

so died for ye elect that, by vertue of ye merit of his death (wch was specially intended for y^m according to gods eternall decree) they not onely **might** but **should** infallibly attaine faith here, & obtaine life eternall hereafter: (and yt wthout any compulsion of their will.)"[33]

Jenison recounted the affair and his battle with the Arminians in letters to Ward. He reiterated his point that "the chiefe effect of the newe Covenant redounds to some onely."[34] With the theological battle so clearly out in the open, Jenison found himself under increasing pressure. In April, 1632, he noted in a letter to Ward that he had been threatened with action by the High Commission.[35] One of the commissioners, Mr. James, had come to hear him preach. By all appearances, the mayor and the rest of the corporation were concerned to keep the affair from developing further. They did their best to get the theological dispute out of the pulpit and into private discussion. Jenison was willing to co-operate with them; he did not see himself as a troublemaker. He wrote to Ward that he was accounted the only contentious one "though I was never first in that."[36] The conditions of the town in the 1630s did not, however, permit Jenison to remain quiet. The Puritan movement in the town had been gaining strength steadily; an unofficial lecturer had been secured, and one of the prominent laymen, the later regicide John Blakiston, had attacked Alvey directly and been summoned before the local High Commission.[37] Moreover, as national affairs deteriorated, Jenison became more and more concerned. In the face of a growing crisis, his principles strengthened rather than weakened.

This is reflected in several ways. In the first place, Jenison's published work during the 1630s began to be marked by a national concern and particularly by a feeling that England was undergoing divine chastisement for her sins. In **The Cities Safetie**, which he published in 1630, he wrote "Let Rome and other Popish Cities abroad, and such Cities and Townes at home as grow wearie of Christs faithfull servants and ministers and thrust them out from among them, looke ere it will be long, for some such direfull judgement and usage from God, unlesse by times they repent, and hold better quarter with Christ and his Messengers."[38] When a crippling plague struck the Newcastle region in 1636, Jenison saw this as a witness to the judgment of God. "Mans sin is the cause of his Sorrowe.... The plague of the heart and soule brings

119

Gods plague upon the bodie."[39] He issued a call for repentance, for a return to the correct path, and into it he mingled his belief in the salvation of the elect. "Yet if the Plague and breaking out of wrath prevent our Humiliation, we must deferre our Humiliation no longer: otherwise, how soon may this spreading evill, and overflowing Scourge, or some other judgement sent to back it, in Gods just wrath make an end of all (save that God will have a remnant in whom hee will glorifie his Mercie, and preserve his Church.)"[40]

In the second place, the Puritan movement in Newcastle began to lean increasingly on the aid of Scottish Covenanters;[41] with this development, some of its leaders began to swing more clearly to the Presbyterian profession. This was especially true of the layman John Fenwick, but Jenison also appears to have been affected. It was never proved that he was involved in the negotiations with the Scots, but it is clear that he was strongly suspected. In any case, he was becoming a marked man, and the ecclesiastical authorities had decided it was no longer possible to allow him to continue in Newcastle. In March, 1639, articles were exhibited by the Commissioners for Causes Ecclesiastical in the Province of York against him.[42] He was attacked over ceremonial issues but chiefly because he preached that "the Saints of God or God's people are persecuted by the great ones and meaning thereby that those factious and schismatical persons who do not observe the rites and ceremonies of the church, commonly called Puritans, are persecuted, that is convented or questioned by those who are in ecclesiastical authority." Jenison answered the charges which were brought to the attention of Secretary Windebank by Archbishop Neile.[43]

Throughout the spring and summer, the investigation dragged on. Neile was confident that Jenison would acknowledge himself "not to have exercised his ministry with such conformity as he ought to have done,"[44] and the confidence seemed justified when, in July, Jenison made an initial submission.[45] The Dean of Chichester, Richard Steward, wrote to Neile on 23 July that the King was pleased by the submission and was willing to allow Jenison to return to Newcastle as a curate, rather than as a lecturer, if "besides his preaching he constantly performs all other canonical duties of his ministry and makes certificate of his performance thereof."[46] Steward amplified the King's views slightly by indicating that at the minimum

120

Jenison was to read the second service throughout in his own person and preach in hood and surplice.

Archbishop Neile confessed within less than a month that too much had been promised on behalf of Jenison when he was reinstated on the condition that he be conformable to the practices of the church.[47] In September, Windebank wrote to Neile that "there is apprehension that Dr. Jenison's return thither [i.e., to Newcastle] will too much countenance the factious party in and about that town."[48] Even the King had begun to doubt the wisdom of reinstating Jenison, and, in September, he was dismissed.[49] He continued to trouble the ecclesiastical authorities in the North for a short while,[50] and then, in 1640, he left England to go to Danzig. Jenison's attitude had considerably hardened by the time he reached Danzig. The letter which he wrote to Ward from there in 1640 foreshadowed the sterner preacher who would return to Newcastle after the war. His new attitude was more militant than before. He wrote bitterly of Newcastle, "that wretched & unthankfull town both to god and man" and drew attention to what he was sure was a judgment of God on it for his deprivation: "they are now fled out of it themselves & their houses plundered & pulpits possessed by others, who were chiefe procurers of my deprivation, yea & removal...from mine own house and native home. God is righteous in all his waies & holy in all his workes."[51]

It is not possible to trace in detail Jenison's career during the Civil War. He published at least one collection of sermons in 1642; part of this was a corrected version of the Good Friday sermon of 1631.[52] He had been impelled to publish it because a pirated edition of it had appeared.[53] The fact that someone took the trouble to publish an unauthorized edition of Jenison's sermon affords clear proof that he was not forgotten even while he was out of the country. In July, 1642, Jenison returned very briefly to England when he was nominated as a member for Durham in the proposed Assembly of Divines, but "arriving and finding that then the King's consent to their assembling was expected and relied upon, and it very unlikely to be got, upon leave obtained, I hastened to return unto my poor flock at Dantzigk."[54] The last phrase would seem to indicate that Jenison had established himself in some sort of ecclesiastical position at Danzig. The town of Newcastle made some effort to get him back in the period between the occupation of the town by the

Scots and seizure of it by the Royalists, but this came to naught.[55]

It was not until the town was reduced to parliamentary hands in late 1644 that Jenison was able to return. By an act of Parliament, Alvey was deprived of his place and Jenison restored.[56] The Common Council of Newcastle had already anticipated the action of the House of Commons concerning Jenison by over a month; on 2 April, 1645, they ordered that a letter should be written in the name of the corporation asking him to return to the town as a preacher.[57] The religious situation in the Newcastle area was, if anything, more bleak than it had been before the war. Yet, in the period between 1645 and 1660, great forward strides were taken, and it is true to say that Newcastle was, in that period, better supplied with educated clergy than it had been at any previous time in the seventeenth century. In this work, Robert Jenison played a major part. As the senior clergyman in the town and the incumbent of St. Nicholas, the only technical parish church in Newcastle in this period, he was in a position of great importance.

The town experienced considerable difficulty in establishing a classical system. This was mainly due to a lack of clergy, but, nonetheless, an organization was begun, and Jenison had four elders associated with him at St. Nicholas.[58] The picture was not encouraging, but it was not so bleak as some contemporary critics, such as Thomas Edwards,[59] made it. Jenison was consulted frequently on matters of importance, such as the selection of a schoolmaster,[60] and, generally, his opinion carried much weight. In the post war period he also found time to continue his writing. In 1648, he produced **The Return of the Sword.** In it he launched a scathing attack on those who now, he felt, were trying to shirk their duties. "The combination of all sorts of Malignants, Papists, Atheists, Prophane, cold, and lukewarm Protestants, against the sincerer sort, and against the Parliament, was thought ground and cause sufficient to unite and enter into a most solemn League and Covenant according to God...And as this our Covenanting was then so occasioned, is there not still the same cause to continue the union, and inviolably, and in conscience to keep close to our Covenant."[61] In the following year, he published his last work, **The Faithfull Depository of Sound Doctrine.** He dedicated it proudly to "The Reverend his Brethren and honoured Friends of the Classis of the Town and County of Newcastle upon Tine." In it, he defended the

Presbyterian system and set forth his standards for the parish clergy. "The true Ministers of Jesus Christ, as they desire and are bound to keep faithfully his Doctrine in purity, so they ought carefully to avoid prophane and vain babblings, and all opposition of their own and other's wit and pretended Knowledge, against the ancient truths of God, delivered to them in the Scriptures."[62]

By the time that Jenison penned these words, he was, of course, an old man. The vigour of his ministry began to be affected by his age. Even as early as 1647, provision had been made for a replacement for him at St. Nicholas when he was unable to preach.[63] In 1650, there was a definite attempt by the town to secure the services of a permanent assistant for him.[64] Jenison retained some of his vigour to the last; in 1651, he joined with six other Newcastle ministers in protesting strongly against an army officer who was preaching Socinian doctrine in the town.[65] In November, 1652, he died. It was, in some senses, the end of an era, for his successor at St. Nicholas, Samuel Hammond, was an Independent and not a Presbyterian. In a more important sense, it was not an ending, for Presbyterianism had struck roots in Newcastle in the seventeenth century; they were strong roots, and their strength owed much to the ministry of Dr. Jenison.

123

NOTES

1. Cal. S.P. Dom., 1639-40, p. 516.

2. Cal. S.P. Dom., 1639, pp. 479-80

3. Cal. S.P. Dom., 1639-40, p. 591. See also HMC 6th Report, appendix, p. 457.

4. These letters are found in a number of volumes of the Tanner MSS in the Bodleian Library. They have been previously noted and used to illustrate the career of Samuel Ward by M.H. Curtis, Oxford and Cambridge in Transition (Oxford, 1957), but have not, to my knowledge, been used to illustrate Jenison's career.

5. Much of the following material is drawn from DNB; R. Welford, Man of Mark 'twixt Tyne and Tweed (London and Newcastle, 1895), 2:629-635; MSS Duke of Northumberland, Bell Genealogical Collection MS 413; A.R. Laws, Schola Novocastrensis (Newcastle, 1925), 1:41-2.

6. See R. Howell, "Puritanism in Newcastle before the Summoning of the Long Parliament," Archaeologia Aeliana, 1962, pp. 135-155; T.G. Bell, Historical Memorials of Presbyterianism in Newcastle upon Tyne (London, 1847); R.S. Robson, "Presbytery in Newcastle-upon-Tyne from the Reformation to the Revolution," Journal of the Presbyterian Historical Society of England, vii (1940-2), pp. 3-23.

7. On Ward, see M.M. Knappen, ed., Two Elizabethan Puritan Diaries by Richard Rogers and Samuel Ward (Chicago, 1933), pp. 37-49 and Curtis, Oxford and Cambridge in Transition, pp. 208 ff.

8. R. Jenison, The Height of Israels Heathenish Idolatrie (London, 1621), sig. A 2v.

9. W.H.D. Longstaffe, ed., Memoirs of the Life of Mr. Ambrose Barnes (Durham, 1867), Surtees Soc., vol. 50, p. 307 notes that Morton was buried 26 July, 1620 and that Jenison preached at the funeral.

10. G. Ornsby, ed., The Correspondence of John Cosin (Durham, 1869-72), Surtees Soc., vols. 52, 55, 1:165.

11. Tanner MS 73/1, f. 29.

12. Cited in T. Sopwith, **A Historical and Descriptive Account of All Saints Church in Newcastle upon Tyne** (Newcastle, 1826), p. 118. Jenison was not, in fact, a Doctor at this time. He did not write to Ward about taking the degree until October, 1628. Tanner MS 72, f. 249.

13. Jenison, **The Height of Israels Heathenish Idolatrie**, sig. A 2v.

14. Tanner MS 73/1, f. 136.

15. **Ibid.**, f. 136.

16. Tanner MS 73/2, f. 437.

17. Jenison, for example, refers to his coal trading in a letter to Ward in 1628. Tanner MS 72, f. 294.

18. Tanner MS 73/2, f. 437v.

19. Tanner MS 71, f. 136v.

20. Tanner MS 73/2, f. 437.

21. R. Jenison, **Directions for the Worthy Receiving of the Lords Supper** (London, 1624), sig. A 2.

22. **Ibid.**, sig. A 5v.

23. **Ibid.**, sig. B 6.

24. **Ibid.**, sig. C 5.

25. R. Jenison, **The Christians Apparelling by Christ** (London, 1625), esp. sig. A 1v and pp. 85-6.

26. Cf. the comments of W. Prynne, **Canterburies Doome** (London, 1646), pp. 166-7, 356, 359.

27. W. Prynne, **Hidden Workes of Darkenes Brought to Publike Light** (London, 1645), p. 188.

28. Tanner MS 73/2, f. 475.

29. Tanner MS 71, f. 30.

30. **Ibid.**, fols. 35, 37. See Curtis, **Oxford and Cambridge in Transition,** pp. 286-7.

31. The following is drawn from a MS vindication of the sermon in Jenison's hand.   It is in the Cambridge Library, MS Dd. xi 49. It has not been, to my knowledge, identified properly before.

32. **Ibid.**, p. 4.

33. **Ibid.**, p. 18.

34. Tanner MS 71, f. 143.

35. **Ibid.**, f. 136v.

36. **Ibid.**, f. 136v.

37. Howell, "Puritanism in Newcastle," pp. 144-6.

38. R. Jenison, **The Cities Safetie** (London, 1630), p. 83.

39. R. Jenison, **Newcastles Call to her Neighbour and Sister Townes and Cities** (London, 1637), p. 97.

40. **Ibid.**, p. 207.

41. Howell, "Puritanism in Newcastle," pp. 147-151.

42. **Cal. S.P. Dom.,** 1638-9, p. 591.

43. **Ibid.**, p. 593.

44. **Ibid.**, p. 593.

45. His submission was dated 14 July, 1639. There is a copy in his own hand in Tanner MS 63, fols. 123-124v.

46. **H M C 6th Report,** appendix, p. 457a.

47. **Cal. S.P. Dom.,** 1639, pp. 445-6.

48. **Ibid.**, pp. 479-80.

49. **Ibid.**, p. 483.

50. **Cal. S.P. Dom., 1639-40,** pp. 11, 21, 183, 321-2.

51. Tanner MS 65, f. 204.

52. R. Jenison, **Two Treatises** (London, 1642).

53. This is the work listed under Jenison's name in Wing as **Soled Comfort**. I have not been able to see a copy of this book.

54. R. Jenison, **The Return of the Sword** (London, 1648), p. 4. See also **CJ** 2:544, 690.

55. H. Hornby, "An Attempt towards Some Account of the Ancient and Present State of the Town of Newcastle," MSS Duke of Northumberland 187A/200, fols. 166-7; **CJ** 2:440.

56. **LJ** 7:395.

57. M.H. Dodds, ed., **Extracts from the Newcastle upon Tyne Council Minute Book** (Newcastle, 1920), p. 37.

58. Tanner MS 58/1, fols. 352-3.

59. T. Edwards, **The Third Part of Gangraena** (London, 1646), pp. 88-9.

60. Newcastle Common Council Book 1645-50, f. 267.

61. Jenison, **Return of the Sword**, pp. 31-2.

62. R. Jenison, **The Faithful Depository of Sound Doctrine and Ancient Truths** (Newcastle, 1649), p. 36.

63. Dodds, **Council Book**, pp. 71-73.

64. **Ibid.**, pp. 123-4; Newcastle Common Council Book 1650-9, f. 13.

65. J. Nickolls, ed., **Original Letters and Papers of State** (London, 1743), p. 81.

VIII

EARLY QUAKERISM IN NEWCASTLE UPON TYNE:
THOMAS LEDGARD'S DISCOURSE CONCERNING THE QUAKERS

In his article on William Coatesworth and the
early Quakers of Newcastle upon Tyne, Henry Cadbury has
drawn attention to the vigorous outpouring of anti-
Quaker literature from the ministers of the town and
from "one Thomas Ledgerd."[1] Although the study of
anti-Quaker literature is an important part of the
history of Friends, Ledgard and his work have received
scant attention. It has long been assumed that none of
his writings have survived, and consequently there has
been little investigation of either him or his views.
In fact, a copy of one of his tracts does exist in the
Library of the Society of Friends in London; this is
the pamphlet A Discourse Concerning the Quakers set out
by T.L. There are, moreover, several references to it
and to its author in contemporary tracts of both Quaker
and non-Quaker origin, and information about the author
and his own views can be extracted from the records
relating to the town of Newcastle during the
Interregnum.

The tract itself is a brief one, containing only
eight pages. No date and no place of publication are
indicated, nor is the author identified except by the
initials T.L. The clue to the date of publication and
the author's name is, however, provided by one of the
tracts written in response to the Discourse, George
Bateman's An Answer to a Discourse Concerning the
Quakers.[2] On the title page of this work, Bateman
identified the initials T.L. by the phrase "or as I
understand the significance of the Letters Tho:
Ledger." This is, without doubt, the Thomas Ledgard
whose name figures prominently in the records of the
Newcastle corporation after 1645 and in the account by
George Fox of his second visit to the town in 1658. At
the end of the tract, Bateman gives the date of 16
July, 1653, which provides certain evidence that
Ledgard's Discourse was written in or before 1653. The
first known Quaker answer to the tract, James Nayler's
A Few Words Occasioned by a Paper Lately Printed stiled
a Discourse Concerning the Quakers was dated by the
London bookseller George Thomason as appearing on 17
March, 1654, but it is apparent from the preface to the
reader that a long enough interval had elapsed since
the publication of the Discourse for the author to have

written another tract.[3] It is also suggestive that the
period 1653-1654 marked the beginning of the steady
stream of anti-Quaker publications written by men with
Newcastle connections. The vast majority of these were
published by the Newcastle press of Stephen Buckley,
and it is possible that Ledgard's **Discourse** may be a
hitherto unidentified product of that press.[4] The fact
that Thomason did not include Ledgard's work in his
collection provides an additional suggestion that the
tract was not readily available in London and that it
probably was not published there.

Who, then, was Thomas Ledgard? The answer, surprisingly enough in view of the lack of attention he
has received, is that he was one of the most prominent
merchants and politicians in Newcastle after the reduction of the town to parliamentary control in 1644. He
had taken up his freedom of the town of Newcastle in
1633 as a draper.[5] At about the same time, apparently,
he became a member of the Hostmen's Company, the guild
of coal traders who were the chief powers in the economic life of the town.[6] Although he does not appear
to have made a great mark as a merchant before the
Civil War, he had achieved some status by the late
1630s when he became a member of the monopolistic South
and North Shields Salt Makers.[7] At the same time,
however, Ledgard became a convert to the Puritan movement which had been growing steadily despite determined
opposition within the town, and he appears as a correspondent of the Puritan lecturer, William Morton.[8] His
Puritan inclinations were well known to the town
authorities, for he was summoned on bond to appear
before the Common Council to answer for them, and, in
1643, he was disfranchised as a supporter of the
Puritans and parliament by the royalist oligarchy of
the town.[9] With the capture of the town by the parliamentarians, Ledgard came into a position of political
prominence. He became an alderman in the Puritan corporation, served as mayor on one occasion, and as
deputy mayor on a later one.[10] His financial position
was secure enough so that he could lend the town ₤450
out of his own pocket, and he had in his possession the
no doubt profitable offices of bailiff of Gateshead and
steward of Whickham.[11]

By 1653, when he wrote **A Discourse,** Ledgard was a
well-established member of the town oligarchy, related
by marriage to one of its most influential families
(the Bonners), and thoroughly representative of the
upper layers of a society which feared the disruptive
effects of spreading sectarianism among the lower

classes. His position of power in the town no doubt
gave the tract added authority with the audience to
whom it was directed, but the arguments which he
produced against the Quakers were hardly original ones.
Even at an early date, anti-Quaker literature had
developed its stereotypes. He alleged that their
"quaking" was either counterfeit or else that it was a
product of the devil;[12] the latter point had been the
main burden of another attack on the Quakers published
in the same year by the Newcastle press, Gilpin's **The
Quakers Shaken**.[13] He asserted that the rule which they
followed was not one which could be justified in the
Gospels, another frequent complaint against the
Quakers.[14] In view of his own position as a town
magistrate, it is not surprising that he particularly
stressed the characteristics of the early Quakers which
were most upsetting to established authority in the
seventeenth century, their refusal to pay "proper"
respect to those in office by taking off their hats to
them and by addressing them as sir and master.[15] In
amplifying this point, Ledgard introduced incidentally
a point which may have been of more significance in the
anti-Quaker literature than is generally supposed. He
drew a connection between their public disavowal of
respect to earthly authority and the relations between
members of the family. It is certain that
patriarchalism had a stronger hold on the general
consciousness than the apparent shortcomings of the
theory would seem to warrant. Historians are becoming
increasingly aware of the fact that family rather than
class was the pre-eminent social institution of the
seventeenth century. Yet, as Ledgard appears to argue,
the failure of the Quakers to show respect to authority
was as damaging to this institution as it was to
society at large. No one would dispute that conversion
to Quakerism could entail a considerable strain on
family ties, and this was obviously strongly marked in
a society which could view the head of the household in
terms of a magistrate.[16]

Ledgard's tract drew three known responses, two
from Quaker sources and one from a sympathizer who was
not a Friend. Although the replies varied somewhat in
length and character, their main arguments were very
similar, those of Fox and Nayler being rather more
outspoken, on the whole, than that of Bateman. In
answering Ledgard's arguments, George Fox did not spare
harsh words:

> Many may have the Scripture and deny the
> power of God which is the Gospel, many had

130

the Scripture and the form, and stood against
the Son of truth, Christ Jesus, the power of
God, the Gospel; And as for thy other lies
and slanders which are not worth mentioning,
which comes from thy drunken spirit, when the
spirit is awakened that suffers by it, thou
shalt feel every word of thy own, thy
burthen, and thou that dost set the
Scriptures above Christ and God, and the
spirit, art a heathen.[17]

Bateman's answer to **A Discourse** was more moderate; he
was not, of course, so personally involved as Fox, for
he was not a Quaker. He challenged Ledgard to find
scriptural support for the view that men should put off
their hats to magistrates, and accused the alderman of
confusing somewhat the ordinances of God and those of
men. His summation of Ledgard's character was not,
however, much kinder than that made by Fox. Ledgard
was, he wrote,

> one of those good thinking Proselytes,
> who thinketh they have God hard Tyed to them
> in the chaines of a faire-seeking Forme, and
> through that great light he may imagine him-
> selfe to have, may become captivated under a
> judgement, whose gates may prove as narrow as
> the eye of a Needle.[18]

The career of Ledgard subsequent to the publication of **A Discourse** is not entirely clear. He certainly remained a determined foe of the Quakers and was
one of those who were, to a large extent, successful in
keeping the Quakers outside the liberties of the town
of Newcastle during the Interregnum. It has been
asserted that he wrote two other anti-Quaker tracts,
one entitled **Another Discourse**, the second called **Anti-
Quaker Assertions.**[19] It does not appear that copies of
either of these tracts have survived. The latter one
was answered by Fox; it appears to have been concerned
mainly with the questions of the nature of sin and the
role of the scriptures.[20] Of the former, nothing is
known, unless perhaps it is that work which Anthony
Pearson referred to as "another paper come forth by the
author of the discourse occasioned by something written
in answer to it."[21]

Although it cannot be precisely documented, it is
extremely probable that Ledgard clashed as well with
the Quakers over the issue of education in Northumberland and Durham. Ledgard certainly displayed a keen

131

interest in education when he was an alderman. He became a visitor of the newly-founded college at Durham in 1657. This was a creation towards which the hostility of the Quakers was strong since they viewed it as an institution for the making of priests. Although Ledgard was not mentioned by name (no laymen were) in the Quaker attacks on Durham College's Newcastle backers, the clergy who were mentioned were men with whom he had close connections.[22]

Ledgard also took an active part in disputing with George Fox when the latter paid his second visit to Newcastle in 1658, although the discussion does not seem to have involved Durham College directly. According to Fox's account, in fact, the Quaker leader came to the town in direct response to the challenge of Ledgard that "ye Quakers would not come Into noe great toundes, but lived in ye ffells, like butter flyes."[23] The meeting of Fox and Ledgard was, not surprisingly, unfruitful. After exchanging mutual accusations, they parted, Ledgard and the rest of the Newcastle magistrates thinking that they had secured the religious peace of the town by keeping the Quakers out. Fox, rather more accurately, wrote that "As I was passing away by ye markett place, ye power of ye Lord risse in mee to warn ym of ye Lord yt was comeinge upon ym. And soe not longe after all those preists of Newcastle and there profession was turned out when ye Kinge came in."[24]

NOTES

1. H.J. Cadbury, "Early Quakerism at Newcastle upon Tyne: William Coatesworth," **Journal of the Friends' Historical Society,** vol. 50, no. 3 (1963), pp. 91-96; see particularly p. 92.

2. G. Bateman, **An Answer to (vindicate the cause of the Nick-named Quakers of such scandalls and untruths as is falsely cast upon them in a lying pamphlet otherwise called) A Discourse concerning the Quakers** [n.p., n.d.]. There is a copy in Friends House Library, London, Wing B 1094.

3. E 731(23). J. Nayler,**A Few words occasioned by a Paper lately printed stiled a Discourse concerning the Quakers** (London, 1654). The interval is mentioned in the preface by A.P. (Anthony Pearson). Wing N 279.

4. On Buckley's press and its products, see R. Welford, "Early Newcastle Typography," **Archaeologia Aeliana,** 3rd Series, iii (1907), pp. 56-58; H.R. Plomer and R.A. Peddie, "Stephen Buckley, Printer," **Library,** New Series, viii (1907), pp. 42-56; R. Davies, **A Memoir of the York Press** (Westminster, 1868), pp. 57-69.

5. M.H. Dodds, ed., **The Register of Freemen of Newcastle upon Tyne chiefly of the seventeenth century** (Newcastle, 1923), p. 17.

6. F.W. Dendy, ed., **Extracts from the Records of the Company of Hostmen of Newcastle upon Tyne** (Durham, 1901), p. 268. His entry is recorded in an undated list of hostmen admitted between 1617 and 1642.

7. C.T. Carr, ed., **Select Charters of Trading Companies** (London, 1913), pp. 143-144.

8. **PRO SP** 16/540/446 no. 33; R. Howell, "Puritanism in Newcastle before the Summoning of the Long Parliament," **Archaeologia Aeliana,** 4th Series, xli (1963), pp. 135-155.

9. W.H.D. Longstaffe, ed., **Memoirs of the life of Mr. Ambrose Barnes** (Durham, 1867), pp. 161, 352; M.H. Dodds, ed., **Extracts from the Newcastle upon Tyne Council Minute Book 1639-1656** (Newcastle, 1920), p. 28.

10. C.H. Hunter Blair, **The Mayors and Lord Mayors of Newcastle upon Tyne** (Newcastle, 1940), p. 68. The

133

first mention of him as an alderman is 4 October, 1645. Newcastle Chamberlain's Accounts 1642-5, f. 167. He officiated as deputy Mayor in March, 1651. Newcastle Council Book 1650-9, f. 69. He had been mayor in 1647-8.

11. Dodds, **Council Book**, pp. 65-66, 138-139; Newcastle Council Book, 1650-9, f. 134.

12. T. Ledgard, **A Discourse concerning the Quakers** (n.p., 1653), p. 1.

13. J. Gilpin, **The Quakers shaken or a Fire-brand snatch'd out of the Fire** (Gateshead, 1653). Wing G 769.

14. Ledgard, **Discourse**, p. 5.

15. **Ibid.**, pp. 6-8.

16. On patriarchalism and the importance of the family, see the suggestive remarks in P. Laslett, ed., **Patriarcha and other political works of Sir Robert Filmer** (Oxford, 1949), pp. 20-33; P. Laslett, "The Sovereignty of the Family," **Listener**, 7 April, 1960.

17. G. Fox, **The Great mistery of the Great Whore unfolded** (London, 1659), p. 257.

18. Bateman, **Answer to a Discourse**, p. 8; Bateman denied being a Quaker, **ibid.**, p. 3.

19. J. Smith, **Bibliotheca Anti-Quakeriana** (London, 1873), pp. 265-266.

20. Fox, **Great Mistery**, p. 257.

21. Nayler, **A Few words occasioned by a paper lately printed**, p. 2.

22. For Ledgard's interest in education, see Newcastle Council Book 1645-50, f. 176. The letters patent to Durham College (15 May, 1657) list him as a visitor, **Allen Tracts** (Darlington, 1777), no. 44. His father-in-law Thomas Bonner was one of those ordered to prepare orders and rules for governing the college. **Cal. S.P. Dom.**, 1655-6, p. 218. For a Quaker attack on the college, see **Some Quaeries to be answered in writing or print by the Masters, Heads, Fellows & Tutors of the Colledge they are setting up at Durham** [n.p., n.d.]. Ledgard had close connections with

134

Samuel Hammond and William Durant, two of the Newcastle clergy mentioned by name in the tract.

23. G. Fox, **Journal**, ed., N. Penney (Cambridge, 1911), i, 310.

24. **Ibid.**, i, 311.

IX

THE NEWCASTLE CLERGY AND THE QUAKERS

In August 1653, James Nayler wrote a letter to
George Fox following a well-attended meeting of Quakers
at the home of Anthony Pearson, secretary to the governor of Newcastle, Sir Arthur Hesilrige; obviously
pleased with the success of the meeting, he told Fox,
"I beleeve it will cause a Shatter in peoples minds in
these parts."[1] The judgment was certainly correct, for
the Quakers were to prove to be a very disturbing
element in the religious history of the Newcastle area
during the Interregnum, both their doctrines and their
attitudes appearing to pose worrying threats to the
oligarchical establishment that ruled the town in the
aftermath of the English Revolution.[2] For all its
importance, however, the history of the early Quaker
movement in the Newcastle area is not well known. The
usual sources on early Quakerism, such as the **First
Publishers of Truth** and Fox's **Journal**, provide tan-
talizing hints rather than a fully documented story; in
the first, there is no local report at all, while the
second contains references to two visits by the Quaker
leader, neither of them fully explicable without reference to other material.[3] But one major source of
information does exist in the form of controversial
writings against the Quakers on the part of the
Newcastle clergy and their supporters. By combining an
analysis of that literature with the scattered references in Quaker sources, newspapers, and official
papers, one can construct a reasonably coherent picture
of the early Quaker movement in the Newcastle area,
and, equally importantly, can identify the expressed
reasons for the high level of animosity that existed
between the Quakers and the clerical and magisterial
establishment of the town.

In understanding both the impact of the Quakers
and the reaction to them by the authorities, it is of
some importance to remember that Newcastle, in the
minds of most Englishmen, was seen as the centre of a
religiously backward area of the country in the seventeenth century. Clearly one of those "dark corners of
the kingdom," the North had been characterized before
the Civil Wars as a place "where God was little better
known than amongst the Indians,"[4] and there was little
in the immediate post-war situation to lead Puritan
observers to think any better of it. Although

strenuous efforts, stemming from both local and
national initiatives, were eventually to provide in the
Newcastle area in the 1650s a more sufficient clerical
provision than had been the case before 1640 (albeit a
restricted one on doctrinal grounds), there is some
validity to the suggestion that the Newcastle area
remained something of a spiritual vacuum, "official"
religion not adequately responding to the spiritual
needs of the population, and thus creating fertile
ground for the emergence of new and enthusiastic
sects.[5] Certainly the early Quaker leaders saw the
Newcastle area as one devoid of genuine spirituality.
James Nayler, for example, described it in the following terms:[6]

> "The thing that was seen concerning
> Newcastle, all his pillars to be dry, and his
> trees to be bare, and much nakedness, that
> they have not scarcely the bark, but are as a
> wilderness where much winde and cold comes,
> where there must be much labour before the
> ground be brought into order; for it's a
> stony ground, and there is much bryers and
> thorns about her, and many trees have grown
> wilde long, and have scarce earth to cover
> their roots, but their roots are seen, and
> how they stand in the stones, and these trees
> bears no fruit, but bears moss, and much
> winde pierce thorow and clatters them
> together, and makes the trees shake, but
> still the rootes are held amongst the stones,
> and are bald and naked."

Nayler's characterization of the spiritual life of
Newcastle is doubtless an exaggeration, but it was not
wholly devoid of truth. It would appear that the
Newcastle clergy, both Independents and Presbyterians,
sensed as well the precarious nature of the Interregnum
religious settlement in the area, and that this realization was a major contributing factor to the
unusually high level of co-operation between the two
major religious factions in the area. In a well-known
passage, Cuthbert Sydenham remarked that at a time
"when all the Nation have been in a puzzle about
errors, sects, and schismes, even almost to bloud, you
have sate as in a Paradise, no disturbances in your
Pulpits, no railings or disputings, Presbyterians and
Independents preaching in the same place, fasting and
praying together, in heavenly harmony, expressing
nothing but kindnesse to each other, in their meetings
ready to help each other."[7] While Sydenham's glowing

picture is, like Nayler's bleak one, not wholly accurate, it does identify an important characteristic in the religious life of the town,[8] and that characteristic of co-operation was to be strengthened decidedly under the impact of the perceived threats in the 1650s to the established religious order by the emergent sects, especially the Baptists and the Quakers.[9]

The main outlines of the emergence of the Quaker movement in the area can be quickly sketched. George Fox visited the region in 1653, passing through Durham, Northumberland, and Newcastle. His visit left few records, but he appears to have secured a number of conversions, and he noted significantly in his journal that "ye preists began to bee in a mighty rage att Newcastle."[10] At about the same time Anthony Pearson, who was to play a key role in protecting and encouraging the nascent Quaker movement, was converted.[11] He was sitting as one of the judges at the sessions at Appleby in January 1653 when James Nayler was examined about his beliefs and activities. The experience was profoundly unsettling. As he noted in a letter several months later, he had long seen himself as serving and worshipping the true God and thought he had attained a high level of religious faith, but now he was confounded and felt his wisdom to be folly; he likened himself to a poor, shattered vessel tossed to and fro, and sought the spiritual aid of Fox and Nayler. "Though I was their Enemy, they are my ffreinds."[12] The process of conversion was swift, and Pearson was soon addressing a statement to Parliament in favour of the Quakers, confidently asserting that "in the Northern Parts of this Nation, God hath raised and is raising up his own Seed in many people, according to his promises."[13] Pearson quickly became the hub of the movement. He visited Fox,[14] Nayler visited him,[15] and by the following year he was calling for a missionary tour by Nayler to the area: "those toward the East Side of Newcastle would faine see Jaimes once; when he comes it were well if he could passe thorough them."[16]

From about the time of Pearson's conversion, the pattern of Quaker activity began a noticeable increase. In October 1653 there was a large Quaker meeting at Bishop Auckland which ended in a riot.[17] In the same year, various Quakers, including John Audland, Edward Burrough, and Miles Halhead, were active in Durham and Northumberland.[18] From the very start, the Quaker spokesmen were faced with a violent antipathy; typical of the reception accorded them was the fate of Edward

Burrough and his colleagues when they disrupted a church service in east Durham: "they knock't ym downe with clubs, as if they had been Beasts, their Hatts were driven off their Heads amongst ye rude Multitude, who appeared as if they had been without limitt to have devoured all before them. Yet Friends were preserved, & a meeting settled at Shotton."[19] Despite resistance that was at times violent, the Quakers were striking roots and gaining permanent converts. Even the other chief sect noted their impact on the area: the Hexham Baptist Thomas Tillam wrote in 1654 to the church at Leominster that "only those deceived souls, called Quakers, have been very active in these parts, and have seduced two of our society and six of Newcastle church."[20] During 1654 Pearson and Nayler held meetings in both Northumberland and Durham,[21] and their followers began to mount a campaign of church visitations in an attempt to spread their views. Thomas Rawlinson reported in a letter from Durham in early March 1654 that eight Quakers had visited churches on the same day, at least one of them being put in the stocks for his efforts, though, Rawlinson added, the Lord soon delivered him out of the hands of "unreasonable" men.[22]

One striking indication of the impact that Quakers were having was the sudden flow of anti-Quaker writings from the Newcastle clergy and their adherents. The first such attack appeared in the summer of 1653,[23] and was followed rapidly by the two main contributions to the debate, both written by a team of five Newcastle area clergymen, Thomas Weld, Richard Prideaux, Samuel Hammond, William Cole, and William Durant; **The Perfect Pharisee under Monkish Holinesse** appeared in 1653 and **A Further Discovery of that Generation of Men Called Quakers** was published in the following year as a response to the protestations the first tract had occasioned on the part of the Quakers themselves.[24] Nor were the attacks solely the province of the clergy, for the prominent alderman and former mayor Thomas Ledgard joined in the literary fray in 1653, and followed up his initial blast against the Quakers by two further publications, both unfortunately no longer extant.[25] Even works not primarily concerned with the controversy were drawn into it; Thomas Weld, writing in the preface to Cuthbert Syndenham's **Hypocrisie Discovered**, went out of his way to attack the Quakers.[26] There was, it might be noted, a fine irony in the fact that the latter publication was dedicated to Sir Arthur Hesilrige, whose secretary Pearson was at the heart of the troublesome Quaker movement.

After the flurry of anti-Quaker pamphleteering in 1653 and 1654, direct mention of the threat occasioned by the Quakers in the vicinity of Newcastle became scanty. But various sources indicate that the movement was continuing a steady and worrying process of gaining converts. It would appear that the movement made more substantial progress in Gateshead than it did in Newcastle, probably as a result of the inability of the Newcastle magistrates to control developments outside the area of their immediate legal authority; in any case, a Quaker meeting in Pipewell Gate appears to have been already firmly established by the time George Fox revisited the area in 1657.[27] Scattered references indicate the continuation of Quaker activity in both Durham and Northumberland. Pearson's home at Rampshaw remained an active centre, while traces of the movement are also to be found at Durham, Heighington, Hartlepool, and Sunderland.[28] Less is known about the activities of the Quakers in Newcastle itself, but there are several indications that they continued their activities vigorously, despite the opposition of clergy and town magistrats. In December 1656 several petitions, including one from the ministers of Northumberland, Durham, and Newcastle, were presented to Parliament, complaining against the "growth and exorbitances" of the Quakers.[29] It would appear that the growth of Quakerism had also become a matter of concern for some of the chartered companies of Newcastle. The Merchant Adventurers' Company, for example, was worried about "a great apostacy and falling off from the truth to Popery, Quakerism, and all manner of heresy and unheard-of blasphemy and prophaness" and passed an order as a result that no Catholics, Quakers, or others who failed to attend public services of the town should be taken on as apprentices.[30] Nor was such concern an idle threat, for there is some evidence to suggest that the company was working on the basis that no known Quaker should be taken as an apprentice as early as 1654, before the passage of the act. In that year, the enrolment of Thomas Turner, apprentice to Edward Hall, was suspended because it was suspected that he was a Quaker; he does not appear to have been able to satisfy the company, for his indenture was not enrolled.[31]

During the winter of 1657-8, it would appear that the Quaker movement was making a sustained effort with respect to Newcastle, and every indication points to Anthony Pearson as being one of the strong moving spirits of the effort. The activity of the Quakers at this point reached a sufficient level of intensity to arouse the interest and concern of national as well as

140

local figures. General Monck wrote to Secretary Thurloe in February, enclosing books and papers to demonstrate the great efforts being made by the Quakers in the North and in the Borders to gain converts.[32] He made a special point of mentioning the role of Pearson and noted that there was an extensive traffic in subversive books between Newcastle and the Scottish Lowlands. References in Quaker correspondence confirm the impression that Newcastle was frequently used as the crucial link in the chain of communication between English and Scottish Quakers.[33] At the same time, Fox made his second and more fully documented visit to Newcastle. It is of some significance that he came as a direct response to the published criticisms of the Quakers by the Newcastle alderman Thomas Ledgard, who had asserted that where churches existed and the saints dwelt, the Quakers dared not appear, for like owls they were bred in "dark places."[34] Fox's own version of the challenge was worded somewhat differently, but the sense was the same: he noted in his journal that he came to prove false Ledgard's assertion that "ye Quakers would not come Into noe great toundes, but lived in ye ffells like butter flyes."[35] As might be expected, Fox's visit amounted to little more than an uneasy confrontation with the authorities. In company with Pearson, he sought a meeting with Ledgard and some of the other aldermen: only Ledgard himself and one unnamed companion attended the meeting, which rapidly degenerated into an exchange of heated words, Fox taunting Ledgard with the term "butterfly," and Ledgard accusing Fox of violating the Sabbath by attempting to hold the meeting. To the latter point Fox retorted that it was the Newcastle magistrates who violated the real Sabbath by celebrating the first day of the week instead of the last. At best it can be described as a distinctly unfruitful encounter, and Fox eventually withdrew from Newcastle and proceeded to the more hospitable ground of Gateshead where a Quaker meeting was well established.[36]

The visit by Fox had an extraordinary aftermath which may, perhaps, be taken as indicative of the tense relations that existed between the Newcastle clergy and magistrates on the one hand and the Quaker meeting in Gateshead on the other. The Quakers in Gateshead seem to have made regular attempts to hold meetings in Newcastle, much to the displeasure of the Newcastle authorities. When Fox departed, he left George Whitehead behind to continue the efforts, and a series of confrontations occurred.[37] William Coatesworth of South Shields and some associates hired a large room in

Newcastle with the intent of holding a Quaker meeting; before the meeting was fully assembled, the mayor and his officers appeared, dispersed those who had gathered, and escorted them to the limits of the town's liberties, charging them in the name of the Lord Protector to "come no more into Newcastle, to have any more meetings there, at your peril."[38] Undeterred, the Quakers were back the next day attempting to hold a meeting out of doors near the river side, and once again the magistrates promptly removed them. The next attempt involved a scheme to rent the Guildhall, a scheme foiled by the intervention of the Newcastle clergyman Samuel Hammond, who was promptly accused by the Quakers of bribing the keeper of the hall to go back on his promise to let it to the Quakers. In the end, a large outdoor meeting was held within the Castle liberties, no doubt to the great consternation of the town authorities. Whitehead himself preached for two or three hours, his voice, as he later claimed, carrying over the Tyne clearly into Gateshead.[39] The meeting passed off without undue incident, though a large and potentially disruptive crowd had gathered. Whitehead himself recalled feelings of gratitude towards the town authorities who escorted him safely through the crowd at the end of the meeting.[40] Having found themselves incapable of preventing the meeting, the town authorities apparently had gone out of their way to avoid its becoming a pretext for violence.[41] This series of confrontrations was followed by a bizarre incident that predictably was featured extensively in subsequent anti-Quaker propaganda. William Coatesworth, a key local figure in the attempt to hold the meetings, took horse for the South in a state which even his Quaker colleagues admitted was one of some discomposure. The Quaker version was that he was on his way to London to appeal to Cromwell against the ill-treatment of the Quakers by the Newcastle clergy and magistrates. The establishment version was that he had gone mad and was fleeing to the South under the delusion that he had murdered the mayor of Newcastle. Both accounts agree that he got no further than Durham where he died within a matter of days.[42] For those opposing the Quakers, it was a sign sent from God; not only had Coatesworth been struck down for his actions, but in his madness he had revealed precisely the sort of dangerous anarchism which they chose to associate with the Quakers.[43]

Concern over the Quakers in the Newcastle area did not end with the excitement of Whitehead's preaching and the confusion of Coatesworth's hurried departure

and death. The movement appears to have gained additional impetus in 1659 when Lambert's army was in
Newcastle. There were a number of Quakers among
Lambert's troops, and they appear to have indulged in
some active proselytizing among the community.[44] Post-
Restoration visitation returns indicate that, for all
the harrassment during the Interregnum and after, the
Quakers had struck permanent roots in Northumberland
and Durham.[45] In any case, the concern expressed by
the clergy of the Newcastle area did not diminish.
John Bewick published in London in the year of the
Restoration a further attack on the attitudes of the
Quakers,[46] and the last, unpublished work of the sometime Newcastle schoolmaster George Ritschel was devoted
to the same theme.[47]

The history of early Quakerism in the Newcastle
area reveals a clear pattern of hostility on the part
of Newcastle clergy and magistrates. On what grounds
was that hostility based and how was the opposition to
the Quakers expressed other than through overt attempts
to prevent meetings from taking place? The anti-Quaker
writings which have already been mentioned and the
replies they called forth provide a useful and informative summary of such concerns, fears, and antagonisms.
The arguments used against the Quakers were not original to the Newcastle area: anti-Quaker literature was,
in many ways, built up from a series of over-lapping
stereotypes, and the hostile assertions made against
Quakers in one area were quickly picked up and copied
in another: the Newcastle clergymen, for example, not
only borrowed positions and information from other
published anti-Quaker writings,[48] but solicited such
information by letter from acquaintances outside the
Newcastle area.[49] In general, the criticisms offered
of the Quakers can be classified under five broad
headings: theoretical or scriptural, social, political, psychological, and single-issue antagonisms.
Though convenient for the purpose of analysis, these
categories should not be seen as rigid or exclusive
ones; a case of single-issue antagonism such as the
question of tithes obviously had scriptural, political,
social and even psychological dimensions. But if the
overlapping is allowed for, the division into categories will provide a useful framework for the analysis
of this literature.

The Newcastle clergy made a strenuous effort to
pitch their argument on scriptural or theoretical
grounds. This is particularly noticeable in the two
combined efforts of 1653-4, **The Perfect Pharisee under**

Monkish Holinesse and **A Further Discovery of that Generation of Men Called Quakers,** but is likewise reflected in Hammond's 1658 tract **The Quakers House Built upon the Sand** and Bewick's 1660 **An Answer to a Quakers Seventeen Heads of Queries.** The first two of these tracts are the most elaborate attempts to argue a scriptural case against the Quakers. Both set out seventeen positions and three principles which were attributed to the Quakers and then attempted to confute them by argument from scripture. There is no doubt that the method employed, while effective as a format for argumentation, was open to considerable abuse. Some of the positions attributed to the Quakers, such as the argument that they postulated an equality of man with God,[50] were at best gross distortions of Quaker teachings, and were simply denied in Quaker replies.[51] Such denials, it must be admitted, had little impact on the Newcastle clergy who simply saw them as a spur to the reiteration of the charges backed up by further circumstantial evidence and citation of scripture. Nayler's attempt to answer the first pamphlet was dismissed out of hand as an exercise in evasion. "There is such palpable shufflings, such miserable weaknesse, and such horrible rayling, as that we should not have medled with it at all, but that we beleeve it is the designe of God to lay more and more open the spirits of these men."[52] Those insinuations which Nayler did not specifically deny but only dismissed in a general way were taken by the Newcastle clergy to be "confessed by him."[53]

The attribution to the Quakers of positions which they did not hold and the treatment of their denials as mere evasion should not disguise the fact that there were genuine theoretical differences between the two groups that could be expressed in the familiar theological language of the day. To the Newcastle clergy, the Quaker views of justification and the inner spirit reduced man to the covenant of works. "Is not this to bring us perfectly under the Covenant of Works, and to make us our own reconcilers, and so to make void the death of Christ?...And so this Antichristian Generation have totally renounced the Lord that bought them: For, this our standing perfect is in that assertion attributed wholly to our own power...these are the people that pretend to lead you to Christ, that thus leave you to the meer strength of your weak and rotten natures, both for life and holiness."[54] The Quakers were quick to respond that the Calvinist emphasis on the sinfulness of man and the importance of scriptures denied the power of faith and neglected the role of the

144

preacher as a physician of the soul. Thus George Fox commenting on **The Perfect Pharisee** noted "You are no more made wise than the Pharisees were by the Scriptures without faith: the Pharisees were not made wise unto Salvation by the Scriptures without faith, neither are you: But who are in the faith, they are made wise to Salvation through the Scriptures."[55] And referring to **A Further Discovery,** he observed sharply, "yee are pleading while men be upon earth they must have a body of sin and he that saith other wayes is a deceiver, and so ye keep them in their wounds and sores, putrifying and imperfect, and not makers up of the breach and binders up of the wounds."[56]

Two aspects of the theoretical argument are perhaps worthy of special note. The first is the attempt by the Newcastle clergy to link the Quakers by association with other religious groups towards whom there would be a predictably hostile response. "Now besides those which we have named, the Readers will easily observe such a masse and heape of Arminian, Socinian, Familisticall errors in their Doctrines layd downe in the **Perfect Pharisee,** that he may clearly observe where the spirit of Antichrist works in all deceiveableness in this last time."[57] In particular, there was an attempt to link the doctrines of the Quakers and the Catholics. Seven "similarities" between the Quakers and the Papists were identified and set forth by the Newcastle clergy. "It is as claere as the noone day...that the Papall Apostacy and State is the Antichrist so often prophesied of in Scripture. Now it is as plaine that the very distinguishing Doctrines and practices of these men are such as are the maine principles of that man of sinne in opposition to Jesus Christ."[58] What was so unambiguously clear to Weld and his colleagues would appear less so to the modern eye; much of the similarity was found in the Quakers' attitudes towards scripture and salvation, both patently misconstrued by the Newcastle clergy, while the laboured attempt to link Catholic monastic practices with Quaker behaviour in renouncing the goods of the world was simply far-fetched.

The second theoretical point to be noted is the response of the Newcastle clergy to the charge that they were in no position to attack the Quaker attitude towards worship when they were themselves, as Presbyterians and Independents divided on the same issue. The response tends to confirm the impression that the outward co-operation between Presbyterians and Independents in Newcastle was the product of perceived

145

threats to their precarious position in an area where puritanism had not been strong before 1640, for it does not deny the existence of differences but attempts to gloss them over as being of the second order and subsumed by a common Christian faith. "Do we not all agree? and is not our reall agreement knowne in all the Doctrines of the Gospel? As for matters of discipline, we doe really confesse there is some difference in judgement amongst us.... Could we not agree in the worship of God? or doth he know what the worship of God is? or what difference is betwixt worship and discipline?"[59] The marginal note introducing the discussion sums up the Newcastle position neatly: "Difference in judgement about discipline no breach of joynt appearance against the methods of Satan."[60]

When the attack on the Quakers moved from theoretical questions of positions to practical questions of principles and actions, the argument frequently achieved a higher level of reality. The scriptural argument need not be dismissed as hypocritical, simply because it was often based on dubious assertions about Quaker beliefs. The perception of important theological distinctions touching the very central issues of Christian faith was real enough, even if the evidence on which it was based was unconsciously distorted or perversely misunderstood. But when it came to Quaker practices, on the other hand, the facts of the dispute were undeniable from both sides. The disruption of church services, the failure to show proper respect to magistrates and others by doffing hats and employing a deferential "sir" or "master," the strong appeal of the Quaker message to members of the lower classes are all documentable phenomena, admitted and defended by the Quakers and feared by the traditional ruling groups. As such, these practices became key ingredients in the anti-Quaker attack both in Newcastle and elsewhere, and far-reaching implications were drawn from what may appear to modern readers to be surface or trivial actions. The social and political objections to the Quakers can be summed up by the observation that they were seen as disruptive to the fine balance of traditional society, a consideration that obviously had special meaning in a society that had just emerged from the confusion of civil war and the toppling of the monarchy.

Though the argument, in Newcastle at least, was seldom couched in precise terms, it is clear that there was concern that Quakerism had appeal among the lower orders. Samuel Hammond for one made the point in his

146

attack that one group to which the doctrines of the Quakers had particular attraction was "the unlearned and unstable."[61] But of even greater concern to those in authority was the unwillingess of the Quakers to observe traditional forms of deference and their plainly anti-social behaviour when it came to making a public demonstration of their beliefs. There was some attempt to argue this point against the Quakers on scriptural grounds. Thomas Ledgard, for example, asked how the Quakers could be expected to be of any "gracious attainment" so long as they walked by another rule than that of the Gospels.[62] Weld and his colleagues attempted to prove that the Quakers were inconsistent in their application of scripture when they would not salute others, arguing that the scripture passage cited by them in defence of this[63] also forbade the wearing of shoes and carrying of purses, which they ignored "as is evident to any that observe them, especially if they be travelling a far journey."[64] In any case, Weld argued, the scriptural passage in question was not a binding example, but a "particular dispensation and command to the seventy Disciples at that time."[65]

Likewise, the Newcastle clergy expressed considerable horror at such Quaker demonstrations as walking through the streets naked. Weld and his colleagues fulminated against "the wickedesse of this practice, besides the impudence and immodesty, even such as nature and ingenuity itselfe abhorres."[66] They went on to lament:[67] "Oh! What a fuell is this to the flames of lust, what accursed fires of Hell doth it kindle in the hearts of men?.... And what is the horriblenesse of the temptation of such wicked practices? This is so loathsome and nauseous to any sober apprehensions, that surely it will make the very practices of such things to be a stinke in their nostrils and to be looked upon as a shame, both to Religion and Humanity, and we are fully certified from severall parts it doth so already." Needless to say, the clergy took a dim view of the interruption of church services, whatever form the interruptions assumed. "While we are carrying on the work of the Gospel in our respective Congregations peaceably, some of them have come no lesse than threescore miles to revile us, and smite us with the tongue of bitter reproaches, in publique Congregations, nay even in the time of exercise to the great hindering of the seed of the Word, which questionlesse is the designe of Satan in those their Confusions. And are we the persecutors?"[68]

147

It is readily apparent that behind the outraged morality and the indignation at being interrupted in their work, there lay deeper and more fundamental concerns. It would do less than justice to the Newcastle clergy to minimize the seriousness with which they viewed the interruption of approved church services. They had a deep calling to be pastors to a sinful mankind; to disrupt their work was both to hinder the work of God in the world and to place their congregations in eternal danger. There was little illusion on the part of the Newcastle clergy that they could persuade the Quakers of the errors of their way; the concern was to guide their flock away from possible seduction. John Bewick expressed the deep conviction of their calling when he noted, "I did not rashly and rawly hasten to be a Pastor: for until I had seriously spent good time and study in the holy Scripture and divine things, being nourished up in the words of faith and of good doctrine, whereunto I had attained, I did not take upon me a Pastoral charge."[69] And Weld and his associates spoke for all the clergy in the expression of determination to carry on established forms and to attack error:[70] "We cannot apprehend that there is any hope of convincing these persons of the error of their way, so farre are they under the very power of the Spirit of delusion, and professed enmity to the Ordinances of Christ Jesus our Lord: Yet for the further securing and fuller satisfying of the people of God, we are induced to Answer...for the clearer manifesting of the wickednesse and folly of these men and their Principles: And though it cost us new revilings and more bitter cursings from this People, which we fully expect: Yet what are we, and our Names, though trodden underfoot, so Jesus Christ may have the glory and his people the advantage of our standing for the truth."

The sense of ministerial calling was deep enough, but the clergy also appreciated and expressed the fact that undoing authority in one sphere could rapidly lead to the undoing of authority elsewhere. In striking secular allusions, the Newcastle writers raised the spectre of the dissolution of the family, the collapse of authority in the army, the questioning of the legality of the Protector's rule, and indeed the crumbling of the whole political structure. Thomas Ledgard, for example, argued that Quaker practices led to the neglect of family duties and the decay of proper respect and authority within the most fundamental of all social units.[71] Ledgard reflected the prevailing patriarchal views of the time, and in a society which

148

could view the head of the family in terms of a magistrate, there is little doubt that he was correct in his assertion that conversion to Quakerism could entail considerable strain on family ties.[72] Others saw an equal threat to the maintenance of army discipline in the Quakers' refusal to give outward respect to those in authority. "This is a high way to poure contempt upon persons in supreme Authority; as if a Souldier should say, He would honour the supreme office in the Army, but would not bear the Lord Gen: Cromwell."[73] Indeed, they reckoned, the application of this principle could undermine the secular authority of Cromwell himself. The reasoning of the Quakers, they maintained, "is as if when the Lord Potector should declare what is treason by Law in publique Proclamation, a Justice of Peace should, when a Person were proved before him guilty of treason, according to the law, but he should appeale from the Law to himselfe for what is treason, though the Law had determined it before."[74] The concern could be extended to embrace the whole area of authority in the state. In an aside directed to Anthony Pearson, Weld and his colleagues accused the Quakers of pursuing an illusory form of political organization in which no one ruled and sin was left to flourish unpunished.[75] "But what becomes of the Justices of Peace, will they be content to be turned out of their being by A.P.? But seriously, A.P., if there be Governments without Governors, who shall punish sin? Who shall make laws? Who shall preserve the Peace? Shall Government? When it is in no bodies hands?... We may leave him amongst the rest of his fancies to study Sir Thomas Moores Eutopia or Platos Common-wealth, where probably he may find a Government without any Persons to Govern or be Governed."

There is a strong indication that concerns for such wider applications of Quaker principles were foremost in the minds of the Newcastle opponents of the Friends. Anarchy in religion could lead to anarchy in the state, and a once ordered commonwealth would be swallowed up in the incoherent strivings of that many-headed monster, the mass of common men. But the grounds for resisting the Quakers did not end here. There was what might be termed a psychological dimension to the opposition as well, a feeling that conversion to Quakerism bordered on diabolism or insanity and that converts were most likely to be found among the unstable, impressionable, or irresponsible elements of the population. The association of the Quakers with the devil was made early in the Newcastle literature and was never totally absent from it. The first

149

anti-Quaker pamphlet to appear in Newcastle, **The Quakers Shaken,** related the temporary conversion of John Gilpin and his subsequent breaking with them on the grounds that it was the devil rather than God who had moved him. "I rest fully persuaded, and I think it doth evidently appear...to persons unprejudiced that my quaking and trembling was of the devill, that I was acted wholly and solely by him whilst in this condition, and I doe really beleeve that others in the like condition which I was then in would be of the same mind with me upon serious tryall of their condition by the principles of Christian Religion and sanctified Reason."[76] Hints that diabolical forces were at work are scattered throughout the two books by Weld and his colleagues.[77] Samuel Hammond indicated a firm belief that Quaker converts were likely to be people of an unstable disposition or young people who had not yet formed clear Christian convictions and were easily seduced, and he took evident pleasure in relating the tale of the alleged madness of William Coatesworth and of a shoemaker in Newcastle who was struck mad after attacking Hammond in a public meeting place.[78]

General opposition to the Quakers was built on grounds such as these, but there were at least two specific issues which also played a part in the Newcastle area, the question of tithes and the movement to establish a university at Durham. Opposition to tithes was by no means confined to the Quakers,[79] but the question became very much a part of the general Newcastle dispute with them. One reason for its prominence in the debate was the fact that the key Quaker leader Anthony Pearson had written a strongly worded attack on the institutions of tithes.[80] But even before that date, during the 1653-4 flurry of pamphleteering, the Quakers attacked the Newcastle clergy for their support of tithes, claiming that they preached for hire, a charge vehemently denied by the clergy.[81] Samuel Hammond was convinced that some were converted to Quakerism because they thought it was a way to get out of paying tithes.[82] Bewick's tract of 1660 was the most extended effort by a member of the Newcastle clergy to answer the Quaker case against tithes. Noting that Christ never spoke against tithes, he argued that tithes "are Gods rent, reserved by himself out of all the increase of every mans lands and goods to be paid by them as an acknowledgement that he is both the soveraign Lord of all the whole earth, and the fulness thereof, of the world, and them that dwell therein."[83] Denying that tithes were a price for preaching, Bewick argued that they were established by divine ordinance for the necessary maintenance of the clergy, and that the Quaker attacks on them were but one more example of the manner in which the Friends sought to disrupt the properly constituted order of things. "The murmure, which is among many in these times against mine and other faithful Ministers maintenance is doubtlesse a murmuring against God, because he did not make us to be creatures, to live without food and raiment, and other temporal necessaries, but made us men like yourselves compassed with the same infirmities, and needing like temporal supplies for back and belly, and other necessaries, as all other men do."[84]

The Quakers were not simply critical of tithes as a means of providing maintenance for the clergy; they were outspokenly critical of the clergy themselves and of the institutions which trained them. It was this latter concern which provided the basis for yet another direct conflict with the governing groups in Newcastle. The early history of Durham College is very much a part of the history of Newcastle as well as that of the neighbouring county.[85] While it is by no means clear who first raised the scheme that a college should be created at Durham out of the property of the dean and chapter,[86] the Newcastle authorities had, by 1656, become deeply interested in the idea and at least four of the most outspoken local critics of the Quakers, William Cole, Richard Prideaux, Thomas Ledgard, and Samuel Hammond, were closely involved.[87] The Quakers generally and George Fox in particular were hostile to the project from the start. It is important in understanding the conflict to be clear about the basis of the Quaker objections. Fox's views were typical of the Quaker position; he was careful to point out that he was not against learning in itself, so long as it was directed to its proper uses, but he was vehemently opposed to learning as a basis for preaching the Gospel and thus it was that he attacked the learning of parish priests as a vain delusion and a reason for not recognizing their authority.[88] Given such an outlook, there is little surprise to be occasioned by the fact that the Quakers denounced the scheme for a college at Durham, vigorously assaulting it as a foundation for the making of ministers, something, in their view, only God could do.[89] Fox joined directly in the onslaught and in fact took personal credit for the destruction of the college, although in doing so he clearly overstated both his own role and that of the Quaker movement.[90]

The clash over education, and particularly over the College at Durham, was but one, and by no means the most important, of a series of frictions between the Quakers and the Newcastle authorities. In the last analysis, all the aspects of the conflict could be summed up under the awareness from both sides that radically different conceptions of order and authority were facing each other. The conservative emphasis on traditional forms and structures which was so much a part of the mental outlook of the Newcastle clergy and the secular authorities there was being challenged by a force that was equally convinced of moral rectitude and which was driven on by an inner light that was, both in theory and practice, a challenge to and a solvent of older conceptions of order, deference, and obedience. Passionately convinced of their own rightness, the two sides simply talked past each other when it came to this point. John Bewick eloquently defended the role of the traditional clergy in opposition to what he could only see as the anarchistic inner light of the Quakers: "I am not in the steps of them who with faire speeches and good words deceive the hearts of the simple.[91]...The doctrines which I have taught them do naturally tend to bring them to Godlinesse, and to have a holy demeanour towards God and man; that impiety of mocking and scoffing, which some have expressed, flowes from the corrupt source of their own corrupt nature, but not from my mouth."[92] But the Quakers were equally eloquent and equally adamant. Anthony Pearson, at the very start of the controversy, delineated clearly the attitudes and convictions that led to the conflict: "The reason why these People above all others are hated by all sorts of men is because the righteous Spirit of God that rules in them, as it will not comply or have fellowship with the wicked in their Pride, lusts, pleasures, customs, worships, fashions, and unfruitful works of darkness, so will it not wink at them, but reprove them where and in whomsoever they are."[93]

The Newcastle clergy and magistrates doubtless thought they had won the battle when they kept the Quakers from meeting in the town. If the existence of the Gateshead meeting place so close to the limits of their authority remained a galling reminder of the Quaker threat, they could at least feel that they had done their utmost to preserve the spiritual purity of Newcastle itself. And yet, they were obviously wrong. Their own authority, nearly as precarious as the revolution on which it was built, was rudely shattered by the Restoration; while Newcastle became, in the post-Restoration period, a centre of dissent, the hegemony

152

achieved during the Interregnum was not preserved. On the other hand, the Quakers had also, despite all the pressure and argument, struck deep roots, and their continued presence in the area after 1660 provides a clear indication of the vitality of the movement. In that sense, Fox's recollection of his departure from Newcastle was both prophetic and to the point: "As I was passing away by ye markett place, ye power of ye Lord risse in mee to warn ym of ye Lord yt was comeing upon ym. And soe not long after all those preists of Newcastle and there profession was turned out when ye Kinge came in."[94]

NOTES

1. Swarthmore MSS. (Friends' Library), iii, 61 (10 August, 1653).

2. For the general background on Newcastle life in this period, see R. Howell, **Newcastle upon Tyne and the Puritan Revolution,** (Oxford, 1967).

3. Cf. H.J. Cadbury, "Early Quakerism at Newcastle upon Tyne: William Coatesworth," **Journal of the Friends' Historical Society,** vol. 50, no. 3 (1963), p. 91. On the origins of the Quaker movement in Durham and Northumberland see also W.C. Braithwaite, **The Beginnings of Quakerism** (London, 1912); W.H. Knowles and J.R. Boyle, **Vestiges of Old Newcastle and Gateshead,** (Newcastle, 1890), pp. 29-39; G.F. Nuttall, "George Fox and the Rise of Quakerism in the Bishoprick," **Durham University Journal,** vol. 36 (1943-44), pp. 94-7; J.W. Steel, **Early Friends in the North** (London, 1905); H. Barbour, **The Quakers in Puritan England** (New Haven, 1964).

4. J.A. Manning, ed., **Memoirs of Sir Benjamin Rudyerd** (London, 1841), pp. 135-6.

5. Cf. Howell, **Newcastle upon Tyne and the Puritan Revolution,** chap. VI.

6. E 738 (16), J. Nayler, **A Discovery of the Man of Sin Acting in a Mystery of Iniquitie** (London, 1654), p. 51.

7. E 1499 (1), C. Sydenham, **The Greatness of the Mystery of Godliness** (London, 1654), dedication to William Johnson, mayor of Newcastle.

8. Sydenham was not the only one to remark on this phenomenon. Cf. also W.H.D. Longstaffe, ed., **Memoirs of the Life of Mr. Ambrose Barnes** (Durham, 1867), Surtees Soc., vol. 50, p. 126. On the other hand, the 1656 order of the Common Council "for settleinge the Ministers in theire preachinge att the severall Churches usque Death etc." mentions sectarian controversy within the town. M.H. Dodds, ed., **Extracts from the Newcastle upon Tyne Council Minute Book** (Newcastle, 1920), p. 225. Likewise an undated petition of James Mirle also seems to indicate some difficulties. Baxter Treatises (Dr. William's

154

Library), vol. 5, fol. 105. Such differences were also raised in the pamphlet controversy with the Quakers discussed later in this paper.

9. On the Baptist threat, see Howell, **Newcastle upon Tyne and the Puritan Revolution**, pp. 248 ff.

10. N. Penney, ed., **The Journal of George Fox** (Cambridge, 1911), 1:141.

11. E 689 (19), G. Fox, **Saul's Errand to Damascus** (London, 1653), pp. 29 ff. Swarthmore MSS. (Friends' Library), iii, 29 (18 May, 1653).

12. Swarthmore MSS. (Friends' Library), i, 87 (9 May, 1653).

13. E 714 (10), A. Pearson, **To the Parliament of the Common-wealth of England** (London, 1653), p. 1.

14. Fox, **Journal**, 1:108.

15. N. Penney, ed., **The First Publishers of Truth Being Early Records of the Introduction of Quakerism in the Counties of England and Wales** (London, 1907), p. 88.

16. Swarthmore MSS. (Friends' Library), iii, 35 (21 February 1653-4).

17. Penney, **First Publishers**, p. 89.

18. **Ibid.**, pp. 89-90, 202, 202-3.

19. **Ibid.**, p. 90.

20. B. Underhill, ed., **Records of the Churches of Christ Gathered at Fenstanton, Warboys, and Hexham 1644-1720** (London, 1854), Hanserd Knollys Soc., vol. 8, p. 352. There is ample evidence that the Quakers found converts in Baptist congregations. Cf. Swarthmore MSS. (Friends' Library), iv, 209 (14 March 1654); 203 (11 February, 1656-7); and 240 (December, 1657).

21. Swarthmore MSS. (Friends' Library), iii, 71, 192 (mid-April, 1654).

22. **Ibid.**, iii, 15 (early March, 1654).

23. **The Quakers Shaken or a Fire-brand snatch'd**

155

out of the Fire (Gateshead, 1653).

24. T. Weld, et al., **The Perfect Pharisee under Monkish Holinesse** (Gateshead, 1653); T. Weld, et al., **A Further Discovery of that Generation of Men called Quakers** (Gateshead, 1654).

25. [T. Ledgard], **A Discourse concerning the Quakers** (n.p., 1653). On the authorship of this tract which exists in an apparently unique copy in the Friends' Library, see R. Howell, "Early Quakerism in Newcastle upon Tyne: Thomas Ledgard's Discourse concerning the Quakers," **Journal of the Friends Historical Society**, vol. 50, no. 4 (1964), pp. 211-16 reprinted above Chapter VIII. Ledgard's two other tracts were entitled **Another Discourse** and **Anti-Quaker Assertions**. See J. Smith, **Bibliotheca Anti-Quakeriana or a Catalogue of Books Adverse to the Society of Friends** (London, 1873), p. 266.

26. E 1504 (2) C. Sydenham, **Hypocrisie Discovered in its Nature and Workings** (London, 1654), preface to the reader.

27. M. Phillips, "Notes on Some Forgotten Burying Grounds of the Society of Friends: Gateshead, Whickham, Boldon, and South Shields," **A.A.**[2], xvi (1891-4), p. 192.

28. Cf. Swarthmore MSS. (Friends' Library), iv, 62; i, 252, 241, 261, 164; iii, 187; iv, 25; i, 277, 278, 282, 283; iii, 78. The listing is chronological; for the dating and attribution of the letters, I am indebted to G.F. Nuttall, "Early Quaker Letters" (London, 1952, duplicated). Cf. also the references to Pearson's activities in A.R. Barclay, **Letters &c. of Early Friends Illustrative of the History of the Society** (London, 1911), pp. 12-13, 17, 33.

29. **C.J.**, 7:470 (18 December, 1656), cf. also **The Publick Intelligencer**, no. 67, 15-22 December, 1656, p. 1067.

30. J.R. Boyle and F.W. Dendy, eds., **Extracts from the Records of the Merchant Adventurers of Newcastle** (Durham, 1895-9), Surtees Soc., vols. 93, 101, 2:128. It is interesting to note that the provision prohibiting Quakers was retained until well into the eighteenth century although other parts of the act were repealed. **Ibid.**, 1:256.

31. **Ibid.**, 1:182-3.

32. T. Birch, ed., **Thurloe State Papers**, (London, 1742), 6:811-12.

33. Swarthmore MSS. (Friends' Library), iv. 64 (15 February, 1656-7); 279 (14 November, 1659).

34. Ledgard, **Discourse concerning the Quakers**, p. 8.

35. Fox, **Journal**, 1:310.

36. **Ibid.**, 1:311; cf. also the brief notice of this visit in **Mercurius Politicus**, no. 399, 14-21 January 1657/8, p. 246.

37. The following is based on G. Whitehead, **The Christian Progress of George Whitehead** (London, 1725), pp. 126-8; **Mercurius Politicus**, no. 399, 14-21 January, 1657-8, p. 246; **Nouvelles Ordinaires de Londres**, no. 400, 24-31 January, 1657-8, as printed in Cadbury, "Early Quakerism in Newcastle upon Tyne," pp. 93-4; S. Hammond, **The Quakers House Built upon the Sand** (Gateshead, 1658), pp. 24-5.

38. Whitehead, **Christian Progress**, p. 126.

39. **Ibid.**, pp. 127-8.

40. **Ibid.**, p. 128.

41. Hammond, **Quakers House Built upon Sand**, p. 24 gives the same impression. While arguing that the magistrates were correct in attempting to prevent the meeting, he also notes that none of the Quakers were hurt because the magistrates had actively sought to prevent violence.

42. The Quaker version is given in Whitehead, **Christian Progress**, p. 129 and is followed in Braithwaite, **Beginnings of Quakerism**, p. 373. The story of his madness appears in essentially identical form in **Mercurius Politicus**, no. 399, 14-21 January, 1657-8, p. 246 and **Nouvelles Ordinaires de Londres**, no. 400, 24-31 January, 1657-8, p. 1606.

43. Cf. Hammond, **Quakers House Built upon Sand**, p. 24 who makes the point explicitly.

44. J. Price, **The Mystery and Method of His Majesty 's Happy Restauration** (London, 1680), p. 32.

45. Cf. the authorities summarized in Howell, **Newcastle upon Tyne and the Puritan Revolution**, p. 261, n. 3. It is striking, however, that the roots were established substantially outside Newcastle, no doubt as a result of the vigorous opposition to the Quakers by the town authorities in the 1650s.

46. E 1038 (1), J. Bewick, **An Answer to a Quakers Seventeen Heads of Queries** (London, 1660).

47. J. Brand, **History of Newcastle** (London, 1789), 2:93; A. Wood, **Athenae Oxoniensis**, 3rd edn. (London, 1813–20), 2:754. On Ritschel, see R. Howell, "Georg Ritschel, Lehrer und Geistlicher: Ein bömischer Vertriebener im England Cromwells," **Bohemia: Jahrbuch des Collegium Carolinum**, vol. 7 (1966), pp. 199–210 and Chapter X below.

48. Cf. the acknowledgment to Samuel Eaton, **The Quakers Confuted Being an Answer unto Nineteen Queries** (London, 1654) in Weld, **A Further Discovery**, p. 3.

49. In January 1653–4 the Newcastle clergy wrote to William Marshall, Michael Althan, and William Baldwinson for testimony about Fox. **Ibid.**, pp. 22–4. At about the same time an unnamed clergyman in Westmorland was writing to William Cole about a Quaker conversion. **Ibid.**, p. 31.

50. Weld, **The Perfect Pharisee**, p. 3; Weld, **A Further Discovery**, p. 18.

51. E 735 (2), J. Nayler, **An Answer to the Booke called The Perfect Pharisee** (London, 1654).

52. Weld, **A Further Discovery**, p. 6.

53. **Ibid.**, p. 9.

54. Weld, **The Perfect Pharisee**, p. 12.

55. G. Fox, **The Great Mistery of the Great Whore Unfolded** (London, 1659), pp. 75–6.

56. **Ibid.**, p. 231.

57. Weld, **A Further Discovery**, p. 11.

58. Ibid., p. 9.

59. Ibid., pp. 12-13.

60. Ibid., p. 12.

61. Hammond, Quakers House Built upon Sand, p. 3.

62. Ledgard, Discourse concerning the Quakers, p. 5.

63. Luke 10:4.

64. Weld, The Perfect Pharisee, p. 32.

65. Ibid., p. 32.

66. Weld, A Further Discovery, p. 86.

67. Ibid., p. 86.

68. Ibid., p. 17.

69. Bewick, An Answer to a Quakers Seventeen Heads of Queries, p. 91.

70. Weld, A Further Discovery, p. 3.

71. Ledgard, Discourse concerning the Quakers, p. 8.

72. On patriarchalism and the importance of the family, see the suggestive remarks in P. Laslett, ed., Patriarcha and Other Political Works of Sir Robert Filmer (Oxford, 1949), pp. 20-33; P. Laslett, The World We Have Lost, 2nd edn. (London, 1971); G.J. Schochet, Patriarchialism in Political Thought (Oxford, 1975); G.J. Schochet, "Patriarchialism, Politics, and Mass Attitudes in Stuart England," Historical Journal, vol. 12 (1969), pp. 413-41.

73. Weld, The Perfect Pharisee, p. 34.

74. Weld, A Further Discovery, p. 69.

75. Ibid., p. 89.

76. The Quakers Shaken, p. 16.

77. Weld, **The Perfect Pharisee**, p. 26. "We can no otherwise look upon this, then the very Hold Satan hath to keep this people under his delusions, by couzening them thus, to stop their eyes against the light." Weld, **A Further Discovery**, p. 9. "Truely these blasphemous Doctrines of these men, with their Diabolicall delusions and quakings, will make it appeare where the man of sin is now working."

78. Hammond, **Quakers House Built upon Sand**, pp. 2-4, 24.

79. On the significance of the debate over tithes in the English Revolution, see M. James, "The Political Importance of the Tithes Controversy in the English Revolution 1640-60," **History**, vol. 26 (1941), pp. 1-18.

80. E 931 (2), A. Pearson, **The Great Case of Tythes truly Stated by a Countryman** (London, 1657).

81. Cf. Weld, **The Perfect Pharisee**, p. 39.

82. Hammond, **Quakers House Built upon Sand**, p. 4. It is interesting to note that among the few documented cases of Quakers in the region suffering at the hands of local justices before 1660, three of the sufferers had cattle distrained for nonpayment of tithes. J. Besse, **An Abstract of the Sufferings of the People Call'd Quakers** (London, 1733-38), 1:82.

83. Bewick, **An Answer to a Quakers Seventeen Heads of Queries**, p. 22.

84. **Ibid.**, p. 67.

85. On the early history of Durham College, see Howell, **Newcastle upon Tyne and the Puritan Revolution**, pp. 330 ff.

86. The idea was in circulation as early as 1649 when George Lilburne suggested to a jury that Durham be made a university. **The Vindication of Edward Colston to a most false and scandalous Remonstrance of George Lilburne** (London, 1649), p. 4.

87. Cole, Prideaux, and Ledgard became visitors of the newly founded college at Durham in 1657, as indicated in the letters patent to the college 15 May 1657. **Allen Tracts** (Darlington, 1777), no. 44. Samuel Hammond was among those empowered to receive subscriptions for the college in 1656. **Publick**

Intelligencer, no. 28, 7-14 April, 1656, p. 480; **Cal. S.P. Dom.**, 1655-6, p. 262.

88. E 731 (20), G. Fox, **A Paper Sent Forth Into the World from Them that are Scornfully Called Quakers** (London, 1654). Cf. also Nuttall, "George Fox and Quakerism in the Bishoprick," p. 95.

89. See, for example, the anonymous **Some Quaeries to be Answered in Writing or Print by the Masters, Heads, Fellows and Tutors of the Colledge they are setting up at Durham** (n.p., n.d.).

90. Fox, **Journal**, 1:311-12. But see also the note in **Journal of the Friends' Historical Society**, vol. 4 (1907), p. 128 which queries the statement that Fox prided himself on suppressing Durham College; there can, despite the argument in this note, be little doubt about his hostile view towards it.

91. Bewick, **An Answer to a Quakers Seventeen Heads of Queries**, p. 72.

92. **Ibid.**, p. 101.

93. Pearson, **To the Parliament of England**, p. 2.

94. Fox, **Journal**, 1:311.

X

A BOHEMIAN EXILE IN CROMWELL'S ENGLAND:
THE CAREER OF GEORGE RITSCHEL,
PHILOSOPHER, SCHOOLMASTER, AND CLERIC

The political events of the seventeenth century brought England and Bohemia into close contact. Although there had been considerable intercourse between the two nations before the Battle of the White Mountain,[1] the common cause of Protestantism led them afterwards into even closer relations. The period of the Thirty Years' War brought a number of Bohemian exiles to England. The best known was the artist Wenceslas Hollar, but there were others of note, such as the humanist poet Jan Sictor.[2] Although there had been contacts between Bohemian intellectuals and the English universities since at least the early fourteenth century,[3] few of the exiles appear to have made their way to either Oxford or Cambridge. In 1635, Comenius referred to some Moravian students then resident in England;[4] of greater interest than these is George Ritschel, a neglected philosopher and teacher who is, next to Hollar, the most significant of the refugees who found their way to the Puritan state formed during the English revolution.[5]

According to his first biographer, Ritschel was born on February 13, 1616, in the village of Deutschkahn in Bohemia, not far from the town of Tetschen.[6] The chief landholder in this area was a Lutheran nobleman who also held lands in Saxony, Count Rudolph von Bunau. It has therefore been suggested with considerable plausibility that Ritschel's father was a Bohemian German of Lutheran views, either a small freeholder or a tenant of Count Rudoph.[7] Not much more than this is known about the family, save for one important relationship which had an obvious bearing on the later stages of Ritschel's career. His father was related by marriage to a Mrs. Butler of Newcastle upon Tyne in England. The Butlers were a prominent merchant family of the important coal-trading centre, and moreover, had close relations with the Puritan movement in the north of England.[8]

Young Ritschel appears to have displayed marked intellectual abilities at an early age. In 1633, he went to the University of Strasbourg, which was at that time a favorite centre of study for the Bohemian and

Moravian Protestants and was generally regarded as one of the most progressive universities in Europe under the Lutheran influence.[9] At the end of January, he matriculated in the philosophical faculty there, along with several other Bohemians. While at Strasbourg, Ritschel received a traditionalist training; even as late as 1640, the university was still dominated by the Peripatetic tradition, and the professor of natural philosphy was still required to base his teaching on Aristotle's **Physics**.[10] The effects of this training in Aristotelian method are marked in all of Ritschel's extant writings. His philosophical writing shows a distinctly Aristotelian bias, as well as precision in the framing of definitions. Ritschel seems to have remained at Strasbourg for about seven years; then the bitterness of the religious passions unleashed in the Thirty Years' War caught up with him. After the Battle of the White Mountain, Bohemia, which had been over-whelmingly Protestant, was converted by the dual pressures of force and propaganda to Roman Catholicism. As early as 1621, some Protestant clergy had been ordered out. Imperial rescripts issued by Ferdinand II in May 1624, and in July 1627, completed the process; under their terms, Roman Catholicism became the only religion besides Judaism tolerated in Bohemia and Moravia; the terms of the rescripts affected not only residence, but also land-holding.[11] Both of these decrees had, of course, been made even before Ritschel went to Strasbourg, but for a considerable part of the war period they had not been enforced in the region around Deutschkahn, because the area had been repeatedly occupied by Protestant Sweden. By 1640, however, the emperor was in a position to enforce the decrees. This fact, combined with the death of Ritschel's father, forced the young student to make some sort of a religious declaration. In the words of Anthony Wood, he "gave a very convincing proof of his zeal for protestantism" by renouncing his share in the family lands to his brother.[12]

Ritschel's immediate reaction to the situation, other than his giving up his share in the family lands, does not seem completely certain. Wood and the accounts which are derived directly from him state that Ritschel moved on to Oxford, where he was admitted as a reader in the Bodleian Library on December 3, 1641.[13] His name is, however, absent from the admission register for that year, and this casts some doubt on the assertion that Ritschel was in Oxford as early as 1641; the only entry concerning him is in the register on December 3, 1646.[14] His epitaph, preserved in an

163

antiquarian history of Newcastle, suggests that he was first at Oxford in 1644, but too much reliance cannot be placed on this either, since it is certain that he was not in England in 1644.[15] The matter must be left unresolved, but the evidence, on balance, would seem to suggest a confusion of dates, a confusion which is emphasized by the date of December 3 mentioned for both 1641 and 1646. The next certain traces of Ritschel which can be found are on the continent. It remains possible, but not proven, that Ritschel went to Oxford in 1641; it might seem to have been a logical time, for in the brief peace of that summer, an exhilaration swept the country. To Stephen Marshall, it was a wonderful year in which God had done more for England than for eighty years past; it was also the year in which the Long Parliament revived the plan to attract Dury and Comenius to England.[16] But the links between Comenius and Ritschel had not yet been forged; to assert firmly that Ritschel had been in England in 1641 and then migrated once again to the continent when the promise of the summer gave way to bitter political strife and the outbreak of the Civil War may be pushing the evidence too far.

Ritschel can be traced in the United Provinces in 1641 and 1642. He appeared at The Hague, Amsterdam, and Leiden. There, while he was serving as tutor to the son of the Prince of Transylvania, it is possible that he made the acquaintance of Christian Rave, the famed Orientalist who later became fellow and librarian of Magdalen College, Oxford.[17] In any case, in 1642 Ritschel was resident in Denmark with Rave's brother, Johann.[18] In this period, Ritschel was for the first time seriously engaged in the teaching end of education. After relinquishing his tutoring post, he joined with Johann Rave in the instruction of young noblemen at the Academy of Soröe. Contact with Rave had profound influence on Ritchel. No doubt it was of considerable importance in formulating his own teaching technique and in shaping his educational ideas. For this purpose, Rave was an exemplary companion. He was later appointed Inspector-General of Schools under the Great Elector and helped to lay the foundations of the Prussian system of public education.

Even more significant is the fact that Rave was in communication with two of the most advanced educational thinkers of the time, Comenius and Samuel Hartlib. In 1644, Comenius invited both Rave and his younger colleague Ritschel to act as his literary assistants in the preparation of material for his didactic and

164

pansophic work. Rave appears to have accepted at once; Ritschel hesitated for a while, but late in the year he joined Rave at Elbing.[19] To Ritschel fell the task of working on the metaphysical portions of the project. For half a year he remained at Elbing, living in the same house with Comenius. Then he left for England to work in the libraries there. He went first to London, where he made contact with one of Comenius's English patrons, Lord Hutton.[20] He experienced considerable difficulty in keeping up his correspondence with Comenius. The latter complained in a letter to him: "Even the process of our communicating with each other is very awkward and unsuccessful, for all that I have worked for your convenience. Your double letter, dated June and July, finally found me around the beginning of December. The next, dated 21 October, in which you wrote that you would expect a reply within two months... was eventually delivered on 19 December as the second month was just expiring."[21] Ritschel burned to get to Oxford. "You write that you are so fired with a desire to see Oxford and gain access to the libraries, and thereby increase our treasures with some choice observations, that you prefer to refuse a glittering opportunity."[22] When Ritschel eventually did get to Oxford, late in 1646, he settled in Kettle Hall and apparently was a member of Trinity College; according to Wood, Ritschel became "a severe and constant student" in the Bodleian.[23] He left practically no trace in the extant records of either the University or of Trinity College, except for the mention of his name in the admissions register of the Bodleian. This is not surprising. In the first place, the records of the period are fragmentary and reflect the unsettled conditions. In the second place, he was probably admitted to Trinity College as a guest, since he was already a member of Strasbourg University.[24]

The life of the young scholar was not an easy one. His English patron Hartlib was often in financial difficulties himself and was therefore limited in his ability to aid Ritschel.[25] These financial straits appear to have been a problem even before Ritschel went to Oxford. On May 24, 1646, Comenius wrote to his patrons in England, commending to their liberality George Ritschel, "now working and in want in their midst."[26] In January 1647, Comenius himself sent fifty imperials to Ritschel, although he confessed that he had scraped it together with some difficulty, and at the same time wrote to the clergy of the Dutch Church, urging them to aid the "young man endeared to me by his singular gifts of intellect."[27] Money was not, however, the only problem which was standing in the way of the completion of Ritschel's metaphysical work. A rift was rapidly growing between him and Comenius over the very nature of the work in hand. Comenius himself viewed metaphysics as as an art rather than a science; what he wanted from Ritschel was a piece of work the substance of which could easily be digested and simplified for young students.[28] One of the first indications of the rift occurred in January 1647, when Ritschel refused to follow Comenius's suggestion that he return to Elbing. At the end of January, Comenius wrote to Ritschel that no more financial aid was likely to be forthcoming. "I can manage no more at present and have no more to promise you. Accordingly I not only set nothing in the way of your looking to your own advantage; rather I urge this upon you."[29] The final break came in June. In the spring of 1647, Ritschel sent to Comenius part of the manuscript of the work on which he was engaged. It was far from what Comenius had anticipated or desired. He wrote in return to Ritschel, expressing his disappointment: "I am pleased with your accuracy, of which I see you make a point, but the work seems to contain more verbosity than is fitting if we wish it to be suited to youth and the schools. Nor does it seem to have that ease of expression which we want if it is to have a ready impact. For you are aware that the intention was to write a metaphysics not for the learned, but for the young and for the general public."[30]

Ritschel's reaction to the strictures of Comenius was to publish the work on his own; his academic pride was above the suggestion that it should be simplified. In 1648 he published the work at Oxford under the title of **Contemplationes Metaphysicae**, in what appears to have been a small printing. It was dedicated to two members of the Hartlib coterie. The first was Sir Cheney Culpepper, a wealthy Kentish landholder, graduate of Oxford and member of the Inner Temple; Culpepper was a man for whom Comenius had a high regard and he was, in addition, a friend of Sir Robert Boyle.[31] The second was Nicholas Stoughton, also a graduate of Oxford and a member of the Inner Temple; he was one of those whom Comenius had asked to help Ritchel.[32] Ritschel's reputation as a philosopher hangs on this single work. There is no doubt that the strictures of Comenius were justified; **Contemplationes Metaphysicae** was far too elaborate and complex to be used as an elementary text. Ritschel was one of those intellectuals who is unable to combine clarity of definition with simplicity of expression; the incisiveness

166

and lucidity of his definitions, on which Leibniz later remarked with favor,[33] were marred by the overall complexity of the whole structure. The work is not, however, without interest, particularly with respect to the question of the hold of Aristotle on philosophical speculation. In the main, the work adheres to the Aristotelian tradition; this is not surprising, considering Ritschel's own background and the prevailing atmosphere at Oxford. Yet even Oxford's defenders maintained that their adherence to Aristotle was not blind idolatry; as Seth Ward put it, "Though we do very much honour Aristotle for his profound judgement and universal learning, yet are we so farre from being tyed up to his opinions, that persons of all conditions amongst us take liberty to dissent from him and to declare against him, according as any contrary evidence doth ingage them, being ready to follow the Banner of Truth by whomsoever it shall be lifted up."[34] Ritschel himself was not totally out of touch with the new scientific thought of the time. In the preface, although not in the text, he refers with evident approval to Bacon's **De Augmentis Scientiarum**, which had been published in 1623, and to the philosophical treatises of Herbert of Cherbury. There is, on the other hand, no evidence that he was familiar with the work of Descartes, but it is possible that he had read Kepler's treatise, **De Harmonia Mundi**.[35] Ritschel would seem, then, to occupy an interesting and not totally insignificant place in the transition from the Aristotelian tradition to the new modes of scientific thought to which he had devoted brief but favorable mention.

Reaction to Ritschel's **magnum opus** was mixed. It seems to have aroused very little interest in England. This is hardly surprising, considering how few copies were printed and in view of its generally Aristotelian form at a time when there was a marked reaction against this, coupled with keen interest in the new scientific developments.[36] On the other hand, it appears to have received an enthusiastic response in Germany. This is of interest because it shows clearly that Ritschel did not abandon his intellectual contacts with the continent even after he had ceased to be associated with Comenius. As late as 1671, Ritschel forwarded a revised edition of **Contemplationes Metaphysicae** to Magnus Hesenthaler, a German professor, for reprinting in Germany.[37] It was, apparently, the German editions of the work that drew Leibniz to Ritschel.[38] The contacts which Ritschel maintained with the continent were largely kept up through the person of Hesenthaler,

167

who appears to have handled the negotiations for the continental printings of all of Ritschel's works.

The publication of his major philosophical work did not solve the pressing problem of Ritschel's livelihood. This was taken care of, however, on August 29, 1648, when he left Oxford to accept the post of headmaster of the Grammar School at Newcastle upon Tyne. The factors which led him to Newcastle are not completely clear, but several suggestions can be made. It has already been mentioned that Ritschel was related, through his father, to a prominent merchant family of the town. Moreover, Newcastle had a long-standing sympathy for exiled Bohemian Protestants; the town had contributed to the voluntary aid for the King of Bohemia in 1620.[39] A number of Newcastle merchants traded with the Eastland region, especially Elbing, a place which had been of some significance in the coming together of Comenius, Dury, and Hartlib.[40] Finally, there appear to have been some close links between the governing body of the town of Newcastle and Samuel Hartlib. Hartlib's son, Samuel, Jr., became one of the town's solicitors,[41] and it seems certain that Hartlib was consulted about the vacancy at the Grammar School, for another candidate considered was that notable exponent of elementary education and associate of Hartlib, Hezekiah Woodward.[42]

Education in the north of England, and in Newcastle in particular, had been severely and adversely affected by the English Civil War. As the Newcastle bookseller, William London, commented, "These counties recorded for Honour, have not yet been worthy to be branded with anything that could truly stick to them so much, as the present want of Studious Gentlemen.... I reckon learning...to be that which the misery of these tempestuous winds of a Civil War...hath made too great a stranger to these parts."[43] At the end of the war, the school was in a seriously decayed condition, the buildings falling down, the standard of work poor. The first postwar schoolmaster tried to remedy the situation, but he made little progress and was forced to retire because of failing health. It was this situation which Ritschel inherited. There is a certain element of mystery about his selection. On the surface, it seems clear what type of man the Newcastle corporation sought: it was, after all, a Puritan corporation, in theory, purged of Royalists and Anglicans, and loyal to the Parliament. One of its influential aldermen, Thomas Ledgard, had stated that the new schoolmaster was to be not only learned and able, but

well-affected to the Parliament.[44] The choice was to
be made in conjunction with the clergy of the town, and
the chief of these, the elderly Presbyterian divine,
Dr. Jenison, was especially to be consulted.[45] In the
final choice, there were two candidates, Ritschel and a
Mr. Webb. The clergy were satisfied that both men were
able, but "taking different circumstances into
account," they felt that Webb would be more useful than
Ritschel.[46] Nevertheless, the Common Council elected
Ritschel, lauding him as "a man of learning and other
abilityes euery way able to execute and discharge the
said place to the good of the schoole and contentment
of this corporation."[47]

The objection of the clergy to Ritschel may have
been because of religion. Although Ritschel subsequently preached in Newcastle on a number of
occasions, at the request of the mayors of the town,[48]
his religious views may not have been completely satisfactory to the Presbyterians and Independents of the
area. In later life, Ritschel denied that he had ever
been an active Puritan, and, in preaching Ritschel's
funeral sermon in 1683, Major Algood stressed that the
Bohemian was "an enemie to all innovation in the
church."[49] It seems likely that Ritschel was and
remained loyal to the Lutheran principles he had
learned in youth.[50] After the Restoration, he noted
that he had never been asked to express disagreement
with the Augsburg Confession.[51]

Although his religious position is not entirely
clear, Ritschel's work for the school is. He took in
hand the matter of the school library, and purchased a
number of books for it.[52] Ritschel was, moreover, in
charge of the school in the period during which its
government was reorganized. The "new" orders for
regulating the school have perished, but references to
them in the Common Council minutes indicate that the
Council was deeply interested in improving the quality
of education.[53] Ritschel further seems to have been
instrumental in seeing that more money was expended for
repairs of damaged school buildings. There can be
little doubt that his headmastership was both wise and
successful. This is attested by the increased number
of students from the school who went on to the universities. It is impossible to calculate the exact
percentage who did go on, for there are no contemporary
registers of the school, but it is suggestive that
during the 1650s, the list of corporation exhibitioners
at the universities began to assume, once again, signs
of regularity; one-half of the corporation exhibi-

tioners elected between 1637 and 1666 fall in the period when Ritschel was master of the school.[54]

In July 1657, Ritschel decided to leave the school. It is not clear what motives induced him to renounce the profession of teaching in favor of that of preaching, but at this time he informed the Common Council that he was shortly leaving "to take up the ministerial function" at the neighboring town of Hexham.[55] By August of the same year, he was fully established in his new post, for at that time he signed as "pastor of Hexham" a declaration of congratulation to the Lord Protector, Oliver Cromwell.[56] Beyond this declaration, Ritschel's early years at Hexham escape the historian: it is only with the Restoration that the threads of the story can be picked up. With the Restoration, Ritschel conformed immediately. He appears genuinely to have been attracted by the comprehensive principle of the Anglican Church and does not seem to have had any qualms about subscribing to the Thirty-Nine Articles; he later complained that German theologians were badly informed about the principles of the Anglican Church and indicated that he was quite content as a member.[57] His happy passage through the difficult years of the Restoration raises the problem of his ordination. There is no direct reference to his ever having been ordained, either as a Presbyterian or as an Anglican, although this may have been done provisionally by the Archbishop of York.[58] In June 1661, Ritschel marked his whole-hearted acceptance of the Anglican Church with the publication of his second and only other surviving work, **Dissertatio de Ceremonii Anglicanae**. It is a well-reasoned defence of the practices of the Anglican Church against charges of idolatry and superstition and contained strong attacks on the Puritans. Anglican opinion was firmly convinced that it was an important defence of their position.[59] The book, like his earlier one, also attracted interest on the continent; within two years, Magnus Hesenthaler was publishing a second edition of it at Stuttgart.

There is little to be learned about Ritschel's last years at Hexham, where he continued until his death in 1683. It is known that he wrote several other books; all have unfortunately perished. At least two manuscript volumes were sent to Hesenthaler, but they do not seem to have printed; this was probably due in large part to the death of Hesenthaler in 1681, for with his death perished Ritschel's last real tie with the continental academic tradition which had nurtured him. Of one of these volumes, **Ethica Christiana,** nothing is known but its title. The other, **Exercitationes Sacrae**, consists of twenty-two essays dealing with the central theological problems of free will, determinism, and supernatural grace. It continues Ritschel's attacks on the Puritans, and is marked by a strenuous attempt to refute the teachings of the Calvinists, especially those of the Scottish theologian Samuel Rutherford.[60] At his death, Ritschel left two further manuscripts with his son. Both appear to have been suppressed. Only the title of the first is known, **De Fide Catholica**; the second was a work against the English Quakers.[61] The latter was well within the tradition of Newcastle religious writing in the mid-seventeenth century.[62]

From all accounts, Ritschel's management of Hexham parish was as active as his literary efforts. Between his arrival there in 1657 and his death in 1683, he completed a career of service to his adopted country. His career had spanned three disciplines: philosophy, education, and religion. In each, he had a measure of success which cannot be ignored. To the end, the formidable Bishop of Durham, John Cosin, gave "venerable respect" to this foreigner who officiated at Hexham, and in his latter days, as Major Algood noted, his "piety which was singular crowned all his other excellencies."[63]

NOTES

1. On Bohemia and England prior to the battle,
see R. Wellek, "Bohemia in English Civilization,"
Central European Observer, vol. 15 (1937), pp. 21-22,
53-54, 107-108; R. Wellek, "Bohemia in Early English
Literature," **Slavonic Review,** vol. 21 (1943), pp. 114-
126.

2. On Sictor's career and writings, see R.F.
Young, **A Czech Humanist in London in the Seventeenth
Century:** Jan Sictor Rokycansky 1593-1652 (London,
n.d.).

3. See R.F. Young, "Bohemian Scholars and
Students at the English Universities from 1347 to
1750," **EHR,** vol. 38 (1923), pp. 72-84.

4. **Ibid.,** p. 75, citing **Opera Didactica,** 1:404.

5. R.F. Young, **A Bohemian Philosopher at Oxford
in the Seventeenth Century:** George Ritschel of
Deutschkahn (London, 1925). Young is the only modern
historian to have made a detailed study of Ritschel, as
far as I know. I am deeply indebted to his work for
much of the information in this paper.

6. A. Wood, **Athenae Oxonienses,** ed., P. Bliss
(London, 1813-1820), 4:124. Wood is a very important
source on Ritschel. He seems to have taken great care
in collecting his material, writing about him to Dr.
Cantar and the Rev. John March, a former pupil of the
Bohemian. A. Clark, **The Life and Times of Anthony Wood**
(Oxford 1881-1895), 3:175, 349.

7. Young, **Ritschel,** p. 4.

8. W.H.D. Longstaffe, ed., **Memoirs of the Life of
Mr. Ambrose Barnes** (Durham, 1867), p. 56. Barnes was
one of the most colorful of the Newcastle Puritans.
The son-in-law of Mrs. Butler, he was an active moral
reformer and one of the chief political figures in the
town during the Interregnum.

9. R.F. Young, **Comenius in England** (London,
1932), p. 1.

10. **Ibid.,** p. 1. There is nothing unusual in
this. Many universities were cold to the new developments in science which were undermining their

172

Aristotelian tradition. There were similar conditions at the liberal Calvinist University of Leiden, and Padua, as well as in the English universities.

11. E. Denis, **La Bohême depuis la Montagne Blanche** (Paris, 1903), 1:71, 83, 89. For Comenius's comments on the rescripts, see Young, **Comenius in England,** p. 26.

12. Wood, **Athenae Oxonienses**, 4:124. There is some discrepancy between Wood's account, which states that Ritschel gave his share in the lands to his brother in return for an allowance for travel, and the account in **Memoirs of Ambrose Barnes**, p. 56, which states that he sold the lands outright to his brother.

13. Wood, **Athenae Oxonienses**, 4:124. Accounts which follow Wood include J. Brand, **History of Newcastle** (London, 1789); H. Hornby, 'Account of Newcastle upon Tyne," MSS Duke of Northumberland, Alnwick Castle, 187A/200-203. Concerning the reliability of Wood, see note 6.

14. Young, **Ritschel**, p. 6.

15. Brand, **History of Newcastle**, 1:93. Ritschel was at Elbing from December 1644 to June 1645. A. Patera, **Jana Amosa Komenského Korrespondence** (Prague, 1892), pp. 93, 101. Cf. also p. 124, which suggests that as late as October 1646, Ritschel had not yet visited Oxford.

16. See H.R. Trevor-Roper. "Three Foreigners and the Philosophy of the English Revolution," **Encounter,** vol. 14, no. 2 (1960), pp. 3-20, especially p. 13.

17. On C. Rave, see **Allgemeine Deutsche Biographie,** 27:396-397. Rave was in London for at least part of 1642, but had apparently returned to he continent before the end of the year. Young suggested that they may have met at Leiden. **Ritschel**, p. 6. Rave matriculated there in 1637, but he had left Leiden in the interval between 1637 and 1642.

18. On J. Rave, see **Allgemeine Deutsche Biographie** 27:397-398.

19. Patera, **J.A. Komenského Korrespondence,** p. 93.

20. **Ibid.**, p. 114.

21. **Ibid.**, p. 123.

22. **Ibid.**, p. 124.

23. Wood, **Athenae Oxonienses,** 4:125.

24. Young, **Ritschel,** p. 9, n. 4.

25. On Hartlib's financial problems, see **BL** Sloane MS 654, f. 350.

26. G.H. Turnbull, ed., **Hartlib, Dury, and Comenius: Gleanings from Hartlib's Papers** (London, 1947), p. 372.

27. Patera, **J.A. Komenského Korrespondence,** p. 129.

28. Cf. **ibid.**, pp. 123, 129; G. Ritschel, **Contemplationes Metaphysicae ex Natura Rerum et rectae Rationis Lumine deductae** (Oxford, 1648), preface, p. 3.

29. Patera, **J.A. Komenského Korrespondence,** p. 129.

30. **Ibid.**, p. 139. The growing rift was also evident on a lower level, that is, the disrespect which Ritschel showed to Cyprian Kinner, who succeeded him as a literary assistant. Ritschel appears to have been skeptical of the attempts to represent things by pictures and models, a way which was characteristic of Comenius's educational work. He also clearly felt that Kinner was very superficial. Cf. Turnbull, **Hartlib, Dury, and Comenius,** p. 432.

31. Young, **Comenius in England,** p. 43, n. 3.

32. Turnbull, **Hartlib, Dury, and Comenius,** p. 372.

33. J. Kvačala, **Korrespondence Jana Amosa Komenského II** (Prague, 1902), p. 153. Leibniz was not above mentioning Ritschel in the same sentence with Plato, Aristotle, Descartes and Hobbes.

34. S. Ward., **Vindiciae Academiarum Containing some Briefe Animadversions upon Mr. Webster's book, stiled the Examination of Academies** (Oxford, 1654), p. 2.

35. Young, **Ritschel**, p. 13., n. 7.

36. See, for example, John Webster's **Academiarum Examen** (1654) or William Dell's **Right Reformation of Learning, Schools, and Universities** (1646). There is useful secondary comment on this point in R. Schlatter, "The Higher Learning in Puritan England," **Historical Magazine of the Protestant Episcopal Church,** vol. 23 (1954), pp. 167-187.

37. J. Kvačala, ed., **Analecta Comeniana** (Dorpat 1910), p. 148.

38. On Leibniz and Ritschel, see especially **ibid.,** pp. 147, 148, 149-150; Kvačala, **Korrespondence J.A. Komenského II,** pp. 151-152, 153.

39. **Cal. S.P. Dom., 1619-1623,** p. 140. See also Tynemouth Vestry Book I, f. 38, which records a contribution received in 1658 for "the distressed protestants in Poland and 20 ffamilyes Bannished out of Bohemia."

40. It is of some interest that at least two of the Newcastle Puritan clergymen went to the Eastland region in times of difficulty - Dr. Robert Jenison in about 1640 and Samuel Hammond in 1660.

41. For evidence of Hartlib as town solicitor as early as 1651, see Newcastle City Archives R 5/1/3.

42. On Woodward, see **DNB**; Wood, **Athenae Oxonienses,** 3:1034-1037; D. Masson, **Life of John Milton** (London, 1871-1880), 3:230-231, 293-296. The election of the schoolmaster is also discussed in the author's article, "Newcastle's Regicide: The Parliamentary Career of John Blakiston," **Archaeologia Aeliana** 1964, reprinted above Chapter IV.

43. W. London, **A Catalogue of the Most Vendible Books in England** (London, 1658), sig. B 1-1v.

44. Newcastle City Archives, Common Council Book 1645-50, f. 176.

45. **Ibid.,** f. 267.

46. **Ibid.,** f. 268.

47. M.H. Dodds, ed., **Extracts from the Newcastle upon Tyne Common Council Minute Book 1639-1656** (Newcastle, 1920), p. 93.

48. Newcastle City Archives, Common Council Book 1650-9, f. 365. He was also on one occasion consulted by the Corporation concerning the stipend of another schoolmaster. **Ibid.**, f. 87.

49. M. Algood, **A Sermon Preached at the Funeral of the Reverend and Learned Mr. George Ritschel** (London, 1684), p. 20.

50. When Ritschel visited Lord Hutton in 1645, the latter remarked on his Lutheranism. Patera, **J. A. Komenského Korrespondence**, p. 114.

51. Kvačala, **Analecta Comeniana**, p. 149

52. Newcastle City Archives, Chamberlains' Accounts, 1651-2, f. 208v; 1654-5, f. 210v.

53. Newcastle City Archives, Chamberlains' Accounts, 1654-50, fols. 351, 355, 363.

54. See A.R. Laws, **Schola Novocastrensis** (Newcastle, 1925), p. 152. The vast majority of the Newcastle students who went to university went to Cambridge, where the town had connections rather than to Oxford, where Ritschel did. Cf. B.D. Stevens, ed., **Register of the Royal Grammar School Newcastle upon Tyne 1545-1954** (Gateshead, 1955), **passim.**

55. Newcastle City Archives, Common Council Book, 1650-9, f. 431.

56. T. Birch, ed., **Thurloe State Papers** (London, 1742), 6:431.

57. Kvačala, **Analecta Comeniana**, p. 149.

58. See Young, **Ritschel**, p. 15., n. 7. All of the livings which Ritschel held were peculiars of York and, therefore, not under the administration of Durham diocese. By the time of his death, he held also Whitley Chapel and Bywell St. Andrews.

59. Bishop Cosin of Durham, to whom it was dedicated, received it favorably. See also W. Kennet, **A Register and Chronicle Ecclesiastical and Civil** (London, 1728), pp. 487, 582; J. Durel, **Sanctae**

Ecclesiae Anglicane Vindiciae (London, 1669), p. 176, wherein Ritschel is referred to as a very erudite man.

60. Kvačala, **Analecta Comeniana**, pp. 149-150; on Rutherford, see **DNB**.

61. Brand, **History of Newcastle**, 1:93, citing Wood, **Athenae Oxonienses**.

62. For a discussion of this point, see above, Chapter IX.

63. Algood, **Sermon**, p. 20.

XI

THE ARMY AND THE ENGLISH REVOLUTION:
THE CASE OF ROBERT LILBURNE

The Lilburne family played a prominent role in the period of the English revolution. Pride of place, both for notoriety and for impact on the unfolding drama, has, of course, been given to the prolific Leveller theorist and organizer, John Lilburne.[1] In more locally oriented annals George Lilburne, the mayor of Sunderland, has his place as a supporter of the parliamentary cause and as an advocate of a preaching ministry,[2] while Henry Lilburne is remembered as a deserter from the parliamentary side who instigated an abortive royalist revolt at Tynemouth Castle in 1648.[3] But next to Free-born John, the member of the family who played the most active role in the wars and the subsequent search for a stable settlement was his brother Robert.[4] It was also a role that was, in some significant respects, ambiguous. Yet its very ambiguities reveal important clues about the movement of opinion in a period of turbulent change. Robert Lilburne made his career as a professional soldier at a time when the army played an unusually central role in the unfolding of events. While it would clearly be a mistake to interpret either his career or his reactions to events as typical of the army as a whole, his response to and participation in these trying circumstances are illustrative of the pressures which weighed on those committed to the parliamentary cause, and they offer a valuable view of certain stages of the revolution as they were perceived and acted upon by a person whose viewpoint was, in important ways, conditioned by his loyalty to the army.

Because of his connection with the rebel cause and particularly because he had been an active participant in the trial of the King and one of the signatories of the death warrant, Robert Lilburne was the target of violent attack after the Restoration. A tract published in 1660 described him as an avid supporter of the Protectorate, indeed tying him closely to Cromwell by suggesting that he was "a pure Bird of Old Noll's Hatching," and condemned him as "a most implaccable Enemy against Kingly Government and a most insolent Infringer of the People's Liberties, one that had more Wit than Honesty, but despised Good Old Law called Magna Charta."[5] Such adverse sentiments were predictably repeated in other early biographical notices. Thomas Gumble thought he was "a great rebel" and inclined to a "violent" Anabaptism.[6] Wood described him as one who sided with "the rout against his Majesty in the beginning of the rebellion" and judged that he was "thorow-paced to Oliver's interests."[7] The Rev. Mark Noble, writing on the lives of the regicides at the end of the eighteenth century, was no less scathing; Lilburne, he argued, had "a prodigious hatred to the court and even the person of his majesty" and, while admitting that Lilburne displayed bravery during the war itself, characterized him as a man well adapted for the "odious undertaking" of imposing military rule on England and one who "was as assiduous in privately ruining the royalists as he had been openly in the field."[8]

Such observations do more than indicate the hostility displayed towards Lilburne, in common with other chief actors in the revolution; they also unwittingly pose some of the problems which are most difficult to resolve in assessing his contribution to and stand on the events of 1640-60. What indeed were his political views? Did he have such a burning hatred of the Stuart monarchy that he was determined from the outset of hostilities to bring the crown to ruin? Is it the case that his puritanism took the form of a violent Anabaptism? Was he truly Cromwell's creature? Not all of these questions can be satisfactorily resolved, but a review of his career, with particular attention to his role in the army in that confusing year of army mutiny in 1647, his role in Scotland in the early 1650s, his activities as a deputy major general in the northern counties in 1655-6, and his actions as the revolution collapsed around him, will provide at least the framework of an answer.

The main events of his life are readily documented and can be quickly summarized. Born in 1613, he was the eldest son of Richard Lilburne of Thickley Puncherdown, Co. Durham.[9] Of his early life, nothing is known, but when the war broke out he was soon engaged on the parliamentary side. His military career was divided between service in the South, where he acted as lieutenant and captain in the armies of the Earls of Essex and Manchester in 1643-4 and as a colonel in the New Model in 1646-7,[10] and service in the North. In the latter area, he raised a regiment of Durham horse in 1644, including several relations and neighbours among his officers.[11] In 1647 he returned to his old regiment in the North and for a brief period served as governor of Newcastle.12 By 1648 he was second in command of the Northern Army under John Lambert, the army colleague with whom he was to be most closely associated throughout the revolution. In 1650-4 and again in 1657-8, he served with the army in Scotland,13 while in 1654-7 and 1658-60, he was in England as governor of York. While his career was thus essentially that of an army officer, he also exercised important administrative functions in conjunction with his military positions; as commander in chief of Scotland between December 1652 and April 1654, he acted as **de facto** chief magistrate, and as deputy major general in the North between 1655 and 1657, he likewise played a role that considerably transcended normal military command. At the Restoration, he surrendered himself to the new regime in accordance with the King's proclamation of 6th June 1660 against the regicides, he having been a member of the High Court of Justice and twenty-eighth signatory to the death warrant.14 He was tried and condemned to death, but the sentence was commuted to life imprisonment, and he lived out his days on St. Nicholas Island where he died in August 1665.

Although his military career had attracted notice before 1647, it was in that year of complicated nego- tiations between King, Parliament, and army that Robert Lilburne first rose to a prominent position.15 Pre- dictably, his role was intimately connected with army grievances, including the fear of abrupt disbanding of the forces before such issues as arrears of pay and indemnity for actions undertaken during the war were firmly settled by parliamentary guarantees. The issue which first forced his hand was the question of the redeployment of troops to Ireland in advance of the settlement of such issues. Lilburne quickly emerged as one of the leaders of the opposition in the army to Parliament. At some point in 1646, Lilburne had been given the command of the Kentish regiment of foot originally raised and commanded by Ralph Weldon; though authorized by Fairfax, it was an appointment which appears from the first to have created dissension and dissatisfaction among the continuing officers of the regiment.16 In the following spring of 1647, when the question of disbanding or serving in Ireland was put before the army by Parliament, Lilburne's new regiment was clearly divided, one group being prepared to under- take the Irish service and urging the appointment of Lt. Colonel Kempson as their commander,17 the other, with which Lilburne was prominently associated, backing the demands for satisfaction of grievances embodied in

The Declaration of the Army.[18] Lilburne's activities
in this regard aroused extreme suspicion in Parliament;
on 27th March the House had ordered Fairfax to suppress
the army petition,[19] but two days later they received
confirmation that not only was the petition still cir-
culating in the army but that a committee of officers
had been formed to take charge of it once it had been
subscribed in the ranks, thus establishing a potentially dangerous link between soldiers and officers.[20]
The reaction of the Presbyterians in the House was both
swift and negative; Lilburne in company with a handful
of other army officers was sent for by the House on
29th March to answer for his behaviour, and the following day both Houses issued a declaration condemning
the petition as "dangerous" and "tending to put the
army into a distemper and mutiny" and adding that
"those who shall continue in this distempered condition
and go on advancing and promoting that petition shall
be looked upon and proceeded against as enemies of the
state and disturbers of the public peace."[21]

While Lilburne was discharged by the House on 25th
May,[22] it is clear that in the interval he continued in
what had been called his "distempered condition." He
bent all his efforts to prevent his regiment from
volunteering for Ireland in the face of what appear to
have been rather underhanded methods employed by
Kempson and the officers loyal to the Parliament to
induce the troops to volunteer.[23] He was reported as
giving numerous speeches to the soldiers attempting to
hinder them from service in Ireland and to draw them
away from obedience to Kempson. On 20th April, for
example, he overtook members of the regiment on the
march through heavy weather, and told them, "Fellow
Soldiers, I am sorry you are marching up and down in
such weather as this; you may thank your Lieutenant
Colonel for it," while one of his companions added,
"They delude you as ignorant men to go to Ireland; no
godly man would desire you to go for that affair."[24]
It appears that his efforts had a marked success; most
of those who had marched with Kempson left him again.[25]
By the time Parliament ordered the regiment disbanded
on 10th June, the whole army was in revolt and had
entered into a Solemn Engagement not to disband until
their demands were granted.[26]

In common with a number of members of the army,
Lilburne appears to have been politicized by this
sequence of events. The rebuff given by Parliament to
the petition for redress of grievances, the labelling
of promoters of the petition as enemies of the state,

his own summoning to the House, and the continued effort to secure volunteers for the Irish service appear to have broadened significantly the scope of Lilburne's demands (or at least of the demands with which he associated himself). As the question was transformed from one of specific grievances to one of the army's honor and its right to petition, Lilburne's position became a more generally political one. On 17th April he was one of the signatories of the vindication of the officers of the army presented to the House of Commons; it argued for the liberty of petitioning for what now concerned the army as soldiers and afterwards would concern them as members of the commonwealth. The call for a vindication of the army's honor, going beyond satisfaction of immediate grievances, was already apparent. "The Sense of such Expressions is so irksom to us, who have ventured whatsoever we esteemed dear to us in this World for Preservation of your Freedom and Privileges, that we cannot but earnestly implore your Justice in the Vindication of us, as in your Wisdom you shall think fit."27 The process of politicization may be seen as complete by the day on which the regiment was ordered disbanded (10th June 1647), when Lilburne signed a letter to the Lord Mayor, Aldermen, and Common Council of London; by that time, the demands for settlement of army grievances had been generalized into a statement about the political interest of the soldiery in the future settlement of the nation. Their demands, the letter stated, "we insist upon as Englishmen, and surely our being Soldiers hath not stript us of that Interest." Arguing that they desired "a Settlement of the Peace of the Kingdom, and of the Liberties of the Subject," the signatories went on to note that "we think we have as much right to demand and desire to see a happy Settlement as we have to our Money and the other common Interest of Soldiers which we have insisted upon."28

During the summer of 1647, Lilburne was detached from his regiment and appointed by Fairfax to be governor of Newcastle, a position he held between the governorships of Skippon and Hesilrige. In that post he seems to have occasioned general satisfaction. The Corporation voted at the conclusion of his appointment that "during the time he hath byn Governor of this Garrison [he] hath shewed many respects and favors to this Corporacion and hath allwaies byn willing to promote what soever might any waies tend to the good and welfare thereof" and presented him with two silver flagons with the arms of the town engraved on them "as a thankful acknowledgement of the respect of this Corporacion to him."[29] What precisely it was he had promoted is unclear, other than his expressed concern for the repair of the town walls.[30] But even though he had been posted to the North, the association of his name and his regiment with army restlessness continued. In November his regiment of foot was referred to as "the most mutinous Regiment in the Army;"[31] it participated more actively than any other in the abortive army mutiny at Ware,[32] at which time its actions revealed that the Leveller ideas of Robert's brother John had spread widely among the rank and file. The incident and Lilburne's reaction to it are revealing with regard to the limits Robert Lilburne would place around direct political action on the part of the soldiers and is suggestive with respect to his attitude towards his more famous brother John.

That Lilburne was unsympathetic to the more radical movement within the army and feared that it would dissolve army unity and hence its overall political influence was readily apparent. If maintaining their rights as Englishmen was one thing, the throwing off of officers by the rank and file was quite another. Writing to Fairfax, Lilburne asserted that as soldiers and members of the army, they owed all obedience and subjection to Fairfax's authority and command, "from which we humbly conceive neither Birthrights, nor other Priviledges whatsoever, whereof we have or ought to have an equal share with others, can or ought in the least to disoblige us." He added significantly, "malcontented Spirits take occasion...to divide the Army into Parties and Factions, endeavouring to turn every Man's Sword against his Fellows, pleading Necessity where there is none," and noting that such things will be more destructive to the commonwealth if granted than refusal would be.[33]

The distancing of himself from the opinions and actions of his brother John is striking and helps to place his own political views in a proper perspective. It raises some doubt about the assertion of Noble that Robert had taken up the parliamentary cause in the war because of a hatred of the King and the court which had its roots in the treatment given to John by the Court of Star Chamber in the 1630s.[34] Although the bonds of family led him to stand by his brother's side during his trial in 1649,[35] for the most part he publicly disassociated himself from him, most notably in this aftermath of his regiment's mutiny, but also by studiedly ignoring John's later trial in 1653. If

183

there was radicalism in the spirit of Robert Lilburne, it was a radicalism that was not in touch with the variety propounded by his brother.

Robert Lilburne's relations with his difficult regiment in 1647 suggest, however, one other possible line of influence. When the officers of the regiment were shuffled in the summer of 1647, Paul Hobson, more distinguished as a preacher than as a soldier, had become major.[36] Hobson had been in trouble as early as 1645 for his contravention of the ordinance forbidding laymen to preach.[37] Described by an admittedly hostile witness as a subscriber to the confession of faith of the Anabaptists, Hobson continued his preaching activities among the soldiery; it was reported by the same source that "the subject matter of his sermons was much against duties and of revelation" and that "he was a means to corrupt some pretious hopefull young men."[38] The obvious Baptist inclinations of Robert Lilburne, which became increasingly evident during his sojourn in Scotland in the early 1650s, when it was noted that Anabaptists were being admitted among his troops through his own favor and intercession,[39] conceivably can be traced to his interaction with Hobson. Without doubt, there is a connection between the foundation of Baptist congregations on Tyneside and the presence in the area first of Robert Lilburne as governor of the town in 1647 and then Hobson as deputy governor in 1648.[40]

Lilburne's stay as governor on Tyneside was relatively brief. With the outbreak of the second civil war, he was to be found once again playing a significant military role, still in the North, when he led the defeat of Colonel Grey, Sir Richard Tempest, and the Northumbrian cavaliers in July 1648.[41] In January, he was an active participant in the central political act of the revolution, the trial and execution of the King. Named as one of the King's judges, he attended the sessions on 15th, 17th, 19th, 23rd, 25th, and 27th January in the Painted Chamber and was present on all days of the trial in Westminster Hall;[42] the judgment given, he was the twenty-eighth signatory to the death warrant.

At the Restoration he would attempt to put a favorable gloss on this involvement, but his active participation in 1649 suggests that at that moment he was convinced of the political necessity of such drastic action.

He was soon again involved in military affairs as
a participant in Cromwell's Scottish campaigns and the
subsequent Worcester campaign. His service was
exemplary from all accounts, his most notable achievement being the utter rout he inflicted on the Earl of
Derby near Wigan on 25th August 1651;[43] it was a stroke
that removed all danger of a royalist rising in the
North and served as a critical step towards the
crowning mercy of Worcester on 3rd September.
Lilburne's letters to Speaker Lenthall and the Lord
General concerning the fight struck a characteristic
note, drawing particular attention to the danger posed
to the revolutionary regime by the Presbyterians. Like
a number of his colleagues in the army, Lilburne had an
acute hostility towards the Presbyterians, and he was
at pains to point out "that assistance the Ministers
and those who are called Presbyterians afforded, and
would more abundantly have appeared, for they are the
men who are grown here more bitter and envious against
you than others of the old Cavaliers' stamp."[44] It was
hardly an attitude likely to stand him in good stead
when he returned to his duties in Scotland. For the
moment, however, he had the openly expressed good
wishes of Cromwell and the gratitude of the Parliament,
which voted him a grant of lands to the value of £300 a
year.[45]

Lilburne's activities in Scotland, where he became
commander in chief on the recall of Richard Deane to
serve as a general of the fleet,[46] were dominated by
the growing violence and disorder occasioned by
Glencairn's rising on behalf of the Stuart cause.[47] As
an officer, Lilburne had had considerable experience of
Scottish conditions. He and his regiment had gone
there with Cromwell in 1650 and had returned following
the Worcester campaign by November 1651; in 1652 he had
been involved in a campaign into the Highlands.[48] The
growing unrest, however, provided deep challenges, both
to Lilburne's grasp of military strategy and to his
comprehension of the needs of the Scottish people. His
attitude towards royalists and Presbyterians complicated his actions, while his capacity for effective
action was further compromised by successive changes of
government in England as the Rump Parliament was
expelled, the Barebones experiment faltered, and the
Protectorate was created. In addition, the diversion
of English attention to the military needs of the
concurrent Dutch war caused many of his pleas for aid
to be given a secondary priority. The normal judgment
of Lilburne's behaviour in these trying circumstances
has been negative; Gardiner argued that "difficult as

the situation was, it is impossible to avoid the conclusion that Lilburne was far from being a resourceful commander,"[49] while the most recent historian of the rising comments "it cannot be said that Lilburne personally stood up to the test well."[50] Both, however, suggest the somewhat paradoxical point that although his performance as a soldier must be found lacking, his counsels as a statesman were far more worthy of attention. The period of Lilburne's command in Scotland thus becomes a critical testing point of his overall ability and both sides of the conventional judgment (his role as a soldier and his advice as a statesman) need careful investigation.

That Lilburne failed as a military commander is, on one level, obvious enough; he failed to put the rising down and it was left to General Monck who succeeded him in April 1654 to suppress the revolt. If there were signs by the time of Lilburne's departure that the rising was on the wane, it is probably the case that this was due more to internal contradictions within the royalist cause itself than it was to any particular efforts on Lilburne's part.[51] The indictment of Lilburne's military efforts goes a step further, however, in the assertion that his command was characterized by irresolution, agonized attention to detail, and consequent rapid fluctuations in his assessment of the military situation.[52] That this is, in large measure, a reasonable judgment of his behaviour under stress cannot be denied; one cannot help but feel in reading his letters from this period and in looking at his pattern of command that one is seeing a man lacking in self-confidence and ultimately overwhelmed by the demands of his assignment.[53] Dow has accurately summed up the situation by commenting that "his letters to the authorities in England became querulous in tone, full of complaints about the failure of the Council and the Committee for the Army to listen to his demands for more men and better supplies, and displaying in general an unwillingness to take responsibility or to exercise his own initiative."[54] Particularly worthy of criticism was Lilburne's slow acceptance of the fact that he had a serious rebellion on his hands; especially in the early stages of the rising, he had a tendency to take a short-term view of the situation and this helps to explain his fluctuating assessment of the danger.[55] It is also probably the case that Lilburne was torn in his letters between emphasizing the seriousness of the situation in order to make compelling his reiterated pleas for reinforcements and other supplies and providing assurance to the authorities that he had the situation under control in order to justify his own handling of affairs. The effort appears to have been too much for him. By the spring of 1654, he clearly conveyed the sense that he was desperate to be relieved of his command[56] and, looking back on his service, he could describe himself as having been "a pure drudge almost these 4 yeares in Scotland."[57] It was manifestly with a sense of relief and gratitude that he turned over his command in the spring of 1654 to assume the post of governor of York.

To be fair to Lilburne, one must qualify this picture of faltering leadership by a recognition of the complexity of the situation facing him. After all, it was Lilburne who had to face the movement while it was still on the rise; the acrid internal divisions and the growing disillusionment which stemmed from the failure to keep promises of aid from abroad would eventually make a failure of Glencairn's rising, but those factors were more characteristic of the revolt that Monck faced and suppressed than of the situation initially confronting Lilburne. Monck may have brought more decisiveness to bear on the situation, but his overall plan of pacification was not radically different from that which Lilburne had sought to pursue.[58] The crucial difference lay in the facts that Monck faced an increasingly divided movement and that he was better supplied to do so. The factor of supply was a far from negligible element in Lilburne's unhappy efforts to cope. It was his misfortune that his offensive against the royalists coincided so closely in time with England's heaviest involvement in the Dutch war; given the logistical realities of the moment, it was simply not possible for authorities in London to provide men and money for both on an adequate scale at the same time. In fact, during the first month of his command Lilburne had to accept a significant reduction in the infantry and lesser reductions in the horse and artillery to free men and money for the Dutch war.[59] There can be little doubt that such decisions weakened his ability to take the offensive the following summer, regardless of any personal shortcomings as a commander. The impression is certainly created that Lilburne, especially when compared with Monck, lacked authority in governmental circles, for all that he was commander in chief in Scotland. When Monck wanted action on civil or military matters from Whitehall, he tended to get prompt attention. Lilburne did not. It was in part the result of the fact that the Council had more time and more money for Monck than they did for

Lilburne, but it was also a measure of the authority their respective names carried with men in London.

On the military level, then, Lilburne's efforts were frustrated and frustrating. But he did appear to have insight into the root causes of the rebellion and he had plans for dealing with the sources of discontent in Scotland; these should not be overlooked simply on the grounds of his military inadequacy. What should be noted about them, however, is that his sound instincts for conciliation were thwarted in part by his own religious preconceptions, which took the form of a marked antipathy to all but a small section of the Scottish clergy, in part by his increasing reliance on coercive measures to control the rising which, of necessity, ran counter to his aspirations for conciliation.

Lilburne had the perception to realize that the rising drew its strength from "the rooted hostility of the Scottish people"[60] to the English government and that such hostility was being fed by grievances stemming from current English policy. He was anxious, as a result, that the circumstances surrounding the revolt should not lead to further estrangement and was quite willing, for example, to issue licences to noblemen and gentlemen to retain their arms in order to protect their property against the depredations of the rebels.[61] In like manner he was much concerned that the army deal fairly with the civilian population; in such a way, he believed, the military regime might commend itself to the people. During the summer of 1653 he issued a series of orders in an attempt to prevent the soldiers from taking advantage of the people over whom they held sway,[62] and he pleaded with authorities in London for money so that he could avoid free quarter, something which he noted would be most "unseasonable" in the circumstances.[63] Likewise, he attempted to deal with the assessment, the chief form of taxation on the Scottish people, in such a manner as to make the burden more acceptable without compromising the financial needs of the administration and his aggrieved complaints about Parliament's decision to levy the assessment to the full only served to underline the complexity of the situation in which he found himself.[64] Lilburne strongly advocated a speedy decision with respect to an act of oblivion for Scotland. He was anxious in this regard to see that people loyal to the regime were restored to their estates;[65] in both this recommendation and his argument that the courts should not be allowed to press too hard

188

in matters of debt against lords whose loyalty he hoped to retain,[66] Lilburne's instincts seem sound. He had realized that sequestration of estates and proceedings with respect to debt had produced a situation of necessity for many in which impoverishment seemed inevitable under English rule, relief only possible by rallying to the royal cause. What he hoped to create instead was a situation in which such individuals had everything to gain by remaining loyal to an English government which protected their interests.

In favouring such policies, Lilburne was making a cool and basically sound appraisal of the situation, but when it came to the matter of assessing the religious loyalties of the Scottish people and dealing with their clergy, his own blind spots led him into great difficulty. Lilburne badly misinterpreted the significance and meaning of the split in the Scottish church between the Protesters and the Resolutioners.[67] On the one hand, he persisted in a belief that the Protesters were potential converts to the cause of Independency, mistaking in the process their antipathy to Resolutioner domination of the institutions of the Presbyterian church for a wavering from the Presbyterian position towards Independency. On the other hand, he was convinced that the overwhelming majority of the clergy, influenced by the Resolutioners, were primarily responsible for instigating support for the royalist cause. It was the latter consideration which led him to take what was perhaps his most controversial action while commander in chief, the dissolution of the General Assembly of the Church of Scotland in July 1653.[68] He had asked Cromwell in advance whether "in regard of the ficklenesse of the times"[69] he should prevent the meeting; receiving no answer in time, he somewhat uncharacteristically acted on his own initiative and had the meeting dispersed by a party of soldiers. It was not a stroke designed to win the hearts of the Scottish people to the English government. Indeed, the Protesters, on whom Lilburne had placed such hopes, condemned the act as vociferously as the Resolutioners themselves.[70]

Even in the absence of such provocative acts, it is doubtful, however, that Lilburne could have successfully steered the treacherous course between conciliation and coercion. While he sensed correctly that the attitude of the people was central to the problem of English administration, once that attitude had become a military problem, he was led perforce to coercive measures, to the passing of edicts against aiding the

189

royalists, and the attempt to control the movement of the people from place to place.[71] And in the end, he got the worst of both sides; the imposition of his coercive measures had a tendency to cancel out the positive effects of his conciliatory overtures and the incapacity of his soldiers to enforce them strictly allowed the continuing opportunity to offer covert aid to the rebels.

If Lilburne left Scotland with his reputation hardly enhanced, he was soon deeply and actively involved in the affairs of the northern counties. Before he had departed from Scotland, he had welcomed the creation of the Protectorate,[72] and in 1655 he found himself involved in the active protection of the new regime against royalist plotters. Since he was in command at York during the attempted insurrection of that year, he took a prominent role in its suppression and more particularly in the subsequent prosecution of those allegedly involved. His actions indicate a ruthless commitment to the preservation of the Protectorate against royalist subversion and totally belie his later pleas that he displayed kindness towards those of the opposite party. To Lambert he wrote about the royalists he was busily hunting down, "I hope the greate estates these blaides leave behinde them will pay for all the charge, if you forgive them not againe."[73] And he was of no inclination to forgive. To Thurloe he complained about the reluctance of the judges to proceed with prosecution on the strength of the Protector's ordinance; holding back in "this weighty case" he attributed to "lameness" and "so much knottiness" and indicated clearly his feeling that the events warranted that "the naile...bee driven into the head."[74] After securing Lord John Bellasis, he quickly wrote for instructions and asked for a speedy reply, adding "I...shall be glad to know what you doe in generall with such kind of cattle."[75] Half a year later, he was still writing on the subject, this time to Cromwell indicating his anxiety to pursue an investigation of the late designs; "Your highness may be confident of a faithful performance of my duty to the utmost of my abilityes, and if I were reduced to a corporall, I should cheerfully undertake it rather than this worke should want my best assistance to carry it on."[76]

It was in the aftermath of the royalist risings of 1655 that Cromwell embarked on the experiment of dividing England into military districts and ruling it through the agency of the major generals.[77] It was a

190

scheme justified as a security measure but ultimately intended to be much more, for the authority of the military was to extend beyond control of the royalist threat to the regulation and supervision of affairs at the local level. Such centralization was unpopular, probably more unpopular, than the attempts to enforce a Puritan morality and to achieve a reformation of English manners that are usually associated with this experiment in military rule. The various major generals responded in differing ways to the challenges presented by their wide authority. Some were obviously more successful than others in working with the local power structures. Lilburne, who at least had the advantage when he undertook his duties of being a local person, was already active as a militia commissioner for Co. Durham in mid-March 1655, charged with enquiring into the conspiracies and secret meetings of the disaffected.[78] From the surviving traces in the central records, it would appear that his actions were energetic and sustained. In April he was to be found acting in conjunction with George Lilburne as a commissioner for trial by oyer and terminer of the rebels in the late disturbances in York, Northumberland, and Durham;[79] later he is to be discovered examining a suspicious stranger detained at Scarborough,[80] and in October order was sent to Lambert to name Lilburne his deputy and to supervise his activity as a major general for the counties of York and Durham.[81]

While evidence of his activity in this office is not abundant, the surviving material is indicative of his range of concerns and shows clearly that he accepted the broader mandate of the major generals to be the agents of reform as well as the arms of repression. This is not to say that he in any way minimized the importance of his security role. In December he supervised the transfer of arms from Raby Castle to the custody of the governor of Tynemouth Castle,[82] while in June he concerned himself with the investigation of a recently elected alderman in Hull who was alleged to be disaffected to the government.[83] In March he reported from York about the securing and conviction of suspected royalists and indicated that sequestration proceedings had been carried out against those of sufficient estate.[84] Two months later he wrote to Cromwell excusing his absence at a meeting to which he had been summoned on the grounds that he had more pressing business at hand in seeing to the sentencing of royalists; "this, I presume, would not have had a dispatch without my attendance."[85] If anything bothered him about the performance of such duties, it was the legal encumbrances which appeared to him to frustrate a more thorough carrying out of the work. He complained to Cromwell, for example, that the income figures set for the decimation tax were too high and urged that they be significantly lowered, "for most of your desperate people, which are a more considerable number then those that are taxt, escape, I may say, unpunished."[86] In like manner, he clearly felt that the effectiveness of his work was compromised by encumbrances on estates due to previous forfeiture and transfer (much of which he suspected to be fraudulent), and he urged clarification of the matter by the central authorities.[87] For all his evident enthusiasm in such work, Lilburne was not, however, without some element of sympathetic understanding for hapless bystanders caught up in the web of such proceedings. He petitioned actively, for example, on behalf of one William Brasse who technically came within the purview of the instructions about delinquents on the basis of a minor offence committed a dozen years earlier; he knew the man as a neighbour, was convinced that he had been proceeded against by a person who sought to derive personal benefit from the composition that Brasse paid, and argued that he was of a sober, honest, peaceable disposition and well affected to the state; his spirit, Lilburne protested, was very different from that of the cavaliers, and he begged his discharge from further harassment.[88]

But such activities, important as they were or seemed to him to be, were not the full measure of Lilburne's activity. He extended his interests to include a number of other concerns. Clearly he was anxious that the major generals might become the instrument through which the magistracy might be improved. He complained to Cromwell about the "wicked carriage" of the excisemen·in January 1656, although it should be noted that in so doing he revealed a characteristic preoccupation by his suggestion that many of those who abused this position were "desperate cavaliers;" in making the criticism, he was moved not only by a concern for the impact of the excise on the common people but equally by a concern that "such untoward people" should not be appointed to positions of authority since they brought contempt and reproach on the present government.[89] He made much the same kind of point in reporting his displeasure at the election of a sheriff who was "noted...as one somewhat of a loose conversation, and one that is addicted to tippling and that which is called good-fellowship." While he could not resist in this case as well hinting that

the man was "somewhat concerned in point of delin-
quency," his main concern was that appointing such men
to responsible positions endangered the hold of the
magistracy on the people; "I doubt not, but it is your
highnes care and advantage rather to call good men to
places of magistracy then such, and I know it will be
more acceptable to godly men, and more honourable to
your highnes, and tending more to the quieting of the
spirit of all good people."[90] In yet another case he
wrote to Secretary Thurloe stressing the identical
point; "It is much against my judgement that any man
justly reputed unworthy, or a cavillier, should in
these tymes have preferment."[91] Just as the magistrates should be worthy of their trust, so should the
clergy, and here too he felt that the major generals
had a role to play. He participated actively with the
commissioners for ejecting scandalous ministers and
complained that not enough commissioners had been
appointed to carry on the work effectively; "I...humbly
intreate your highnes to give some order in this, that
the worke of purging corrupt ministers may not sticke
for want of commissioners for the more effectual
carrying on of that affaire."[92] At a more humble
level, he intervened with the government to procure a
patent to change the market day at Thirsk from Monday
to Tuesday; his explanation for the requested change
was characteristically religious, that it would help to
avoid profaning the Lord's Day. "I am senceable it
will bee a very greate obligation to the well affected
of these parts, and begett a greater esteeme of his
highnes and government and be thankfully acknowledged
by the towne."[93] In common with other major generals,
he was concerned about and active in connection with
the reformation of manners by the suppression of excessive alehouses and what he saw as "unlawful pastimes
dishonourable to God and disturbing the peace of the
Commonwealth."[94] Finally, one should note his interest
in and work on behalf of that great educational experiment of the Protectorate, the college at Durham. He
was appointed a member of the committee for Durham
College in May 1656[95] and wrote enthusiastically to
Thurloe about the project, urging him to further the
address about the college and adding "I doubt not but
it will turne to the great renowne of his highnes and
very much affect the inhabitants of that poore county
and citty to him and the government."[96]

     For all his efforts, Lilburne's role in the
northern counties was no more popular there than that
of his colleagues elsewhere in the country, a point
made clear as the elections for the 1656 Parliament

approached. On 9th August he wrote to Thurloe that a spirit to keep out the friends of the government had infected the people of Durham and Northumberland; they "are perfect in their lesson, saying they will have noe swordsman, noe decimator, or any that receives sallary from the state to serve in Parliament."[97] He was inclined to think that Sir Arthur Hesilrige was behind the agitation, a suspicion perhaps influenced by the fact that he had clashed with Hesilrige earlier in the summer over charges that Sir Arthur was an oppressive landlord.[98] In any case, his former good relations with Newcastle appear to have been somewhat strained by a suspicion that the town was co-operating with Hesilrige, even if they had decided against his standing as a parliamentary candidate; he noted darkly that the town clerk of Newcastle had been meeting with Hesilrige, though he admitted ignorance as to what the meetings were about.[99] A week later he wrote to Cromwell in a similar vein, noting that "many at home are fraught with perverse spirits and labour to sett up some new interest," but adding his hope they would be disappointed and that "there will be sober men enough to ballance such."[100]

Lilburne himself was returned to the Parliament for the East Riding, and though he was far from an active participant in debate,[101] the Parliament itself led to a decisive turn in his position. It was during the Parliament of 1656 that Cromwell was offered the crown.[102] In common with many in the army, Lilburne was decidedly opposed to such a move and by May 1657 he had openly broken with Cromwell over the issue. As a soldier Lilburne had to this point accepted the successive political changes of the revolution without reservation; he had served the Rump, accepted the Barebones Parliament, welcomed the Protectorate. But even though he did not resign his commission, he could not accept Cromwell's flirtation with the kingship. He wrote angrily about the matter to Luke Robinson, expressing his hope that the opposition to the kingship would come to "some good issue at last" and urging that care be taken to counteract the propaganda spread by any "new royalist" among the troops in the North.[103] A year later he was reported to be still "a malcontent" because of the changes that were made among his officers in the aftermath of the army resistance to the kingship scheme.[104]

As the revolution wound its way to a chaotic close in 1659, the position of Lilburne became increasingly untenable. Given his consistent adherence to the cause

194

of the army, it is hardly surprising to find that he sided with his long-time colleague Lambert in the last ditch efforts of the army to hold on to its revolutionary position. Indeed, he applauded Lambert's turning out of the Parliament; identified by this time as "altogether his [i.e., Lambert's] creature," he was alleged to have commented "that he hoped never a true Englishman would name the Parliament again and that he would have the house pulled down where they sat, for fear it should be infectious."[105] The attitude reflects a central ambiguity in his career, an ambiguity shared in common with many others associated with the army cause; originally a soldier in the service of the parliamentary cause, he had come to see the army as more embracing of, more faithful to the original goals of taking up arms than its master, the Parliament. Just as events in 1647 had seemed to make a newly politicized army a vehicle more representative of the interests of the nation than the Parliament itself, so again in the dying days of the revolution, Lilburne echoed that dubious and dangerous creed. In the last analysis Lilburne's loyal support of Lambert was futile. At the end his own regiment deserted him; he was forced to surrender York, and the command of his regiment was transferred by Monck to Major Smithson, who had been chiefly responsible for its defection.[106]

The final public act of Robert Lilburne was his trial before the High Court of Justice in October 1660. His was no heroic performance, no act of final defiance; the fiery spirit of a regicide like Harrison did not burn within him. Already before the trial, Lilburne had petitioned for a pardon on the grounds that he had engaged in the late wars only in the hope of promoting an accord between King and Parliament, that he had acted benevolently towards the royalists during the war, and that he was no contriver of the King's death, indeed would have prevented it if he could.[107] That the plea scarcely rings true in view, for example, of what is known about his attitudes towards the investigation and prosecution of alleged royalists in 1655-6, is obvious enough, and even if he could subsequently produce a certificate from a royalist vouching for the kindness shown to him by Lilburne when he was made a prisoner of the parliamentary forces in 1651,[108] such a defence had little chance of success, especially in the heated atmosphere of the time. Lilburne persisted, however, in this line of defence at his trial. "I shall not wilfully nor obstinately deny the matter of fact, but my Lord I must and I can with a very good conscience say that what I did, I did it very

195

innocently without any intention of murther, nor was I ever plotter or contriver in that murther. I never read in the Law, nor understood the case thoroughly; whatever I have done, I have done ignorantly."[109] Indeed, Lilburne suggested that he had favoured the King's motion for the withdrawal of the court and, thinking of the day on which the King was put to death, he recalled how "I was so sensible of it, that I went to my Chamber and mourn'd and would if it had been in my power have preserved his life."[110] The man who had declared a year earlier that he hoped no true Englishman would ever name the Parliament again solemnly assured the court "I was not at all any Disturber of the Government; I never interrupted the Parliament at all."[111] When he argued that he had had no hand in such things, either in 1648 or "at any other time," he was being technically correct; his had not been the hand that did the act, but such technical correctness hardly seems to extend to the question of attitudes. Lilburne was found guilty and at once petitioned for pardon again.[112] Though formally sentenced to death, he achieved a partial response to his pleas when the sentence was commuted to life imprisonment. Lilburne's stance at the trial is, of course, understandable; he was struggling to save his life. At the same time, however, it has a pathetic quality about it that underlines the extent to which Lilburne was an ambiguous revolutionary. The heroism of the battlefield did not extend in the end to a defence of what he had done.

On 31st October 1661, Lilburne was ordered to be sent prisoner to either Plymouth or St. Nicholas Island.[113] It was at the latter place he died in August 1665. Even in his last months the ambiguity remained. The contrite prisoner of 1660, who had announced his intention to lead a loyal and peaceable life,[114] was reported in 1665 to be expecting a speedy alteration of government and was suspected by the authorities of being involved in a plot for a new revolution based on the landing of foreign troops in Scotland.[115] What truth there was in such suspicions is impossible to say, but if nothing else, they indicate that the government had little faith in the sincerity of his submission at the Restoration.

How should one judge Robert Lilburne? The impression is often that of a man caught up in events that are too sweeping, too complex, too challenging for him to cope with either comfortably or certainly. The sense of inadequacy that he displayed as commander in

196

Scotland is seemingly echoed by the lack of conviction for the revolution he displayed at his trial. His politics remain difficult to characterize; what one knows about them is substantially negative, namely that he disassociated himself from the radical ideas of his brother. For the rest, he accepted the changes of regime as they came, only balking at the offer of kingship to Cromwell. But the latter action scarcely makes him a confirmed republican; it is a reflection of his loyalty to the army, not a statement of his abstract political views. In religion, the position is more clear and consistent. There seems little reason to doubt either his Baptist orientation or his deep-rooted hostility to the Presbyterian position. That he was a creature of Cromwell is true enough up to a point, but in the end he broke with him, and the break appears to have been decisive. His attitude to the monarchy he resisted and the King whose death warrant he signed remains most ambiguous of all. It was easy for the supporters of restored monarchy to see one of the regicides as "a savage Creature in the midst of civil People,"[116] but there remains an impression of a lack of resolution in Robert Lilburne when he is viewed in the guise of radical regicide. And therein lies the central paradox and ambiguity of many of the men involved in the English revolution. The fanaticism of a man like Robert Lilburne was never so all-embracing as later critics were to suggest; the radicalism of the regicide and the apparent moral certainty of the major general masked but did not eradicate the sense of ambiguity and uncertainty that was part of the revolution in which he was a major actor.

NOTES

1. On John Lilburne see the standard biographies M.A. Gibb, **John Lilburne the Leveller: A Christian Democrat** (London, 1947) and P. Gregg, **Free-born John** (London, 1961).

2. On George Lilburne see H.L. Robson, "George Lilburne, Mayor of Sunderland," **Antiquities of Sunderland and Its Vicinity**, vol. 22 (1960), pp. 86-132.

3. On Henry Lilburne and the revolt at Tynemouth Castle see R. Howell, **Newcastle upon Tyne and the Puritan Revolution** (Oxford, 1967), pp. 200 ff. and the sources cited p. 200, n. 3.

4. There is a brief life of Robert Lilburne by Sir Charles Firth in **The Dictionary of National Biography.** A biographical notice of him by J.S. Morrill will appear in the forthcoming **Biographical Dictionary of Seventeenth Century English Radicals;** I am grateful to the editors of this work for allowing me to see a copy of this entry in advance of publication.

5. **A Declaration Concerning Colonel H. Martin** (London, 1660), p. 4.

6. T. Gumble, **The Life of General Monck Duke of Albemarle** (London, 1671), pp. 80-81, 206.

7. A. Wood, **Athenae Oxonienses** (3rd edn., London, 1817), 3:358.

8. M. Noble, **The Lives of the English Regicides** (London, 1798), 1:378-80.

9. **DNB**, s.v. Lilburne, Robert. He was two years old at the visitation of Durham in 1615.

10. Sir Charles Firth and G. Davies, **The Regimental History of Cromwell's Army** (Oxford, 1940), 1:264.

11. **Ibid.**

12. Lilburne served as governor of Newcastle between the appointments of Skippon and Hesilrige. The exact dates on which he was in Newcastle are not

certain. The corporation was considering a petition to parliament desiring that Skippon remain as governor on 5th April 1647. The earliest reference in the town records to Lilburne's presence as governor is a letter of his dated 11th August 1647. On 22nd February 1648 it was noted that Hesilrige "is shortly to come downe to this Garrison." Tyne and Wear Archives Dept., Newcastle Common Council Book 1645-50, fols. 138 (5th April 1647) and 163 (12th August 1647); M.H. Dodds, ed., **Extracts from the Newcastle upon Tyne Council Minute Book 1639-1656** (Newcastle, 1920), p. 83 (22 February, 1648).

13. On Lilburne's career in Scotland see Sir Charles Firth, ed., **Scotland and the Commonwealth** (Edinburgh, 1895) and **Scotland and the Protectorate** (Edinburgh, 1899); F.D. Dow, **Cromwellian Scotland 1651-60** (Edinburgh, 1979).

14. J. Nalson, **A True Copy of the Journal of the High Court of Justice for the Tryal of King Charles I** (London, 1684), p. 110.

15. On the situation in the army in 1647 see I. Gentles, "Arrears of Pay and Ideology in the Army Revolt of 1647" in B. Bond and I. Roy, eds., **War and Society** (London, 1976); M.A. Kishlansky, "The Army and the Levellers: The Roads to Putney," **Historical Journal**, vol. 22 (1979), pp. 795-824; M.A. Kishlansky, **The Rise of the New Model Army** (Cambridge, 1979), chap. 7; J.S. Morrill, "The Army Revolt of 1647" in A.C. Duke and C.A. Tamse, eds., **Britain and the Netherlands**, vi (The Hague, 1977).

16. Firth and Davies, **Regimental History of Cromwell's Army**, 2:453.

17. **Cal. S.P. Dom., Addenda 1625-49**, p. 706.

18. E 390 (26), **The Declaration of the Army** (London, 1647).

19. **C.J.**, v:127.

20. **L.J.**, ix:115.

21. **Ibid.; C.J.**, v:129; 669 f.9(84), **A Declaration of Parliament** (London, 1647).

22. **C.J.**, v:184.

23. On the underhanded methods of Kempson see Firth and Davies, **Regimental History of Cromwell's Army**, 2:454-55.

24. **L.J.**, ix:153-4.

25. Firth and Davies, **Regimental History of Cromwell's Army**, 2:455.

26. S.R. Gardiner, **History of the Great Civil War 1642-1649** (London, 1910-11), 3:280 ff. gives an account of the circumstances surrounding the Solemn Engagement.

27. J. Rushworth, **Historical Collections: The Fourth and Last Part** (London, 1701), 1:471.

28. **Ibid.**, 1:554.

29. Dodds, **Newcastle Council Minute Book**, p. 85.

30. Tyne and Wear Archives Dept., Newcastle Common Council Book 1645-50, f. 163.

31. Rushworth, **Historical Collections Part IV**, 2:875. It is interesting to note that Lilburne had to defend his then regiment against a charge of being "the beginners of Mutinies" in 1645. E 302 (17), **Col. Lilburne's Letter to a Friend** (London, 1645).

32. On the events at Ware see Gardiner, **Great Civil War**, 4:21 ff.

33. Rushworth, **Historical Collections Part IV**, 2:913-14.

34. Noble, **Lives of the English Regicides**, 1:378.

35. Gibb, **Lilburne**, pp. 279, 288, 291; Gregg, **Free-born John**, p. 298.

36. Firth and Davies, **Regimental History of Cromwell's Army**, 2:436.

37. **Ibid.**

38. T. Edwards, **Gangraena** (1646, reprint edn., Exeter, 1977), pt. I, p. 90.

39. Gumble, **Life of Monck**, pp. 80-1.

40.   Howell, **Newcastle and the Puritan Revolution,** p. 248.

41.   Rushworth, **Historical Collections Part IV,** 2:1177.

42.   Noble, **Lives of the English Regicides,** 1:379.

43.   G. Ormerod, ed., **Tracts Relating to Military Proceedings in Lancashire during the Great Civil War** (Manchester, Chetham Soc., 1844), 2:296-307, reprinting the text of **A Great Victory by the Blessing of God Obtained** [1651] and two letters from Robert Lilburne to Lenthall and Cromwell.

44.   **Ibid.,** 2:301.

45.   **C.J.,** viii:247; W.C. Abbott, ed., **The Writings and Speeches of Oliver Cromwell** (Cambridge, Mass., 1937-47), 2:296-7.

46.   Firth, **Scotland and the Commonwealth,** pp. 62, 72 n. 1; The appointment was only intended to be a temporary one, but the pressure of the Dutch war meant that a replacement was not provided until May 1654.

47.   On Glencairn's rising see Firth, **Scotland and the Commonwealth;** Firth, **Scotland and the Protectorate;** and Dow, **Cromwellian Scotland,** chaps. 4-5.

48.   Dow, **Cromwellian Scotland,** p. 78.

49.   S.R. Gardiner, **History of the Commonwealth and Protectorate** (reprint edn., New York, 1965), 3:97.

50.   Dow, **Cromwellian Scotland,** p. 78.

51.   **Ibid.,** p. 114.

52.   **Ibid.,** p. 98.

53.   On Lilburne's lack of confidence see his letter to Cromwell on 20th December 1653. "I hope a happy conclusion with the Dutch will putt an end to these unhappy peoples distempers, and that things may come to a settlement againe, though being jealous of my owne weaknes [I] am doubtfull soe great affaires as are here to be managed may suffer for the want of one more fitt to wrastle with them." Firth, **Scotland and the Commonwealth,** pp. 302-3.

54. Dow, **Cromwellian Scotland**, p. 78.

55. **Ibid.**, pp. 80 ff.

56. Cf. his letter to Monck 21 January 1654. Firth, **Scotland and the Protectorate**, pp. 20-1.

57. **Ibid.**, p. 82. It is perhaps significant that it was to Lambert that he addressed this disillusioned comment.

58. On Monck's scheme of pacification see Dow, **Cromwellian Scotland**, chap. 6 and M. Ashley, **General Monck** (London, 1977), chap. 9.

59. Dow, **Cromwellian Scotland**, p. 79.

60. The phrase is from Gardiner, **Commonwealth and Protectorate**, 3:97.

61. Dow, **Cromwellian Scotland**, pp. 107, 300 n. 35.

62. Firth, **Scotland and the Commonwealth**, pp. 139, 141-2, 154-5.

63. **Ibid.**, p. 149.

64. **Ibid.**, pp. 287-8; Firth, **Scotland and the Protectorate**, p. 22. On the assessment see Dow, **Cromwellian Scotland**, pp. 109 ff.

65. Firth, **Scotland and the Protectorate**, pp. 19, 21, 44.

66. Firth, **Scotland and the Commonwealth**, pp. 267, 289, 295-6.

67. Dow, **Cromwellian Scotland**, pp. 99 ff. Contains a useful discussion of Lilburne and the Scottish church.

68. **Ibid.**, p. 103.

69. Firth, **Scotland and the Commonwealth**, p. 161.

70. Dow, **Cromwellian Scotland**, p. 103.

71. Firth, **Scotland and the Commonwealth**, p. 259; T. Birch, ed., **A Collection of the State Papers of John Thurloe** (London, 1742), 2:221.

72. Thurloe State Papers, 2:18.

73. Ibid., 3:226-7.

74. Ibid., 2:359-60.

75. Ibid., 3:587.

76. Ibid., 4:294.

77. On the nature of the rule of the major generals see D.W. Rannie, "Cromwell's Major-Generals," EHR, vol. 10 (1895), pp. 471-506 and I. Roots, "Swordsmen and Decimators: Cromwell's Major-Generals" in R.H. Parry, ed., The English Civil War and After (London, 1970), pp. 78-92.

78. Cal. S.P. Dom., 1655, pp. 77-8.

79. Ibid., p. 117.

80. Ibid., p. 201.

81. Ibid., p. 387.

82. Cal. S.P. Dom., 1655-6, p. 56.

83. Ibid., p. 387; Cal. S.P. Dom., 1656-7, p. 4.

84. Thurloe State Papers, 4:614.

85. Ibid., 5:33.

86. Ibid., 4:321.

87. Ibid., 4:541.

88. Ibid., 4:364.

89. Ibid., 4:468.

90. Ibid., 4:397.

91. Ibid., 5:229.

92. Ibid., 4:643.

93. Ibid., 5:296.

94. Ibid., 4:541.

95. **Cal. S.P. Dom.**, **1655-6**, p. 325.

96. **Thurloe State Papers**, 4:442.

97. **Ibid.**, 5:296.

98. **Ibid.**, 4:229, 234.

99. **Ibid.**, 5:296.

100. **Ibid.**, 5:317.

101. This judgment is based on the minimal trace of his speaking recorded in Burton's diary. J.T. Rutt, ed., **Diary of Thomas Burton** (reprint edn., New York, 1974).

102. On Cromwell and the crown see Sir Charles Firth, "Cromwell and the Crown," **EHR**, vol. 17 (1902), pp. 429-42 and vol. 18 (1903), pp. 52-80.

103. **Thurloe State Papers**, 6:292.

104. **Ibid.**, 7:85.

105. **Cal. S.P. Dom.**, **1659-60**, p. 295.

106. Sir Richard Baker, **A Chronicle of the Kings of England** (London, 1670), pp. 688-9, 699, 700. Cf. F.J. Routledge, ed., **Calendar of the Clarendon State Papers**, vol. IV (1657-60) (Oxford, 1932), pp. 338, 455, 459, 501 for royalist reports on these events.

107. **Cal. S.P. Dom.**, **1660-1**, p. 8.

108. **Ibid.**, 318.

109. **An Exact and Most Impartial Accompt of the Indictment, Arraignment, Trial and Judgment...of Nine and Twenty Regicides** (London, 1660), p. 253.

110. **Ibid.**, p. 254.

111. **Ibid.**

112. **Cal. S.P. Dom.**, **1660-1**, p. 318.

113. **Cal. S.P. Dom.**, **1661-2**, p. 130.

114. **Cal. S.P. Dom.**, **1660-1**, p. 8.

115. Cal. S.P. Dom., 1664-5, pp. 235, 236, 271.

116. A Declaration Concerning Colonel Martin, p. i.

XII

CROMWELL AND THE IMAGERY OF NINETEENTH CENTURY
RADICALISM: THE EXAMPLE OF JOSEPH COWEN

Joseph Cowen was one of the best known figures of
nineteenth century Newcastle.[1] Indeed, his reputation,
especially in radical circles, extended far beyond his
native area; he was a friend and correspondent of many
of the influential figures in the European radical
movement, including Mazzini, Blanc, Kossuth, Herzen,
and Bakunin. His active support of the Chartists and
membership of the Northern Reform League were natural
counterparts to his interest in revolutionary movements
on the continent, while his journalistic activities as
editor of the **Newcastle Chronicle** and **The Northern
Tribune** afforded considerable opportunity for the dis-
semination of his views. Likewise his career as a
Liberal member of Parliament for Newcastle (1873-1885)
gave him ample occasion to comment on the major issues
of the day. Concerning the perspective from which he
commented, Cowen had no doubts: "I am not a conventional adherent of the fashionable Liberalism of the
hour, but I am a life-long Radical by conviction,
sympathy, training, and taste."[2]

As a convinced radical and also "a devourer of
histories,"[3] Cowen had to come to terms with England's
own revolutionary past.   While one's attitude towards
the protagonists of the seventeenth century Civil War
was no longer the political touchstone that it had been
in the eighteenth century, the events of the 1640s and
1650s were frequently referred to in the political
language and imagery of the nineteenth century.[4] The
figure of Oliver Cromwell himself was obviously central
to such references and while a general (and on the
whole favourable) reassessment of his role was well
under way by the middle of the nineteenth century, it
is of significance that evocation of his name was
frequently associated with radical causes of the sort
that Cowen championed such as the Chartists.[5] Cowen,
in his writings and speeches, provides a telling illustration of the use of Cromwell as a radical image, an
illustration all the more striking since Cowen's formal
education appears to have stressed the more traditional
picture of the Lord Protector as an ambitious hypocrite
and tyrant.

Cowen's notes as a student at Edinburgh University survive. Though the entries with respect to Stuart England, made in 1846, are brief, the ideological orientation is clear enough. Charles I was "tried by a mock Parliament." The period of the Commonwealth was "full of faction and caprice," while Cromwell's reign was characterized as "one continued scene of bloodshed."[6] In his notes regarding the characters of the King and Cromwell, Cowen recorded that Charles I was "a good Master, a kind husband, a generous foe, and gracious sovereign" while the Lord Protector's qualities were summed as "deceit, cunning, pride, jealousy, and haughtiness."[7] The contrast between such a view and the evocation of Cromwell to praise Garibaldi on his visit to Tyneside only eight years later could not be more striking: "When they who drive out the Austrian build up again a Republican capital upon the Seven Hills, the heirs of Milton and Cromwell will not be the last to say, even from their deepest heart, God speed your work!"[8] The student notes from Edinburgh echo the still prevalent condemnation of Cromwell and the revolution by David Hume;[9] the address to Garibaldi suggests the radical's identification with the Puritan revolutionary hero.

If Cowen nowhere set down systematically his views on Cromwell, there is ample evidence both for his favourable assessment of him and for his identification of Cromwell with the sort of moral radicalism he himself advanced. It is suggestive that among the discussion topics in the first year (1848) of the Winlaton Literary and Mechanics Institute, an institution in which Cowen took a lively personal interest,[10] appeared the question "Was [sic] Cromwell and his party justified in beheading Charles the first?"[11] Three years later, in his notes for a lecture on the study of history, Cowen commented "the history of England shows the futility of Physical force if not backed by moral and intel[lectual] power" and illustrated the point by reference to Cromwell and Chartism among other examples.[12] In 1876 in a speech made at the ordination of the Reverend H.E. Radbourne at the West Clayton Street Chapel, Cowen spoke feelingly of the greatness of Cromwell at home and abroad in connection with the theme of an alliance between dissenters and Liberals to secure religious and civil liberties:[13]

He begged to remind these supercilious critics [of the dissenters] that this country was once ruled by Nonconformists and that never in her history was her influence

greater or her power more respected.
(Cheers) "A king without a sceptre and a
prince without a throne" swayed the destinies
of this great country, and never was that
power wielded with more dignity in the long
period of her history as an independent
state.... His authority at home was as potent
and effective as it was abroad: he enforced
submission from the aristocracy, the priest-
hood, and the factions that then disturbed
the country. Ashamed to be a Nonconformist!
For his own part, he gloried in the name.
(Cheers). Achievements in the past had won
for it the renown of history and the gratitude of the nation and there was still a
nobler future in reserve if its adherents
walked in the way of their forefathers.
(Loud cheers).

In the following year, speaking at the Nonconformist
Conference, Cowen reiterated the point. While the Nonconformists were not the strongest section of the
Liberal party they were, he said, "without question the
most trustworthy and reliable" and he added, "They have
been the backbone of the party for centuries. Like
Cromwell's soldiers, they make a conscience of their
politics."[14]

It is likewise noticeable that Cromwell received
frequent and favourable reference in Cowen's journal
The Northern Tribune. In volume one a sympathetic
brief biography of the Lord Protector appeared as the
sixth in a series on "Britain's Worthies"; others in
the series had been Milton, Drake, Bernard Gilpin,
George Stephenson, and John Wyclif.[15] Paxton Hood,
later the author of a highly commendatory biography of
Cromwell,[16] contributed pieces periodically to the
journal; they included "The Battle of Dunbar" with its
reference to "our glorious Cromwell" and its hope that
his spirit might reform the present "days of shame"[17]
and "The Farmer of St. Ives" with its similar theme
that Cromwell's name "shall return to light our world
to future liberty."[18] Even more aggressively radical
was the printing of "Cromwell's Sword," one of the
"Songs for the People" by W.J. Linton. Designed to be
sung to the tune of "The Marseillaise," it linked
Cromwell to the nineteenth century struggle for freedom
and equality:[19]

Awake, thou sword of England's glory!
The day of strife dawns on thy grave:

Gleam again as in our old story:
  Let thy flash light the brow of the slave!
  Bright flash! light the brow of the slave.
Too long, O sword hast thou lain sleeping:
  Leap forth from thy tomb to the fight!
  The nations depend on thy might.

Yet another issue reprinted a speech by Charles Larkin, originally delivered during the agitation over the Reform Bill in 1832, in which Cromwell was evoked as a person who "brought a treacherous, a perfidious, a tyrannical, a promise-breaking, anti-reforming king to rthe block."[20] When **The Northern Tribune** criticized the Aberdeen ministry for its conduct of foreign affairs, the image of Cromwell was once again employed; "Oh for one hour of Alfred or Coeur-de-Lion, of Cromwell or of Chatham, to burst the bonds that hinder this nation's energies and give free scope and fair play to its mighty moral and material power!"[21] And evoking Cromwell's image in a matter of considerable local concern, the paper linked the Protector and Ralph Gardner with the nineteenth century battle over the conservancy of the Tyne.[22]

One theme particularly elicited Cromwellian echoes and imagery in the speeches of Cowen, the theme of empire and the exercise through it of moral strength in foreign relations. Speaking on "The British Empire" at the Mayor's Banquet on 26 June 1897 in connection with the Diamond Jubilee celebrations, Cowen raised a characteristically Cromwellian note:[23]

> Once we stood forth as liberators, and always threw our influence, and often our sword, into the scale of people struggling to be free. (Cheers) We encouraged and subsidized neighbouring nations during their periods of despondency and destitution. But we have retired from this gratuitous protectorship and abandoned the pretension to restrain all the wicked, to defend all the weak, and guide all the foolish.

That the time Cowen was referring to was that of Cromwell seems abundantly clear when the passage is compared with Cowen's earlier summary of Cromwellian achievement in foreign policy as expressed in a speech of 1876:[24]

> The Protestant residents of an Alpine valley were at that time treated as the Bulgarian

shepherds have recently been by their Moslem
rulers. And what was his action? The
memorable message that Cromwell sent to the
Catholic Powers of Europe to secure protection for these suffering co-religionists was
in very different terms, and couched in a
very different spirit from the half-hearted
and hesitating remonstrances addressed by our
present Foreign Secretary to the Sultan.
(Hear, Hear) The Tories boasted of their
spirited foreign policy. There never was a
Tory stateman who manifested the energy,
courage, and determination that the Puritan
Protector showed. There were three great
powers in Europe--France, Spain, and Holland:
he intimidated one, coerced the other, and
beat the third. (Cheers)

He made similar statements in speaking on foreign
policy in January 1880: "I contend, therefore, for
these two principles--the integrity of the Empire, and
the interest, the right, and the duty of England to
play her part in the great battle of the world, as did
our illustrious ancestors, the forerunners of European
freedom."[25] And in speaking on the empire in February
1885, he likewise stressed the moral obligation of
Englishmen to spread the benefits of liberty and law:
"One of the duties demanded of Englishmen is the extension of the benefits conferred by liberty and of the
security conferred by law to the communities created by
their enterprise."[26]

That Cowen found inspiration in the example of
Cromwell is perfectly clear. To his mind Cromwell provided an example of the struggle for liberty and of the
exercise of foreign policy on the basis of moral principles. The imagery and the example came readily to
him. Indeed, it is possible to say that Cromwell, in
company with other radical heroes, presided over the
composition of some of his most eloquent statements.
Cowen's biographer has given us a picture of the
library at Stella in which "his best speeches" were
composed; it is a telling vignette of the heroes of
Cowen's own radicalism. "The room is a large, lofty
oblong, abundantly supplied with books and decorated
with portraits and busts of Cromwell and Milton,
Mazzini, Garibaldi, and Lincoln, and the demi-gods who
have lived to some purpose."[27]

NOTES

1. There is a life of Cowen by William Fraser Rae in **DNB: First Supplement** (1901); the only extended study of his career is an adulatory nineteenth century study, E.R. Jones, **The Life and Speeches of Joseph Cowen M.P.** (London, 1886).

2. Speech on foreign policy, 31 January 1880 in Jones, **Life and Speeches of Cowen,** p. 175.

3. "He cultivated the Classics, became a devourer of histories, with a passion for the poets and a turn for public debate." **Ibid.,** p. 11.

4. The point will be explored at length in my forthcoming study of the posthumous reputation of Cromwell. See also J.P.D. Dunbabin, "Oliver Cromwell's Popular Image in Nineteenth Century England" in J.S. Bromley and E.H. Kossmann, eds., **Britain and the Netherlands,** vol. V (The Hague, 1975), pp. 141-163; O. Anderson, "The Political Uses of History in Mid-Nineteenth Century England," **Past and Present** no. 36 (1967), pp. 87-105; T.W. Mason, "Nineteenth Century Cromwell," **Past and Present** no. 40 (1968), pp. 187-191.

5. Henry Vincent provides a good example of a Chartist using Cromwell as a favourable image. Cf. the report of his lectures in May 1850 in PRO HO 45, 3136. Cf. also reports on his speeches at Sheffield in **Sheffield and Rotheram Independent,** 26 September 1846, and at York in **York Herald,** 9 and 16 December 1846. I am indebted for the last two references to Dr. Brian Harrison.

6. Tyne and Wear Archives Office, Cowen Papers F 14 ("Notes on Stuart and Hanover"), f. 1v.

7. **Ibid.,** f. 2v.

8. Cowen Papers D 87, **Northern Tribune,** 1:174.

9. Cf. D. Hume, **The History of Great Britain vol. II: Containing the Commonwealth and the Reigns of Charles II and James II** (London, 1757). On Hume's treatment of Cromwell's character see the perceptive comments of L. Braudy, **Narrative Form in History and Fiction: Hume, Fielding, and Gibbon** (Princeton, 1970), pp. 40 ff.

211

10. Cf. Jones, **Life and Speeches of Cowen,** pp. 95 ff.

11. Cowen Papers D 25 ("Report Read at the Annual Soiree of the Winlaton Literary and Mechanics Institute, 10 July 1848"), f. 4v.

12. Cowen Papers D 46 ("Notes of a Lecture on the Study of History"), f. lv.

13. Cowen Papers B 178 ("Speech on Civil and Religious Liberty, October 18, 1876"), pp. 12-13.

14. Cowen Papers B 181 ("Speech on Religious Equality, February 27, 1877"), p. 6.

15. Cowen Papers D 87. **Northern Tribune,** 1:409-414.

16. E.P. Hood, **Oliver Cromwell: His Life, Times, Battlefields, and Contemporaries** (London, 1882).

17. Cowen Papers, D 87, **Northern Tribune,** 2:31-33.

18. **Ibid.,** 1:251-253.

19. **Ibid.,** 1:147.

20. **Ibid.,** 1:380. The speech was delivered 15 May 1832.

21. **Ibid.,** 1:317.

22. **Ibid.,** 1:104, 295-301.

23. Cowen Papers B 409 ("The British Empire"), p. 5.

24. Cowen Papers B 178 ("Speech on Civil and Religious Liberty, October 18, 1876"), p. 12.

25. Speech on foreign policy, 31 June 1880 in Jones, **Life and Speeches of Cowen,** p. 157.

26. Speech on empire, 14 February 1885, **ibid.,** p. 262.

27. **Ibid.,** p. 104.

Coulson, William, 79

Cowen, Joseph, 10, 206, 207, 208, 209, 210

Creagh, Sir William, 31, 32, 33

Cromwell, Oliver, Lord Protector, 10, 26, 55, 102, 142, 149, 170, 178, 179, 185, 189, 190, 191, 192, 194, 197, 206, 207, 208, 209, 210

Culpeper, Sir Cheney, 166

Danzig, 121

Davenant, John, 118

Dawson, Henry, 26

Deane, Richard, 185

Delaval, Ralph, 79

Derby, Earl of, 185

Deresleye, Margaret, 84

Downing, Emmanuel, 90

Durant, William, 98, 139

Durham, 49

Durham College, 102, 132, 151, 193

Edwards, Thomas, 95, 122

Elbing, 165, 166

Elizabeth I, 19, 28, 47

Eliot, John, 86, 102

Emerson, John, 27

Farmer, Sir John, 53

Fenwick, John, 49, 120

Fox, George, 128, 130, 131, 132, 136, 138, 140, 141, 145, 151, 153

Gardner, Ralph, 5, 9, 10 47, 59, 76, 77, 79, 80 81, 209

Gataker, Thomas, 118

Gateshead, 49, 58, 79, 80, 81, 83, 95, 96, 97, 98, 99, 100, 101, 102, 103, 129, 140, 141

Gilbert, Elizason, 97

Gilpin, John, 150

Grand Lease, 18, 58

Grey, Colonel, 184

Gumble, Thomas, 179

Halhead, Miles, 138

Hall, John, 78

Hall, Richard, 79

Hammond, Samuel, 98, 123, 139, 142, 144, 146, 150, 151

Harrison, Henry, 77, 79

Hartlib, Samuel, 59, 164, 165, 168

Harvard College, 86, 88, 90, 91, 102

Hedwin Streams, 76

215

216